Acing

Evidence

A Checklist Approach to Solving Evidence Problems

Second Edition

Aviva Orenstein
Professor of Law & Val Nolan Fellow
Indiana University Maurer School of Law

Series Editor
A. Benjamin Spencer

ACING SERIES®

Acing Series is a trademark registered in the U.S. Patent and Trademark Office.

© 2014 LEG, Inc. d/b/a West Academic
© 2016 LEG, Inc. d/b/a West Academic
      444 Cedar Street, Suite 700
      St. Paul, MN 55101
      1-877-888-1330

West, West Academic Publishing, and West Academic are trademarks of West Publishing Corporation, used under license.

Printed in the United States of America

ISBN: 978-1-63460-605-9

*"Take nothing on its looks; take everything on evidence.
There is no better rule."*
— Charles Dickens, Great Expectations

*For Sylvia Orenstein,
a loving mother, dedicated appellate public defender,
and indomitable spirit whose acts of loving-kindness
enrich everyone who knows her*

Acknowledgments

Thanks to Alexandra Block, Jocelyn Bowie, Mary Beth Boyer, Ryan Kelly, Sylvia Orenstein, and Caroline Wong for their moral support and excellent help in editing this manuscript. Thanks also to Laura Buchanan, Elliot Edwards, and Hannah de Keijzer for their terrific help on the second edition. I am indebted to my coauthors of *Evidence Law: A Student's Guide to the Law of Evidence as Applied in American Trials,* Roger Park, Steven Goldstein, and the late David Leonard, who taught me much about evidence.

Acknowledgments

Introduction

Studying evidence rewards both detail-oriented and creative types. To understand evidence law, you need to master intricate and occasionally counterintuitive rules. Then you must put together everything you have learned to analyze a single piece of evidence that may present multiple questions regarding admissibility. The chapters in this book are arranged to replicate the order in which a lawyer would consider a piece of evidence, starting with relevance and ending with questions for appeal. Such an analysis requires a methodical approach. A checklist will help you organize the order of inquiry and ensure that you did not omit an important step. Checklists are essential tools in many disciplines. They "provide a kind of cognitive net,"[1] helping pilots work systematically and making surgeons less likely to leave a sponge inside a patient. By routinizing the inquiry, checklists allow you to organize your approach, navigate the rules, notice patterns, and identify what might be unique about a challenging question.

Evidence checklists provide advocates with the structural foundation to build creative arguments. Once the technical aspects of evidence have been parsed and organized using your checklist, you will be able to make creative arguments, crafting compelling theories about relevance, prejudice, and evidence policy.

Acing Evidence prepares you for your evidence exam by reviewing key concepts and walking you through a checklist that assists you in applying the Federal Rules of Evidence to a fact pattern or problem. Examples in the text and sample problems at the end of every chapter illustrate how to apply the various checklists. In addition to the checklists at the end of individual chapters, this book provides a Meta Checklist that traces the entire process of admitting or excluding a piece of evidence.

Acing Evidence can also help you prepare for the evidence portion of the bar exam, which is currently the only upper-class subject that is tested on the Multistate Bar Exam. Later in your professional career, the checklists can assist you in drafting summary judgment motions (where the evidence is restricted to what is admissible), arguing motions in limine, preparing for trial, arguing a point of evidence at trial, and formulating an effective appeal.

---

[1] ATUL GAWANDE, THE CHECKLIST MANIFESTO: HOW TO GET THINGS RIGHT 48 (2009).

Although this book occasionally refers to common-law principles, it centers on the Federal Rules of Evidence, which the vast majority of states have adopted as their template, though, significantly, not California and New York. Even the states that model their evidence rules on the federal standards may choose not to adopt a particular rule or may use language identical to the federal rule but apply their own interpretation. Therefore, be sure to check for state variations if you are using this book to navigate evidence in state court.

Finally, it is important to note that the evidence rules do not apply in every situation. Some administrative law courts operate with relaxed evidence rules and the Federal Rules of Evidence do not apply to sentencing.

I hope you find *Acing Evidence* useful. I welcome any suggestions. If you choose to delve more deeply into an issue or need to find case law support for evidence arguments, I recommend that you consult the one-volume hornbook, Park, Leonard, Orenstein & Goldberg, *Evidence Law: A Student's Guide to the Law of Evidence as Applied in American Trials.*

Aviva Orenstein
Professor of Law & Val Nolan Fellow
Indiana University Maurer School of Law
aorenste@indiana.edu

Note on the Second Edition

This edition corrects some errors in the first edition, adds more examples, and reflects recent amendments and proposed changes to the Federal Rules of Evidence. I am grateful for students' kind reception of *Acing Evidence*. Thanks especially to my students at Indiana University Maurer School of Law for helping me improve this study guide and making evidence law so much fun to teach.

Note on the Use of the Third-Person Feminine

Although it is becoming more common to refer to an individual as "they," I have decided to use the single-person feminine. I thereby avoid both the cumbersome construct "he or she" and the sexist assumption that all lawyers and judges are male. The unknown woman, that elusive "she," will regularly appear as an unnamed judge, attorney, witness, party, or accused.

About the Author

Aviva Orenstein, Professor of Law and Val Nolan Fellow, teaches Evidence and Civil Procedure at Indiana University Maurer School of Law. After graduating Cornell Law School, Professor Orenstein clerked for the late Edward R. Becker of the U.S. Court of Appeals for the Third Circuit. Her academic writing addresses the nexus of evidence and culture, with a focus on gender. Professor Orenstein volunteers as a pro bono attorney in family law cases, particularly those involving guardianship, domestic violence, and abuse and neglect of children. She has three wonderful adult sons, David, Michael, and Benjamin Greenberg, who were not abused (and hardly neglected) in the writing of this book. Her debut novel, *Fat Chance*, which is much more fun to read than *Acing Evidence*, came out in February 2016.

Table of Contents

Acing

Evidence

Second Edition

CHAPTER 1

Relevance

§ 1.1 *Logical Relevance: An Easy-to-Meet Standard*

[Fed. R. Evid. 401]

Relevance is a core concept of evidence. It is the first of many questions one asks about a piece of evidence to determine its admissibility. Fed. R. Evid. 401, which addresses logical relevance, defines relevant evidence as evidence that has *any* tendency to make a material fact (a "fact of consequence") more or less likely. Thus, Rule 401 is a very loose and porous standard—lots of evidence will be deemed relevant, and only in a few areas will there be a serious debate as to the logical relevance of the evidence that a party wishes to introduce.

The common law divided logical relevance into two distinct categories:

(1) *Materiality*, which is to say whether the evidence logically relates to a point in the case. Evidence is immaterial when it is offered to prove a fact that is not in issue; and

(2) *Relevance*, which is to say whether the logical inferences actually make sense. Evidence is irrelevant if it cannot logically establish the fact that the proponent asserts it will prove.

Fed. R. Evid. 401 does not distinguish between materiality and relevance, and instead combines them into one rule.

The mere fact that an issue is not in controversy (and a party is willing to stipulate to it) does not mean, under the low standard of Fed. R. Evid. 401, that the evidence is irrelevant. However, sometimes a fact will simply not be relevant.

EXAMPLE

Plaintiff sues the Johnny-Be-Good Company in product liability for negligent design of an infant child car seat.

Evidence that the workers on the assembly line were regularly drunk and high would not be relevant (under the old common law, we would say it was not material). Such evidence would be relevant in an action for negligence, but has no tendency to make the fact of consequence, product design, more or less likely.

§ 1.2   When Is Relevant Evidence Inadmissible?

[Fed. R. Evid. 402]

Fed. R. Evid. 402 provides that all relevant evidence is admissible *unless* some other provision—that is, a constitutional provision, statute, or rule—excludes the evidence. Consequently, Fed. R. Evid. 402 creates a large pile of relevant evidence that is deemed admissible unless it is excluded some other way, most typically by some other evidence rule. When analyzing an evidence problem, one must decide whether relevant evidence is somehow otherwise inadmissible. Because of this design, most evidence rules are rules of exclusion.

§ 1.3   Fed. R. Evid. 403: The Most Important Evidence Rule

[Fed. R. Evid. 402]

It would be overwhelming, unfair, and impractical to admit all logically relevant evidence. Therefore, Fed. R. Evid. 403 further limits the amount of admissible evidence by screening evidence for practical relevance. Even if evidence passes the admission-happy relevance test of Rule 401, the trial court may nevertheless exclude evidence that is unfairly prejudicial, confusing, distracting, or simply not worth the bother. Rule 403 excludes relevant evidence only if the probative value of the evidence is *substantially* outweighed by the dangers of unfair prejudice, confusion of issues, distraction, or waste of time. Although many Federal Rules of Evidence exclude specific types of evidence, Rule 403, which applies to both civil and criminal cases, is a more general and pervasive rule. Its balancing test allows an attorney to argue that the court should exercise its discretion to exclude otherwise admissible evidence for reasons of fairness, confusion, distraction, or waste of time. Thus, the scope of Rule 403 is much broader than the other rules; it may be applied to *any* piece of evidence.

To understand Fed. R. Evid. 403, imagine a set of balance scales, where the left side is probative value and the right side is one of the Rule 403 "dangers" (unfair prejudice, confusion, distraction, or waste of time).

If the probative value and "dangers" are equal, the trial judge should admit the evidence.	If the "dangers" somewhat outweigh the probative value, the trial judge should admit the evidence.	If the probative value is slight, but the "dangers" are also slight, the trial judge should admit the evidence.	If the probative value is great and the "dangers" are also great, the trial judge should admit the evidence.	Only if the "dangers" substantially outweigh the probative value should the trial judge exclude the evidence.

Reduced to a formula, the rule provides that a trial judge should exclude the evidence only if:

$$\text{[Dangers]} \quad \text{substantially} > \quad \text{[Probative Value]}$$

It is insufficient for the court to find that one of the enumerated dangers simply exists or somehow outweighs the probative value of the evidence. To exclude the evidence, the danger must *substantially* outweigh the probative value. Thus, the greater the probative value of the evidence, the more difficult it will be to exclude the evidence under Fed. R. Evid. 403. The converse is also true: if the probative value of the evidence is slight, the degree of danger necessary to satisfy the Rule 403 standard can be less.

In conducting the Rule 403 balance, the district court will also weigh the effect of giving the jury a limiting instruction under Fed. R. Evid. 105.[1] A limiting instruction restricts the evidence to its permissible use and warns about the impropriety of using the evidence for a prohibited purpose.

§ 1.4   *Understanding the Rule 403 Dangers*

The primary aim of Fed. R. Evid. 403 is to minimize jurors' consideration of marginally relevant but emotionally powerful facts. Rule 403 grants the trial judge wide discretion to exclude evidence on grounds that it will prejudice, confuse, or mislead the jury. The trial judge operates with tremendous discretion because any ruling under Fed. R. Evid. 403 must be contextualized within the other evidence

---

[1]   *See* § 1.7.

of the case, and the trial judge is in the best position to make that decision. However, the trial judge should not use Fed. R. Evid. 403 to exclude evidence based on her personal assessments of persuasiveness or witnesses' credibility.

Four Rule 403 "dangers" can render otherwise relevant evidence inadmissible:

- "Unfair prejudice" means an appeal, often an emotional one, that invites the fact-finder to dislike a party, punish someone for an action not at issue in the case, or decide on a basis prohibited by another rule;

- "Confusion" means that the evidence, while logically relevant, may cause the jury to misunderstand key issues or facts in the case;

- "Distraction" means that the evidence, while logically relevant, may misdirect the finder of fact, shifting the focus to an immaterial issue or a prohibited line of reasoning; and

- "Waste of time" refers to tangential matters and cumulative evidence that add nothing new and use up precious court time and resources.

Fed. R. Evid. 403 also serves a vital function in determining what to do with evidence that is admissible for one purpose but is inadmissible for another. It provides a mechanism for exclusion if the danger that the jury will misuse the evidence substantially outweighs the probative value of the evidence's permissible use.

Some other rules, such as Rape Shield (Fed. R. Evid. 412) and Impeachment by Evidence of a Criminal Conviction (Fed. R. Evid. 609), use language deceptively similar to that in Fed. R. Evid. 403. Watch out; these other rules function very differently.

§ 1.5   Old Chief v. United States

In *Old Chief v. United States*, 519 U.S. 172 (1997), the Accused was charged with being a felon in possession of a firearm, assault with a deadly weapon, and using a firearm in connection with a crime. He had previously been convicted of assault causing serious bodily injury, placing him within the scope of a federal statute prohibiting some felons from possessing firearms. The court held that the trial court abused its discretion in admitting the details of the Accused's prior crime, given that the Accused was willing to stipulate to the fact of his felony status. Though logically relevant under Rule 401, admission of the facts relating to his prior felony failed Rule 403 because of the unfair prejudice.

The court explained that in assessing the probative value of a piece of evidence, the judge should consider available substitutes for that evidence. Given the Accused's willingness to stipulate to his status as a felon, the specific nature of his prior crime had low probative value. On the other hand, the unfair prejudice of having the jury learn about the details of his prior crime was substantial, creating the risk that the jury would convict based on their beliefs about the Accused's propensity to assault or their desire to prevent him from committing future crimes, regardless of his guilt in the present case.

Acknowledging that "a syllogism is not a story," the court conceded in dicta that the prosecution is entitled to tell a colorful story with descriptive richness. The court also noted that in some cases the absence of proof can cause the jury to draw unfair inferences unfavorable to the prosecution. Nevertheless, the court held that these principles did not apply in *Old Chief*, because proof of felony status was not probative for any other point and left no gap in the narrative.

As a practical matter, the requirement that the prosecution must accept an accused's stipulation has been limited to cases like *Old Chief* where the stipulation relates to status and the underlying facts of the former conviction have no relevance. By contrast, when evidence is admitted to show intent, motive, plan, etc.,[2] the underlying facts of the prior bad act may indeed increase relevance and the prosecutor may not be required to accept the stipulation.

§ 1.6   *Motions in Limine*

Any party may make a motion in limine, which requests the court to make an evidentiary ruling before trial. Although sometimes the rulings are preliminary and may be revisited by the judge at trial, parties will often structure their trial strategy based on the court's rulings. Sometimes, based on a court's ruling in limine, an accused will choose to take a guilty plea or a party will choose to settle.

§ 1.7   *Limiting Instructions*

[Fed. R. Evid. 105]

If an out-of-court statement is admissible for one purpose but not for another, under Fed. R. Evid. 105 the objecting party is entitled to a limiting instruction telling the jury the proper purpose and the forbidden purpose.

---

[2]   *See* § 2.11 (discussing Fed. R. Evid. 404(b)(2), use of other crimes, wrongs, or acts for non-propensity purposes).

If the danger that the jury will misuse the statement substantially outweighs the probative value of the statement when used for its limited purpose, then the trial judge may exclude the statement altogether under Rule 403.

Sometimes an out-of-court statement can be redacted to remove inadmissible portions or to avoid the danger that the jury will use the statement for an impermissible purpose. For example, the patient's account of who was at fault in an automobile accident can be removed from a hospital medical record, or references to the guilt of a co-defendant might be removed from a confession. The remaining portion of the statement would then be admissible.

As a practical matter, seasoned litigants often decline to ask for limiting instructions, believing that they sometimes draw attention to the questionable evidence and, ironically, remind the jury of the inadmissible purpose.[3]

RELEVANCE CHECKLIST

1. Does the evidence proffered have *any* tendency to make a material fact more or less likely? (Remember, this is an easy standard to satisfy. The argument does not have to be ultimately persuasive on the point in question, it just has to have some small probative value.)

   If yes: The evidence is relevant under Fed. R. Evid. 401 and the judge should weigh the admissibility of the evidence under Fed. R. Evid. 403. Go to Step 2.

   If no: The evidence is not relevant under Fed. R. Evid. 401 and should not be admitted.

2. In setting out the factors for the Rule 403 balance, determine how much probative value the piece of evidence has standing alone. Go to Step 3.

3. Is there alternative evidence in the case that proves the proposition in question in a less prejudicial or distracting manner?

   If yes: The probative value of the evidence is diminished by the availability of other evidence on the same point. Go to Step 4.

---

[3] See J. Alexander Tanford, *Thinking About Elephants: Admonitions, Empirical Research and Legal Policy*, 60 U.M.K.C. L. REV. 645 (1992).

If no: The probative value of the evidence is arguably enhanced. Go to Step 4.

4.   In setting out the factors for the Rule 403 balance, consider the unfair prejudice/confusion/distraction/waste of time that the evidence might generate. Go to Step 5.

5.   Are the Rule 403 "dangers" diminished by a limiting instruction under Fed. R. Evid. 105?

     If yes: Discount the unfair prejudice in conducting the Rule 403 balance. If the evidence is ultimately admitted, use a limiting instruction. Go to Step 6.

     If no: Go to Step 6.

6.   Conduct the Rule 403 balance: Does the unfair prejudice/confusion/distraction/waste of time *substantially* outweigh the probative value?

     If yes: The evidence is excluded.

     If no: The evidence is admissible subject to other rules (such as character and hearsay).

ILLUSTRATIVE PROBLEMS

■ PROBLEM 1.1 ■

Q: Agatha, an investment banker with a high six-figure salary, is accused of mail and wire fraud in connection with a scheme to bilk elderly investors of their monthly social security benefits. To show why Agatha needed the money despite her large income, the Prosecutor wishes to introduce Agatha's extravagant spending habits, including her purchase of expensive designer clothes and jewelry, her taste in high-end restaurants, and her indulgence in first-class world travel. Agatha objects that evidence of her high-spending lifestyle is irrelevant and unfairly prejudicial. How should the court rule?

A: Evidence of Agatha's spending habits is logically relevant because it helps to explain why a woman with such a high income might still feel the need to amass more money. Therefore, evidence of Agatha's extravagant lifestyle is relevant under Fed. R. Evid. 401 because it makes a fact of consequence—her motive to get more money—more likely.

     Turning to practical relevance under Fed. R. Evid. 403, however, the trial court will probably exercise its discretion to exclude at least some of the evidence. The probative value is slight because a jury generally will not require reasons or need to hear about specific expenditures to imagine why a person might want more money. Most people like money.

On the other side of the balance, the unfair prejudice is potentially high. The jury may simply dislike or be envious of Agatha because of her extravagant lifestyle. Her extravagant lifestyle may make her less sympathetic, particularly in contrast to the elderly pensioners whom she is accused of defrauding. The jury may adopt an "eat the rich" attitude. Also, the distraction caused by all the bling, furs, fancy meals, and jet-setting travel would substantially outweigh the probative value of the evidence. Therefore, the distraction and unfair prejudice of Agatha's lifestyle would substantially outweigh the minimal probative value of the evidence of her high-flown lifestyle. To the extent Agatha made a direct argument, that as a wealthy woman, she had no need to defraud the elderly, her spending and expenses become more probative. Even so, using Rule 403 the judge should avoid waste of time and limit detailed and inflammatory evidence of her purchases and lifestyle.

■ PROBLEM 1.2 ■

Q: Dr. Sheppard is on trial for murdering his wife, who died of poison ingestion. Dr. Sheppard claims that his wife took her own life. The Prosecutor offers evidence that before her death, Mrs. Sheppard accused Dr. Sheppard of poisoning her. The prosecution claims that the statement, though inadmissible to prove the truth of what it asserted (to prove that Dr. Sheppard actually poisoned her),[4] should be admitted for the limited purpose of showing that Mrs. Sheppard possessed a "vital urge" and was not in a suicidal frame of mind.

A: In this case, we have a piece of evidence that is inadmissible for one purpose (the assertion that Dr. Sheppard was the poisoner) but admissible on another theory (to prove Mrs. Sheppard's will to live and therefore contradict Dr. Sheppard's defense). Certainly, the evidence is logically relevant under Fed. R. Evid. 401 because it makes the fact of Mrs. Sheppard's suicide less likely. However, the evidence will probably be excluded under a Rule 403 balance. The probative value of Mrs. Sheppard's state of mind is substantially outweighed by the unfair prejudice of the impermissible use of a powerful accusatory voice from the grave, condemning Dr. Sheppard as a murderer. Although, under Fed. R. Evid. 105, the judge could give the jury a limiting instruction directing the jurors to consider the evidence only to prove Mrs. Sheppard's state of mind, and not to prove that Dr. Sheppard poisoned her, the instruction would be ineffective. The highly emotional and evocative accusation by the

---

[4] This is a hearsay objection. *See* §§ 5.1–5.5.

dying woman would overwhelm the legitimate purpose of proving her state of mind, and the trial judge should use Fed. R. Evid. 403 to exclude the evidence.

■ PROBLEM 1.3 ■

Q: Don is accused of driving carelessly and causing an accident. Is the fact that Don had a fight with his husband on the morning of the accident relevant to his liability for the car accident?

A: Under Fed. R. Evid. 401, the fact that Don had a fight with his husband has some tendency to make a fact of consequence more likely. Don's argument at home may have increased his agitation or distraction. It therefore passes the test of logical relevance. However, Don's fight with his husband will probably not survive the Rule 403 balance. Although it is minimally probative of a fact at issue (indicating anger or distraction because of thoughts about domestic problems), the probative value is low because the chain of inference is attenuated. The trial court should use its discretion to exclude the evidence under Fed. R. Evid. 403 because of the waste of time and possibly unfair prejudice that might result if the jury were to see Don as angry or unlikeable, or if the Plaintiff is trying to tap into any homophobic bias. The waste of time and the unfair prejudice would substantially outweigh the minimal probative value of evidence of his domestic dispute.

POINTS TO REMEMBER

- Relevance is the first question one must ask about any piece of evidence.

- Logical relevance, governed by Fed. R. Evid. 401, is an easy standard to meet, requiring that the evidence has some tendency, no matter how small, to make a fact of consequence more or less likely.

- Sometimes a piece of evidence is not relevant because it does not address a fact of consequence. In the older parlance of the common law, it is not material. To figure out what is a fact of consequence one must know the substantive law.

- Even when evidence is logically relevant, the trial judge may exclude it if the probative value of the evidence is substantially outweighed by unfair prejudice, confusion, distraction, or waste of time.

CHAPTER 2

Character

§ 2.1   *General Rule*

[Fed. R. Evid. 404(a)(1); Fed. R. Evid. 404(b)(1)]

Evidence of a person's character trait or predisposition is generally not admissible to show that she acted according to her character on a particular occasion, Fed. R. Evid. 404(a)(1). Such evidence is called "propensity evidence" and is generally prohibited in both criminal and civil cases, though, as outlined below, there are some important exceptions.

EXAMPLE

Evidence that Charlene is generally a careless driver is not admissible to show that Charlene was therefore more likely to have caused the traffic accident at issue.

Similarly, specific crimes, wrongs, or acts cannot be admitted to show that a person tends to commit that type of behavior and therefore probably engaged in similar acts again, Fed. R. Evid. 404(b)(1).

EXAMPLE

Evidence that Audrey has a previous arrest for drunk driving is not admissible to show that she was probably intoxicated when she operated the heavy machinery that caused the accident at issue. Even multiple previous drunken incidents, including convictions, are not admissible to show Audrey's propensity to drink.

§ 2.2   *Reasons for the Ban on Character Evidence*

Traditionally, Anglo-American law rejects character evidence, expressing a preference for judging people on their actions regarding the event in question, rather than on their personalities, tendencies, or past acts. Character evidence tends not to be particularly probative (at least that is what psychologists tell us). However, despite its slight probative value, character evidence may disproportionately influence jurors, who tend to give it too much credence. Negative character traits can induce the trier-of-fact to dislike a party or witness, perhaps even to the point of—consciously or not—punishing the person for prior misconduct that is not charged in the present case. Finally, Americans have a basic belief in the possibility of change and self-reinvention, and therefore, as an acknowledgement of the idea that people can change, it makes sense to reject character evidence.

§ 2.3 Exceptions to the General Ban on Propensity Evidence

It is crucial to appreciate the scope of the general ban on character evidence; most character evidence is simply not admissible. However, there are five categories of exceptions:

(1) Character of the accused in a criminal case, Fed. R. Evid. 404(a)(2)(A);

(2) Character of the victim in a criminal case, Fed. R. Evid. 404(a)(2)(B);

(3) Character of the accused for sexual misconduct in a case charging a sex crime,[1] Fed. R. Evid. 413–414;

(4) Impeachment of a witness for truthfulness, which is available in both civil and criminal cases, Fed. R. Evid. 608; and

(5) Impeachment of a witness by evidence of the witness's criminal conviction, which is available in both civil and criminal cases, Fed. R. Evid. 609.

Two important general principles govern character evidence introduced under the exceptions provided in Fed. R. Evid. 404(a)(2) (the first two exceptions above). First, except for homicide cases where the accused claims that the victim was the first aggressor, Fed. R. Evid. 404(a)(2)(C), any discussion of character evidence begins with the accused's strategic decision to introduce it. It must be the accused who gets the ball rolling. However, the accused need not take the stand to do so; the accused could get the ball rolling by calling a witness with personal knowledge regarding the accused's or the victim's pertinent character trait. The prosecutor cannot introduce

---

[1] This book discusses only Fed. R. Evid. 413–414, the rules for sexual propensity in criminal cases. Fed. R. Evid. 415, the analogous civil rule, which is used most often in sexual harassment cases, provides another exception to the general character ban for propensity to engage in sexual misconduct. Rule 415 is not covered in this book.

character evidence unless the accused does so first, and then the prosecutor can "rebut same."

Second, the Rule 404 exceptions are governed by Rule 405, which governs how character evidence may be introduced. Only evidence of reputation and opinion may be admitted on direct examination, but specific instances may be inquired into on cross-examination.

§ 2.4 *Character of the Accused in a Criminal Case*

[Fed. R. Evid. 404(a)(2)(A), (C)]

Offered by the Accused

The accused may introduce a pertinent trait of her own character, Fed. R. Evid. 404(a)(2)(A), which she may do only via reputation or opinion evidence, Fed. R. Evid. 405(a); she may not introduce specific instances for this purpose.

EXAMPLE

Alice is accused of aggravated assault. At her criminal trial:

- Alice may testify herself or offer *opinion* evidence from others that she is a gentle person;

- A witness called by Alice may testify that Alice has the *reputation* of being nonviolent; but

- A witness called by Alice may not testify that Alice failed to fight despite being provoked one night at a local bar. This last example is a prohibited *specific instance*.

Offered by the Prosecutor

If an accused has raised a pertinent issue of her good character, the prosecutor may then rebut that evidence, Fed. R. Evid. 404(a)(2)(A). In rebutting the Accused's character evidence, the prosecutor may offer testimony of reputation or opinion, but not specific instances, Fed. R. Evid. 405(a).

EXAMPLE

Once Alice, the Accused in an aggravated assault case, offers testimony that she is a gentle person, the Prosecutor can call a witness to testify that, in the witness's opinion, Alice tends to be violent.

Additionally, the Prosecutor also may introduce evidence of the Accused's character regarding the same trait that the

Accused introduced about the Victim, Fed. R. Evid. 404(a)(2)(B)(ii).[2]

EXAMPLE

The Accused, Alice, calls a witness to testify to Victoria's reputation as a violent person. The Prosecutor may call a witness to testify that in the witness's opinion, *Alice* is violent, even if Alice never introduced testimony about her own character.

On Cross-Examination

If a party in a criminal case introduces pertinent character evidence, the opposing party may then question the witness regarding specific instances of the party's trait on cross-examination, Fed. R. Evid. 405(a). To do so, the cross-examiner must have a good-faith belief that the specific instance actually happened, and cannot introduce extrinsic evidence (that is to say, other witnesses or documents) to contradict the witness's testimony on cross-examination, Fed. R. Evid. 403. That is, the cross-examiner may inquire about specific instances, but she must take the witness's answer.

EXAMPLE

After a witness for the Accused testifies that, in her opinion, Alice is very gentle, the Prosecutor may cross-examine concerning whether the witness is aware of a specific incident when Alice was violent. The Prosecutor must have a good faith belief for asking the question. Additionally the Prosecutor must accept the witness's answer and may not introduce extrinsic evidence of the specific incident to contradict the witness.

§ 2.5 *Character of the Victim in a Criminal Case*

[Fed. R. Evid. 404(a)(2)(B)]

Offered by the Accused

The accused may introduce a pertinent trait of the victim's character, Fed. R. Evid. 404(a)(2)(B), using reputation or opinion evidence, Fed. R. Evid. 405(a). This exception does not apply to rape victims, Fed. R. Evid. 412(a).

---

[2]   See § 2.5 (Character of the Victim in a Criminal Case).

EXAMPLE

The Accused, Alice, claims that she attacked the Victim, Victoria, because Victoria lunged at her with a knife. Alice may call a witness to testify to Victoria's reputation as a violent person. Alice may also call a witness to testify that in the witness's opinion, Victoria is very violent.

Offered by the Prosecutor

The prosecutor may rebut evidence of the victim's character, Fed. R. Evid. 404(a)(2)(B)(i). This rebuttal can take the form of reputation or opinion evidence, Fed. R. Evid. 405(a).

In homicide cases, where the accused's defense is that the victim was the first aggressor, the prosecutor may introduce evidence that the victim was peaceable, Fed. R. Evid. 404(a)(2)(C). This is the only time under Rule 404 that the prosecutor may initiate a discussion of the accused's propensity. Otherwise, the decision rests with the accused whether to introduce propensity evidence.

EXAMPLE

The Accused, Alice, claims that the Victim, Victoria, threw the first punch. Evidence that Victoria started the fight is not character evidence—it is just a contested fact in the case. Nevertheless, such testimony in a homicide case, where Victoria is dead and unavailable to tell her side of the story, triggers the Prosecutor's ability to introduce character evidence about Alice's peaceable tendencies.

On Cross-Examination

Specific instances may be inquired into on cross-examination regarding the character of the victim. The questioner must accept the witness's answer and cannot introduce extrinsic evidence to contradict the witness's testimony, Fed. R. Evid. 405(a).

§ 2.6   *Rape Shield*

[Fed. R. Evid. 412]

The Rape Shield rule prohibits the examination of the victim's promiscuous character or the victim's sexual proclivities, including what the victim was wearing at the time of the alleged assault, Fed. R. Evid. 412. It restricts information about the victim's sexual history, behavior, and preferences in order to limit irrelevant inquiries that may embarrass or traumatize the victim. Rape Shield operates as an exception to Fed. R. Evid. 404(a)(2)(B), which generally allows the accused to raise a pertinent character trait of the victim. Essentially, Rape Shield is an exception to an exception that reverts to the general rule prohibiting propensity evidence.

Although every jurisdiction has a Rape Shield rule, many state versions diverge significantly from the federal rule.

Federal Rape Shield is not absolute, and allows some prior evidence of the victim's sexual conduct in a criminal trial.[3] Fed. R. Evid. 412 recognizes three exceptions:

- Evidence that a person other than the accused was the source of semen, injury, or other physical evidence, Fed. R. Evid. 412(b)(1)(A);

- Evidence of the Victim's prior sexual relationship with the accused to prove consent, Fed. R. Evid. 412(b)(1)(B); and

- An ill-defined safety-net exclusion that provides for admitting evidence about the victim's sexual history and propensities where failure to admit such evidence "would violate the constitutional rights of the defendant," Fed. R. Evid. 412(b)(1)(C).

Rape Shield is intended to counteract the unfair prejudice that arises when the jury adopts sexist stereotypes and jumps to conclusions based on the victim's sexual activities, dress, or sexual history. Rape Shield is also intended to facilitate rape prosecutions by making the trial itself less of an ordeal for the victim.

§ 2.7 Propensity of the Accused to Commit Sex Crimes

[Fed. R. Evid. 413–414]

In sex crime cases, under Fed. R. Evid. 413 (which deals with sexual assault) and Fed. R. Evid. 414 (which deals with child molestation), the prosecutor may introduce against the accused any prior, similar, wrongful sex act (whether convicted conduct or not) for any purpose, including propensity. The prosecutor may argue that the accused has a tendency to make sexual attacks and probably did so on the occasion in question. Fed. R. Evid. 415 applies in civil cases in which there is a claim for relief based on a party's alleged sexual assault or child molestation and is not discussed in this book.

---

[3] The Rape Shield rule was extended in 1994 to civil cases. It excludes evidence of sexual behavior and propensity otherwise admissible in civil cases unless the probative value of that evidence "substantially outweighs the danger of harm to any victim and of unfair prejudice to any party," Fed. R. Evid. 412(b)(2). The issue mainly arises in employment cases where the defendant wishes to introduce plaintiff's prior sexual conduct as a defense to sexual harassment.

Rules 413–414 contravene evidence law's long history of banning propensity evidence. Unlike under the exceptions in Rule 404(a)(2), the prosecutor does not have to wait for the accused to initiate a discussion of character. In fact, the prosecutor may raise the evidence of the accused's prior sexual misconduct in the prosecution's case-in-chief. Only specific incidents are allowed—not opinion or reputation evidence. Evidence of the prior similar sexual misconduct must pass the *Huddleston* test,[4] which requires that the trial judge determine that a jury could find that the other act actually occurred. The prosecutor must give advance notice of the sexual propensity evidence. There is no time limit regarding how long ago the prior similar sexual misconduct occurred.

EXAMPLE

Alfred, age 43, is charged with rape. Evidence that Alfred raped someone when he was 21 is probably admissible to show that Alfred tends to rape. This is true even if Alfred was never convicted of the alleged first rape.

Courts have resisted due-process challenges to Fed. R. Evid. 413–414, holding that these rules are limited by Fed. R. Evid. 403 and that the Rule 403 judicial balancing of probative value against unfair prejudice guarantees due process. As a practical matter, however, most prior sexual misconduct by the accused is admitted. Because propensity has been designated a permissible purpose and because prior sex crimes are (mistakenly)[5] considered highly probative, judges almost always admit the evidence.

Many states that have adopted the Federal Rules as their template for their evidence rules have rejected Rules 413–414.

§ 2.8   *Exception for Character of Witnesses for Honesty or Dishonesty*

[Fed. R. Evid. 608]

This form of impeachment involves an exception to the ban on propensity evidence for one trait: the character of honesty. It applies to all witnesses in criminal and civil cases who take the stand. This rule is discussed in the chapter on impeachment.[6]

---

[4]   *Huddleston v. United States*, 485 U.S. 681 (1988). *See* §2.11.

[5]   *See* Tamara Lave and Aviva A. Orenstein, *Empirical Fallacies of Evidence Law: A Critical Look at the Admission of Prior Sex Crimes*, 81 U. CINN. L. REV. 795 (2012).

[6]   *See* § 4.4.

§ 2.9   *Exception for Impeachment by Evidence of Criminal Conviction*

[Fed. R. Evid. 609]

This form of impeachment involves another exception to the ban on propensity evidence, this time for convicted conduct of witnesses who take the stand. The logic is that one who has broken the law is more likely to lie on the stand. Within a time limit of ten years, all convicted conduct concerning crimes involving dishonesty (such as identity theft, fraud, perjury, tax evasion, embezzlement, etc.) is admissible to impeach any witness. Certain other convictions are also admissible to impeach witnesses, though the crimes must be felonies and must pass various balancing tests. Crimes older than ten years are very unlikely to be admitted. This rule is discussed more fully in the chapter on impeachment.[7]

§ 2.10   *When Character Is an Essential Element*

[Fed. R. Evid. 405(b)]

In extremely limited cases, character evidence is admissible because character forms an essential part of the charge, claim, or defense. In such cases, character is not being used circumstantially, but instead, character is itself an issue in the case. Fed. R. Evid. 405(b) covers those limited cases where character is actually in issue.

Examples include:

- Moral fitness to practice law;

- Truth as a defense in a libel action;

- Fitness of a parent in a custodial matter or in an action to terminate parental rights;

- The driving ability and driving history of a driver where the car owner is sued for negligent entrustment of the vehicle to the driver; and

- Mental capacity in a commitment hearing or guardianship.

In all these examples, the character traits are essential pieces of evidence that are directly, not merely circumstantially, relevant.

Students sometimes mistakenly over-apply Fed. R. Evid. 405(b). Rule 405(b) does not apply to cases where the evidence is being used

---

[7]   *See* § 4.5 (discussing impeachment of witnesses based on their criminal convictions).

for a non-character purpose;[8] rather, it applies in the very rare cases where character is directly in issue.

EXAMPLE

Amy is accused of embezzling money from her employer. The Prosecutor cannot ·introduce evidence in the prosecution's case-in-chief concerning Amy's character for cheating and stealing because character is not an essential element of the claim against Amy. She would be just as guilty of the crime if she had an impeccable character up until the moment that she uncharacteristically acted on an impulse to embezzle. The character issue would not be necessary to the indictment because in charging the elements of embezzlement, the Prosecutor need not prove that Amy possesses the character of an embezzler. Therefore, character is not "in issue" and Fed. R. Evid. 405(b) does not apply. The only ways Amy's character can come up are: (1) if she raises her character herself under Fed. R. Evid. 404(a)(2)(A); (2) if Amy is a witness and her character for honesty is raised under Fed. R. Evid. 608; or (3) if Amy is a witness and the court admits a prior crime under Fed. R. Evid. 609.

§ 2.11   *Evidence Used for a Non-Character Purpose*

[Fed. R. Evid. 404(b)(2)]

Sometimes evidence that looks like impermissible character evidence can nevertheless be admitted because the evidence serves a different, legitimate purpose and is not being introduced as character evidence at all. In other words, the evidence is not being offered to prove propensity. Fed. R. Evid. 404(b)(2) provides that certain uncharged misconduct—other wrongs, crimes, or acts—may be admissible for "other purposes" beside propensity.

Rule 404(b)(2) does not provide an exhaustive list of "other purposes," but does specifically mention:

- Motive;
- Intent;
- Preparation;
- Knowledge;
- Absence of mistake;

---

[8]   *See* § 2.11 (discussing Rule 404(b)(2), where evidence, though susceptible to a character use, is being used for a non-character purpose).

- Identity;

- Opportunity; and

- Common plan or scheme.

Often such non-propensity purposes overlap, and the evidence will fit into more than one of the above categories. Courts often add *modus operandi* to the non-exhaustive list of potential "other purposes."

Prior acts admitted under Fed. R. Evid. 404(b)(2) need only pass the *Huddleston* standard, under which a judge will admit the prior crime, wrong, or act if a jury could believe the act actually happened.[9]

Fed. R. Evid. 404(b)(2) is always moderated by Fed. R. Evid. 403, which balances unfair prejudice, confusion, distraction, and waste of time against the probative value of the evidence.[10] Even if the proponent of the evidence of the other crime, wrong, or act can show another purpose, the evidence is not admissible if, under Rule 403, the unfair prejudice, confusion, or distraction it generates substantially outweighs the probative value of that other purpose.

The prosecution may offer Rule 404(b)(2) evidence in its case-in-chief. Such evidence can be offered whether or not the accused chooses to testify. When a prosecutor wishes to introduce evidence under Fed. R. Evid. 404(b)(2), she must, upon request of the accused, give notice.

Although Rule 404(b)(2) applies most often in criminal cases, it also applies to civil cases.

EXAMPLES

Amy is accused of embezzling money from her employer. Her defense is that she did not do it, and the elaborate scheme was too complex for her limited financial abilities. Evidence that Amy was arrested three years previously for executing a similar scheme is not admissible to show that she tends to embezzle or has a propensity for cheating people. It is, however, admissible under Fed. R. Evid. 404(b) to show Amy's *knowledge* of such sophisticated schemes. Had Amy not raised the defense of lack of knowledge, then her previous arrest for embezzlement would still be logically relevant under Fed. R. Evid. 401, but the probative value would be significantly lower. Additionally, the low probative value would probably be substantially

---

[9]   *See Huddleston v. United States*, 485 U.S. 681 (1988); § 2.11.

[10]   *See* § 1.3 (discussing Fed. R. Evid. 403).

outweighed by the danger that the jury would use the evidence for an impermissible purpose and think that Amy just tends to steal people's money. However, even without Amy's lack-of-knowledge defense, a court might potentially find the evidence of the sophisticated knowledge important enough to pass the balance test of Fed. R. Evid. 403 despite the potential unfair prejudice. Any determination by the court in such a close case would probably be affirmed on appeal, given the abuse-of-discretion standard of review.

* * *

Agatha is accused of murdering Vicky to silence her. Vicky was about to inform the police of Agatha's plot to kill Zenobia. If the Prosecutor mentions Agatha's plot to kill Zenobia to show that Agatha is a serial murderer and has no respect for human life, then that would be an impermissible propensity use of the uncharged misconduct evidence. However, if the Prosecutor, after providing the requested notice, introduces evidence of Agatha's plan to kill Zenobia to show Agatha's *motive* for killing Vicky, then that is "another purpose" under Fed. R. Evid. 404(b)(2) that could justify admission of Agatha's plan to kill Zenobia. Using Fed. R. Evid. 403, the trial judge would weigh the unfair prejudice of the impermissible propensity purpose against the high probative value of the permitted purpose of demonstrating motive. The judge would probably conclude that the unfair prejudice of the use as character evidence does not substantially outweigh the probative value of the motive evidence and would admit the evidence.

* * *

Arnold posted an ad on craigslist seeking fathers who would allow Arnold to have sex with their underage daughters in exchange for payment. (This is based on a real case. Unfortunately, you cannot make these things up.) A police officer posing as "Don," a dad of a fourteen-year-old girl, engaged Arnold in an online discussion in which a deal was made for Arnold to have sex with Don's daughter. Arnold is charged with a federal crime of using the Internet to attempt to induce a minor to have sex. (This crime is not covered by Fed. R. Evid. 414.) Arnold claimed that he merely posted the ad to confront child-abusers and not to actually have sex with underage girls. Uncharged evidence (that is to say, evidence that the Prosecutor would like to use against Arnold but that is not the subject of this indictment) that Arnold solicited sex online from other

underage girls would be evidence of intent negating
Arnold's defense. The Prosecutor could therefore present a
non-propensity purpose of *intent* that has high probative
value. However, on the other side of the balance, the
evidence of Arnold's soliciting sex directly from a minor is
highly unfairly prejudicial. It leads directly to an
impermissible propensity inference that Arnold is a child
molester and it is also unfair because the uncharged
misconduct is more egregious than the conduct charged,
given that it involves direct discussion with a minor. It
would be fair to worry that once jurors hear that Arnold
contacted minors directly, they would not use the
information merely to negate his intent with "Don," but
instead just loathe him and wish to punish him for the
uncharged misconduct, even if they were not certain he was
guilty of the crime charged. Although there is a nontrivial
argument that the evidence could be unfairly prejudicial,
given Arnold's motive defense, it is highly probative and
would probably pass the Rule 403 test.

§ 2.12 *Habit*

[Fed. R. Evid. 406]

Habit evidence is admissible to show that the witness acted in
accordance with that habit on a particular instance, even if no
eyewitnesses testify and there is no corroboration (two requirements
of the common law that the Federal Rules of Evidence reject). Habit
evidence consists of repeated, almost semiautomatic responses to the
same stimulus. It tends to be nondramatic and, in fact, boring.
Therefore, habit evidence usually passes Fed. R. Evid. 403 because
the unfair prejudice tends to be very low.

Be careful about using the notion of habit colloquially and of
over-applying the concept.

Examples of Habit:

A person always takes the stairs rather than the elevator.

* * *

A person always takes the outgoing mail with her to mail
on her way to lunch.

Examples That Are Not Habit:

A person is in the "habit" of getting drunk on football
weekends.

* * *

A person has the unfortunate "habit" of seducing married men.

These last two examples of evidence that do not qualify as habit are certainly not boring or low prejudice. Furthermore, such conduct, though perhaps distressing and regular, is not semi-automatic.

 CHARACTER CHECKLIST

1. Is the evidence propensity evidence? That is to say, is it being used circumstantially to show that a person behaved in conformity with a general character trait or with past conduct?

    If yes: This is traditional character evidence and unless it fits into an exception or has another legitimate non-character use, it will be excluded. Go to Step 2.

    If no: The evidence is not traditional character evidence and may be admissible because:

    •   It is being used for another (non-character) purpose under Rule 404(b)(2). Note that often evidence is susceptible to both an impermissible propensity use and another, legitimate purpose. The trial judge should conduct a Fed. R. Evid. 403 balance to see if the probative value of the other purpose is substantially outweighed by the dangers of unfair prejudice, distraction, or confusion caused by an inappropriate character use.

    •   It is one of the very rare occasions, occurring only in civil cases, when character is "in issue" and specific-incident evidence of character is admissible under Fed. R. Evid. 405(b). The evidence is admitted not for circumstantial evidence of general propensity but as direct evidence of character because the trait or character is an essential element of the claim, crime, or defense.

    •   It is habit evidence under Fed. R. Evid. 406.

2. If you deem the evidence propensity evidence, next determine whether various exceptions apply. Does the propensity evidence relate to a witness's character for truthfulness or credibility?

    If yes: The propensity of witnesses (in both civil and criminal cases) to be honest may be admissible under Fed. R. Evid. 608.

Additionally, the witness's general credibility and willingness to abide by social norms can be raised via impeachment for convictions for certain crimes under Fed. R. Evid. 609. Continue to Step 3.

If no: Go to Step 3.

3. Is this a homicide case where the accused contends that the victim was the first aggressor?

If yes: The prosecutor may introduce reputation and opinion evidence of victim's character for peaceableness.

If no: Continue to other exceptions for criminal cases. Go to Step 4.

4. Is this a criminal sexual assault or child molestation case?

If yes: All relevant prior bad acts of the accused are admissible under Fed. R. Evid. 413–414. There is no time limit on the remoteness of the prior offense, and the prior act need not be convicted conduct; it only must meet the *Huddleston* standard, which provides that a reasonable juror could find that the prior event occurred. The check on admission of this evidence is Fed. R. Evid. 403. In conducting the Rule 403 balance, note that propensity use of a prior bad act is by definition not "unfair prejudice."

If no: Go to Step 5.

5. Is this a pertinent character trait of the accused offered by the accused?

If yes: It may be proved by reputation or opinion evidence by the accused herself or by a character witness for the accused. The prosecutor may then:

- Rebut the accused's character evidence with contrary reputation and opinion evidence regarding the same character trait; or

- Cross-examine the witnesses for the accused (including the accused herself) regarding specific instances of pertinent behavior. However, the prosecutor must have a good faith belief that the specific instances occurred and may not introduce extrinsic evidence to contradict the witness's answer.

If no: Go to Step 6.

6. Is this a pertinent character trait of the victim offered by the accused?

If yes: Go to Step 7.

If no: The propensity evidence is not admissible.

7. Is this evidence of sexual disposition or sexual history, including the victim's dress?

If yes: Go to Step 8.

If no: It may be proved by reputation or opinion evidence by the accused herself or by a character witness for the accused, unless it involves a rape victim. The prosecutor may then:

- Offer pertinent character evidence about the victim to rebut the evidence offered by the accused about the victim;

- Offer character evidence on the same trait about the accused; or

- Cross-examine the witnesses for the accused (including the accused herself) regarding specific instances of pertinent behavior. However, the prosecutor must have a good faith belief that the specific instances occurred and may not introduce extrinsic evidence to contradict the witness's answer.

8. Does it fall under one of the following exceptions for Rape Shield?

- Evidence that a person other than the accused was the source of semen, injury, or physical evidence, Fed. R. Evid. 412(b)(1)(A);

- Evidence of the victim's prior sexual relationship with the accused to prove consent, Fed. R. Evid. 412(b)(1)(B); or

- An ill-defined safety-net exclusion that provides for admitting evidence about the victim's sexual history and propensities where failure to admit such evidence "would violate the constitutional rights of the defendant," Fed. R. Evid. 412(b)(1)(C).

If yes: The character evidence is admissible.

If no: The character evidence is not admissible.

ILLUSTRATIVE PROBLEMS

■ PROBLEM 2.1 ■

Q: Peter is suing Donald for tortious battery arising out of a fistfight at Bunny's Restaurant. Will evidence of Peter's two previous fights at Bunny's be admissible if they did not result in convictions?

A: In this civil case, previous specific instances of fights at Bunny's are not admissible to show Peter's propensity to fight. As a general rule, evidence of propensity is inadmissible in civil cases, except for certain types of impeachment. Even if Peter took the stand, Peter could be impeached only for his character for dishonesty or his previous criminal conduct, not for his violent tendencies. (Note that if this were a criminal case against Donald, Donald would be able to raise Peter's pertinent tendency towards violence under Fed. R. Evid. 404(a)(2)(B), but there is no such exception in civil cases.) Furthermore, character is not "in issue" in the sense of Rule 405(b) because it does not form an essential element of the tort or of a defense. Unless there was some question about the identity of the person who hurt Peter and the Defendant had a "signature crime" that was unique enough to indicate his identity, the other two incidents would not be admissible under Rule 404(b)(2). Finally, even if one might say colloquially that Peter is in the habit of starting brawls at Bunny's, such behavior is not semi-automatic and regular, and therefore would not qualify as habit under Fed. R. Evid. 406. The ban on propensity is intended to focus the trier-of-fact on the facts in the case and not on the personalities or tendencies of the individuals involved.

■ PROBLEM 2.2 ■

Q: Carl and Siggy were heatedly discussing the nature of human creativity and the fight became physical. Siggy is charged with criminal assault and battery. Which of the following will be admissible?

> **Q1:** The Prosecutor calls Joseph Campbell as a witness in the state's case-in-chief. Campbell testifies: "My personal dealings with Siggy have led me to believe that he is dangerous and has homicidal tendencies."
>
> **A1:** This is impermissible character evidence. Only the Accused may initiate discussion of the Accused's character under these facts, and the prosecution can then rebut same, Fed. R. Evid. 404(a)(2)(A). The Prosecutor is calling Campbell in the case-in-chief, which means that the Accused has not yet had a chance to call witnesses.

Q2: In his case-in-chief, Siggy, the Accused, calls Anna, who testifies: "In my opinion, Carl is a belligerent bully who is absolutely intolerant of people with other views. Carl is violent and capable of hurting someone."

A2: This evidence, offered by the Accused about a pertinent character trait of the Victim and presented in the form of opinion testimony, is admissible under Fed. R. Evid. 404(a)(2)(B) and 405(a).

Q3: If the Judge admits Anna's testimony that Carl is violent, should the Prosecutor be permitted to offer reputation evidence that Carl is peace-loving?

A3: Yes, the Prosecutor may rebut the negative character evidence about the Victim, Fed. R. Evid. 404(a)(2)(B)(i) and 405(a).

Q4: If the Judge admits Anna's reputation evidence that Carl is violent, should the Prosecutor be permitted to offer evidence that Siggy is also violent?

A4: Yes, the Prosecutor may counter the negative character evidence about the Victim with the same negative character evidence about the Accused, Fed. R. Evid. 404(a)(2)(B)(ii). Such evidence may take the form of reputation or opinion evidence, Fed. R. Evid. 405(a).

Q5: Assume that instead of calling Anna to describe the character of Carl, Siggy calls an eyewitness who claims that Carl struck the first blow. Could the Prosecutor then introduce evidence that Carl was, by disposition, peaceable?

A5: No. Siggy's evidence is not character evidence, but direct factual evidence concerning the incident, and does not trigger the Prosecutor's ability to rebut with character evidence.

Q6: Assume that Carl died shortly after the fight and Siggy is charged with homicide instead of assault and battery. Siggy calls an eyewitness who states that Carl struck the first blow. Could the Prosecutor then introduce evidence that Carl was, by disposition, peaceable?

A6: If Carl dies and this becomes a homicide case, and Siggy persists in portraying Carl as the first aggressor, then the Prosecutor may introduce reputation or opinion evidence that Carl was of peaceable disposition, Fed. R. Evid. 404(a)(2)(C). This is the one example under Rule 404 where the Prosecutor can initiate character evidence.

Q7: During the Accused's case-in-chief, Siggy calls Rabbi Debra Orenstein to the stand as a character witness. May the Rabbi discuss Siggy's reputation as a renowned surgeon?

A7: The Rabbi may testify about any pertinent trait, so the question is whether Siggy's renown as a surgeon would be pertinent to this case. Perhaps counsel for Siggy could argue that a surgeon might tend to be very protective of his hands and unlikely to throw the first punch in a fight. This is questionable, but if it is admitted, it will be under Fed. R. Evid. 404(a)(2)(A).

Q8: May Siggy call the Rabbi to testify about Siggy's failure to fight when provoked at the "I'm OK, You're OK" annual picnic?

A8: No, the Rabbi, in her direct testimony, is restricted to reputation and opinion evidence. She may not testify about specific instances on direct, Fed. R. Evid. 405(a).

Q9: If the court allows some or all of Rabbi Orenstein's character testimony, can the Prosecutor call Joseph Campbell during the state's case-in-rebuttal to testify that Siggy once pulled Campbell's hair at a conference on rediscovering the inner child?

A9: No, Campbell is limited to reputation and opinion evidence. He cannot testify about a specific instance in his direct testimony.

Q10: During the Accused's case-in-chief, Rabbi Orenstein testifies that Siggy is a "peaceable, non-violent fellow." On cross-examination, may the Prosecution ask the Rabbi if she is familiar with a previous violent altercation involving Siggy?

A10: Yes, specific instances may be inquired upon in cross-examination, Fed. R. Evid. 405(a). The Prosecutor, however, is stuck with the witness's answer and may not introduce extrinsic evidence to contradict the Rabbi.

POINTS TO REMEMBER

- Character evidence offered for propensity purposes is generally not admissible.

- When propensity evidence is admissible, it concerns:

  o Prior sex offenses by an accused in sexual assault or child molestation cases (civil and criminal);

  o A pertinent trait of the accused offered by the accused (criminal only);

- ○ A pertinent trait of the victim offered by the accused, excluding sexual behavior and sexual character of a rape victim (criminal only);

- ○ Prosecutor's evidence rebutting the accused's character evidence (criminal only);

- ○ Character of witnesses for honesty or dishonesty, used to impeach (civil and criminal); and

- ○ Prior convictions of witnesses that reflect on their credibility, used to impeach (civil and criminal).

- If character evidence is admissible, it may be presented in the following manner:

  - ○ *For sex crimes*: Evidence of specific past instances is allowed.

  - ○ *For exceptions in criminal cases under Fed. R. Evid. 404(a):*

    - Opinion;

    - Reputation; and

    - On cross, the opposing party may inquire into specific instances, but must accept the answer and may not dispute the witness's answer with extrinsic evidence.

  - ○ In the rare cases where character is an essential element of a charge, claim, or defense, each of these forms of evidence is allowed:

    - Opinion;

    - Reputation; and

    - Specific instances

  - ○ *For a witness's character for honesty:*

    - Opinion;

    - Reputation; and

    - On cross, the opposing party may inquire into specific instances, but must accept the answer and may not dispute the witness's answer with extrinsic evidence.

  - ○ *For prior convictions*: If the evidence is about a witness's prior conviction, that evidence may be proved by a public record of the conviction or testimony of the witness.

- Habit evidence—routinized, semi-automatic behavior—is distinct from character evidence. Habit evidence tends to be boring and uncontroversial.

- Evidence of past wrongs, crimes, or acts may be admitted for other, non-propensity purposes, such as identity, motive, or absence of mistake, Fed. R. Evid. 404(b)(2). Admission of such evidence:

    o   Must pass the *Huddleston* test, which requires that the court finds by a preponderance of the evidence that the jury could believe that the crime, wrong, or act occurred;

    o   Must pass the Rule 403 balancing test; and

    o   Must, in criminal cases, have been the subject of notice by the prosecutor to the accused.

CHAPTER 3

Other Relevance Rules

§ 3.1 *Introduction*

The additional relevance rules described in this chapter—rules on insurance, plea bargains, compromises, and remedial repair—reflect outcomes that theoretically could be determined just by using Rule 403's balancing test. However, experience at common law indicated that the balance should result in exclusion in these cases. When offered for the impermissible purposes enumerated in these relevancy rules, the potential unfair prejudice, distraction, or confusion has been categorically deemed to substantially outweigh the probative value of the evidence.

Note, however, that the evidence may still be admitted if it is offered for "another purpose." If the party proffering the evidence can articulate a valid other purpose for admitting the evidence, the evidence may be admitted if it passes a Rule 403 balancing test. For instance, as will be seen below, although evidence of insurance is not admissible to show negligence, the very same evidence might be admissible to show ownership or control. The trial court would have to apply Rule 403 to balance the unfair prejudice of the impermissible purpose (showing negligence) against the probative value of the permissible purpose (showing ownership or control).

§ 3.2 *Subsequent Remedial Measures Rule*

[Fed. R. Evid. 407]

<u>Prohibition of Evidence of Remedial Measures</u>

Fed. R. Evid. 407 excludes evidence that the defendant made repairs or took other remedial measures when such evidence is offered to prove negligence or other culpable conduct. Rule 407 excludes measures taken after an incident that, if taken before that incident, would have made the incident less likely to occur. In federal court, the exclusion of remedial measures clearly applies to product liability cases because of an amendment in 1997. Some states, however, do not include product liability within the ambit of the exclusion.

31

Any remedial measure that would have made the accident less likely to occur falls under the scope of the rule. This includes actions beyond repairing a defect, and reaches conduct such as firing a harassing supervisor, changing a product's design, recalling a defective item, or installing lights in a dark parking lot.

The primary policy behind the rule is to encourage defendants to make needed improvements or repairs by eliminating the possibility that evidence of such remedial measures will be used against defendants in litigation. The rule excludes evidence that often has low probative value but tends to be overvalued by juries. The remedial measures rule also promotes fairness to the repairing party. It seems unfair to punish a party engaged in useful, accident-preventing conduct by turning that conduct against her in litigation.

EXAMPLE

The Plaintiff slipped and fell on the Defendant's stairs. The Plaintiff alleges that the Defendant was negligent because she failed to provide a handrail. After the accident, the Defendant installed a handrail on the stairs in question. Evidence of the Defendant's subsequent improvement is not admissible to prove that the Defendant was negligent at the time of the accident. This result could have been reached by using Rule 403: the probative value of the repair as demonstrating fault is small but the jury might overvalue it when assessing negligence. Rule 407 represents a categorical assessment that such evidence is substantially more unfairly prejudicial, confusing, and distracting than it is probative.

Requirement That the Measure Occur *After* the Event

The subsequent remedial measures rule excludes only evidence of action taken *after* the accident at issue occurred. If the remedial measure was taken before the incident, the exclusion of Rule 407 does not apply.

EXAMPLE

In 2013, a manufacturer redesigns a toaster so that it does not emit an electric shock. A customer purchased the toaster in 2012 and received a shock from it in 2014, after the newer model was produced. Rule 407 does not limit this customer from presenting evidence of the redesign because the change predated the accident. The policy of encouraging repair would not apply because the repair has already been undertaken and was not implemented in response to the accident.

Remedial Measures That Fall Outside the Rule

The subsequent remedial measures rule excludes evidence of safety measures only when the evidence is offered for the forbidden purpose of showing negligence or culpable conduct. Subject to Rule 403 balancing, such evidence may be offered for any other purpose that is actually in controversy, including ownership, control, and the feasibility of taking a remedial action.

Offered to Show Feasibility

If the defendant merely testifies that a product was safe or in "normal condition" when the accident occurred, this does not open the door to evidence of the subsequent remedial measure. If, however, the defendant argues that no change was possible, or that the design was the best possible one, then feasibility is controverted and the subsequent measure is admissible.

EXAMPLE

The Plaintiff was injured while operating a lawnmower and claims that the lawnmower should have included a protective toe guard. The Defendant asserts that installing a toe guard was not feasible because it would have interfered with the lawn cutting operation and was prohibitively expensive. Subject to Rule 403, evidence that the Defendant subsequently installed a toe guard would be admissible to show feasibility, because feasibility was controverted by the defendant.

Fed. R. Evid. 407 Is Subject to Rule 403 Balancing

Even if evidence of remedial measures fits one of the categories for which it is admissible, such as impeachment or to demonstrate feasibility, its value for this purpose must still pass the Rule 403 balancing test. The unfair prejudice, confusion, or waste of time of evidence introduced for another purpose must not substantially outweigh its probative value.

§ 3.3   *Offers to Compromise (Settlement Negotiations and Agreements)*

[Fed. R. Evid. 408]

Exclusion of Evidence of Settlement Agreements and Settlement Offers

Settlement offers, agreements, and negotiations relating to a settlement offer are generally inadmissible to prove the validity of a claim. Fed. R. Evid. 408 applies to settlements or attempted settlements between the parties as well as settlements between parties and nonparties. This rule does not apply in a suit to enforce the terms of a settlement contract itself.

EXAMPLE

Harry sues Sally for $100,000 for breach of contract. Sally tries to settle the claim for $50,000. Rule 408 prohibits Harry from introducing Sally's settlement offer to prove either that Sally acknowledges that she owes Harry something or that his claim is valid.

Rule 408 Shields Surrounding Statements

In addition to the offer itself, Rule 408 also shields from admission any conduct or statement made during compromise negotiations. Statements made in settlement negotiations cannot be used to impeach a witness through a prior inconsistent statement or impeachment by contradiction.

EXAMPLE

In negotiations, Sally says, "Look, I know I owe you money for the contract, but $100,000 does not account for the labor I already put in. How about $50,000 and you drop this suit?" In addition to prohibiting the fact of a settlement offer, Rule 408 prohibits Harry from introducing Sally's statement, "Look, I know I owe you money for the contract," to prove the validity of the contract. This is true even if Harry wishes to introduce Sally's statement merely to impeach Sally's claim that the contract claim is invalid and she owes him nothing.

Offers That Fall Outside the Rule 408 Exclusion

This rule of exclusion applies only to offers of compromise and statements made in seeking compromise of *disputed* claims. If there is no dispute as to validity or amount, Rule 408 does not apply.

Rule 408 also does not apply when the evidence is offered for another purpose, that is to say any purpose other than to prove the validity or amount of the claim. Such other permissible purposes include:

- Demonstrating witness bias;

- Negating a claim of undue delay; and

- Proving an effort to obstruct justice.

The Rule clearly prohibits use of statements made in negotiation merely to impeach a witness. Allowing impeachment to serve as a permissible "other purpose" would undermine the Rule.

EXAMPLE

Jocelyn and her passenger, Walter, are injured when Jocelyn's vehicle collides with Dan's truck. At trial, Walter testifies that Dan's truck ran the red light and struck Jocelyn's vehicle. Dan wishes to present evidence that previously, Walter had made a claim against Jocelyn, and that Jocelyn had paid Walter to settle the claim. This evidence is most likely admissible to demonstrate that Walter might have been biased toward Jocelyn, and his favorable attitude could cause Walter to shade his testimony to Jocelyn's benefit.

Exception to Rule 408 for Statements Made to Government Agents

An exception to Rule 408's general principles, Fed. R. Evid. 408(a)(2) provides that conduct or statements made in compromise negotiations concerning a claim by a public office or agency in the exercise of its regulatory, investigative, or enforcement authority are admissible when offered in a subsequent criminal case.

EXAMPLE

Martha, CEO of a hedge fund company, admitted in discussions with the SEC that her company knowingly sold worthless junk bonds to clients, telling the clients the collateralized debts were rated AA. Martha negotiated with the government agency for a way to repay investors in the hopes of lessening civil penalties. If the company is later charged with a crime, any statement made by Martha to SEC agents could be used as evidence against the company even though the statements were made in compromise negotiations. Martha's statements are admissible because they fall under the exception for statements made to government agents in the exercise of their regulatory, investigative, or enforcement authority.

Policy Justification for Excluding Compromise

Rule 408 is primarily justified by the public policy of encouraging settlement. Additionally, Rule 408 rests on the notion that sometimes evidence of compromise is minimally relevant, and that in making the settlement offer, the offeror may have been seeking peace or an end to litigation rather than admitting a weak legal position. Finally, it seems unfair to punish a party who acts in a socially useful way by seeking to resolve disputes privately.

§ 3.4   *Evidence of Payment of Medical and Similar Expenses*

[Fed. R. Evid. 409]

Fed. R. Evid. 409 excludes evidence of "furnishing, promising to pay, or offering to pay medical, hospital, or similar expenses resulting from an injury" in order to prove liability for the injury. This rule primarily affects insurance companies that issue checks before they determine fault. The primary policy behind Rule 409 is to encourage such payments. Furthermore, payment of medical expenses is often not particularly probative of belief in fault. Unlike the much more expansive Rule 408, Rule 409 does not apply to surrounding statements made in conjunction with payment of medical expenses.

§ 3.5   *Plea Bargains/Nolo Contendere and Statements Made in Plea Bargaining*

[Fed. R. Evid. 410]

Fed. R. Evid. 410 excludes from evidence in both civil and criminal suits:

- A withdrawn guilty plea;

- A plea of nolo contendere;

- Statements surrounding a withdrawn guilty plea or a plea of nolo contendere; and

- Statements made during plea bargaining with a prosecuting attorney.

To be excluded, the accused must negotiate with the prosecutor or the prosecutor's agent, not the police. Rule 410 generally does not allow the use of statements made during plea negotiations to impeach the accused. Some jurisdictions apply Rule 410 to prohibit the use of statements by the prosecutor, though the plain language of the rule does not so require.

Rule 410 has two exceptions to its ban on evidence from plea bargains. First, statements made in a plea negotiation may be admitted when another statement from the same plea or plea discussions has been introduced, and in fairness the statements ought to be considered together, Fed. R. Evid. 410(b)(1). Second, statements made in plea negotiations will also be admissible in the accused's subsequent criminal proceeding charging perjury or false statement if the accused made the statement in plea negotiations under oath, on the record, and with counsel present, Fed. R. Evid. 410(b)(2).

Rule 410's primary purpose is similar to that of Fed. R. Evid. 408 (the rule on compromise): to encourage full disclosure during negotiations and to promote settlement. Like Fed. R. Evid. 408, Rule 410 protects not only the fact of the attempted compromise, but the surrounding conversation as well.

As a practical matter, many prosecutors circumvent part or all of Rule 410, negotiating for waivers of Rule 410 protection before they will engage in a plea bargain. In *United States v. Mezzanatto,* 513 U.S. 196 (1995), the United States Supreme Court held that prosecutors may require as a precondition that the accused agree that anything she says in plea negotiations may be used to impeach her. Some circuits allow prosecutors to undo Rule 410 entirely by recognizing agreements that allow all of the accused's statements to be admissible if plea negotiations fail, even if the accused does not take the stand.

§ 3.6   *Evidence of Liability Insurance*

[Fed. R. Evid. 411]

Fed. R. Evid. 411 excludes evidence concerning liability insurance when offered on the issue of whether the insured party acted negligently or wrongfully.

The relevance of insurance to the issue of liability is questionable and has great potential for prejudice. For instance, if the jury finds out that a defendant corporation is insured, it might be more likely to hold it liable because of the insurance company's deep pockets. If the jury finds out that a plaintiff is not insured, then the jury might provide the plaintiff with an undeserved award out of concern that the plaintiff will suffer without access to the defendant's greater resources. Conversely, if the jury learns that the plaintiff is insured, it may unfairly discount deserved damages.

Even though inadmissible at trial, evidence of insurance is discoverable. The underlying facts regarding parties' insurance will be known to the opposing parties and are usually available in initial disclosure under Fed. R. Civ. P. 26(a).

As is typical with the 400 Rules, under Fed. R. Evid. 411 evidence of insurance may be received for other purposes, such as proving agency, ownership, or control of an item or demonstrating bias or prejudice of a witness. As with other evidence that is admissible for one purpose but not for another, the trial judge must use Rule 403 to weigh the danger of unfair prejudice against the probative value of the evidence in deciding whether to admit it.

      OTHER RELEVANCE RULES CHECKLIST

Remedial Repair [Fed. R. Evid. 407]

1. Does the evidence involve a remedial measure taken in a civil case that would have made the accident or event less likely?

    If yes: Go to Step 2.

    If no: Rule 407 does not apply. Consider other relevance rules.

2. Was the remedial measure or repair taken after the accident?

    If yes: Go to Step 3.

    If no: Rule 407 does not apply. Consider other relevance rules.

3. Did the evidence of the remedial measure show the defendant's negligence, culpable conduct, or, in federal courts and the majority of states, product liability?

    If yes: Rule 407 bars admission of the evidence unless it is being used for another purpose. Go to Step 4.

    If no: Rule 407 does not apply. Consider other relevance rules.

4. Do other valid reasons render the evidence admissible, such as:

    - Feasibility of repair;

    - Proof of ownership; or

    - Proof of control?

    If yes: Go to Step 5.

    If no: You lack a theory for admitting the evidence other than the prohibited purpose of proving negligence or culpability. The evidence is inadmissible under Rule 407.

5.   Has the other purpose been controverted?

If yes: Go to Step 6.

If no: The evidence is inadmissible under Rule 407.

6.   If one of these controverted "other purposes" exists, does it pass a Rule 403 balance test? That is, will the trial court find that the probative value of such other purpose is not substantially outweighed by the unfair prejudice, confusion, distraction, or danger that the jury would misuse the fact of repair to prove negligence or culpability?

If yes: The evidence is admissible.

If no: The evidence is not admissible under Rule 403. (Note: A Rule 403 balance is conducted at the beginning of your analysis to assess practical relevance—*see* §§ 1.3–1.4—and again later to balance permissible and impermissible uses of the evidence.)

Compromise [Fed. R. Evid. 408]

1.   Does the evidence arise in a civil case out of:

-   A compromise;

-   An offer to compromise; or

-   Surrounding statements in the course of the negotiation?

If yes: Go to Step 2.

If no: The evidence is not excluded under Rule 408.

2.   Did the statement relate to a genuine dispute as to validity or amount?

If yes: Go to Step 3.

If no: The evidence is not excluded under Rule 408 and may be otherwise admissible as a statement by an opposing party.[1]

3.   Is the statement offered in a subsequent criminal case, and did the negotiations concern a claim by a public office or agency in the exercise of its regulatory, investigative, or enforcement authority?

If yes: This is an exception to the exclusion of Rule 408, and the evidence in these limited circumstances is admissible unless excluded by another rule.

If no: Go to Step 4.

4.   Is the fact of compromise, offer to compromise, or surrounding statement in negotiation being offered to demonstrate a purpose

---

[1]   *See* § 6.6 (Statements of a Party-Opponent).

other than the party's belief in the validity of the claim or amount?

If yes: The evidence is not being used for the purpose prohibited by Rule 408, and Rule 408 may not exclude it. Be sure in your analysis to specify what other purpose the evidence is being used for. Examples include:

- Demonstrating witness bias;
- Negating a claim of undue delay; and
- Proving an effort to obstruct justice.

Note: impeachment is not an appropriate other purpose.

If you think the evidence is admissible for a valid purpose other than proof of validity or consciousness of liability, go to Step 5.

If no: Rule 408 will preclude admissibility of the fact of compromise or offer to compromise and any surrounding statements made during the negotiations.

5.   If you have postulated a valid other purpose for the evidence, but the jury might also improperly use the evidence to find validity or consciousness of liability, examine whether the evidence passes Rule 403. In other words, do the confusion, distraction, and unfair prejudice caused by Rule 408's impermissible purpose substantially outweigh the probative value of the valid other purpose?

If yes: The evidence is excluded under Rule 403.

If no: The evidence is admissible.

Plea Bargain [Fed. R. Evid. 410]

1.   Does the evidence arise out of any of the following?

- A withdrawn guilty plea;
- A plea of nolo contendere;
- Surrounding statements concerning a withdrawal of a guilty plea or a plea of nolo contendere; or
- Statements made during plea bargaining with a prosecuting attorney in a criminal case?

If yes: Go to Step 2.

If no: The evidence is not excluded under Rule 410, but it is likely hearsay. If it involves statements or actions made by a party, it may be admissible if offered by an opposing party under Fed. R. Evid. 801(d)(2).

2. Has another statement from the same plea discussions already been introduced, and if so, would fairness dictate that this plea statement also be admitted?

If yes: The statement made in plea discussions is admissible.

If no: Go to Step 3.

3. Is the statement made in a plea discussion being offered in a criminal prosecution for false statement or perjury?

If yes: If the statement was made under oath, on the record, and with counsel present, then the evidence is not excluded under Rule 410 and will be admissible as a statement by an opposing party.

If no: The statement is excluded by Rule 410.

Insurance [Fed. R. Evid. 411]

1. Does the evidence relate to whether a person possessed liability insurance?

If yes: Go to Step 2.

If no: The evidence is not excluded under Rule 411.

2. Does the evidence concerning liability insurance potentially go to prove whether a person acted negligently or otherwise wrongfully?

If yes: It may be prohibited by Rule 411 unless another valid purpose can be supported. Go to Step 3.

If no: Rule 411 does not apply.

3. Is evidence of insurance being offered to demonstrate a purpose other than to prove that a person acted negligently or otherwise wrongfully?

If yes: The evidence is not being used for the purpose prohibited by Rule 411 and Rule 411 will not exclude it. Be sure in your analysis to specify the other purpose for which the evidence is being used. Examples include:

- Proving agency, ownership, or control of an item; and

- Demonstrating bias or prejudice of a witness.

If you think the evidence is admissible for a purpose other than proof of negligence or wrongful conduct, go to Step 4.

If no: The evidence is excluded under Rule 411.

4. If you have postulated another purpose for the evidence, but the jury might also improperly use the evidence of insurance to find

negligence or wrongdoing, does the evidence pass Rule 403? In other words, do the confusion and unfair prejudice caused by the purpose barred by Rule 411 substantially outweigh the valid other purpose?

If yes: The evidence is excluded under Rule 403.

If no: The evidence is admissible.

ILLUSTRATIVE PROBLEMS

■ PROBLEM 3.1 ■

Q: Ernie was injured on January 27, 2010, when the gas pedal in his 2005 Toyota Camry became stuck and he hit a tree. Ernie's attorneys learn in discovery that the problem was known to Toyota, and starting in 2006, Camry cars in Europe were fitted with a small metal stent that prevented this acceleration problem. Will Ernie be able to introduce evidence of Toyota's European stent in his lawsuit?

A: As a general matter, anything a party says or does can be admitted by an opposing party if it is relevant under Rule 401 and not unfairly prejudicial under Rule 403. Ernie will be able to introduce Toyota's European repair program because it is relevant, not particularly prejudicial, and not barred by the language or policy of Fed. R. Evid. 407.

Rule 407 only prohibits evidence of *subsequent* remedial repair, and the repair in this case was implemented prior to the injury. There is no point in depriving Ernie of the evidence of the repair because Rule 407's policy of shielding remediation in order to encourage repair does not apply in this case.

Toyota could argue that the jury may overvalue the evidence, but the court is unlikely to exclude the evidence under Rule 403. The European stent is relevant and probative of Toyota's knowledge as well as the ease of remediation. The probative value of learning about an inexpensive fix that the company already knew about is high. Such probative value is probably not outweighed by the danger of the jury overvaluing the evidence. It also does not raise issues of confusion or distraction. The evidence is certainly prejudicial against Toyota, but not unfairly so.

■ PROBLEM 3.2 ■

Q: You complain to your landlord at Hoosier Pride Apartments that the roof is leaking, the music students next door practice their brass instruments during the early morning hours, and you are being billed by a very unfriendly computer for $100 more per month than the agreed rent. The landlord's representative, a lovely old army sergeant named Bubba, assures you that you only owe $650, not $750, per month, but also says that to avoid a computer error, you should just pay the billed amount. Bubba says: "Do not worry. We'll credit it to your last month's rent. We know that you do not really owe the full $750." Unfortunately, it turns out that when your last month's rent comes due, you are charged the full amount and given no credit. In a suit to recover the overpayment, is Bubba's statement admissible?

A: Bubba's statement, though hearsay, will be admissible as a statement by a party-opponent under 801(d)(2)(D),[2] as Bubba was working for Hoosier Pride Apartments. The statement is not precluded by Fed. R. Evid. 408 because there is no dispute about liability or amount. Bubba fully acknowledges the debt and his statement is not part of a protected negotiation.

■ PROBLEM 3.3 ■

Q: Patty, a pedestrian, is injured in an accident and sues Delia, whom Patty claims is the owner of the vehicle that hit Patty. Delia claims that, at the time of the accident, she no longer owned the car that hit Patty, and had sold the car to David, a poor graduate student. May Patty introduce evidence that Delia was still paying car insurance premiums on the vehicle when the accident occurred?

A: Patty may introduce evidence that Delia was paying the insurance on the vehicle when the accident occurred because the evidence is being offered to show ownership, not to imply anything about Delia's ability to pay an award or Delia's level of care. Therefore, it is probably not prohibited by Fed. R. Evid. 411. However, the judge would have to conduct a Rule 403 balance to check the probative value of Delia's ownership-proving insurance, and to ensure that it is not substantially outweighed by the unfair prejudice of the jury's learning that Delia was insured. The probative value of the insurance would depend on what other evidence of Delia's ownership was available. For instance, if public records from the Bureau of Motor Vehicles conclusively show that Delia still owned the vehicle, the probative value of her insurance to prove ownership would be low and would probably fail the Rule 403 balance. However, if little other available evidence pointed to Delia owning the vehicle, the fact of her paying for the insurance would not be excluded by Rule 403.

---

[2]   *See* § 6.6 (Statements of a Party-Opponent).

POINTS TO REMEMBER

- All the relevance rules in this chapter concerning:

  o   Subsequent remedial repair;

  o   Compromises;

  o   Payment of medical expenses;

  o   Plea bargains; and

  o   Insurance

  reflect the common law's assessment that the Rule 403 balance between probative value and unfair prejudice should result in exclusion. These relevance rules also stem from important policy concerns designed to influence social behaviors outside the courtroom, such as encouraging compromise (Rule 408) and promoting safety improvements (Rule 407).

- If the party proffering the evidence can articulate a valid "other purpose" for admitting the evidence, the evidence may be admitted if it passes a Rule 403 balancing test, that is to say, if the risk of unfair prejudice posed by the prohibited use does not substantially outweigh the probative value of the permitted use.

Subsequent Remedial Repair [Fed. R. Evid. 407]

- Fed. R. Evid. 407 excludes evidence that the defendant made subsequent repairs or took other subsequent remedial measures when such evidence is offered to prove negligence or other culpable conduct.

- Measures taken before the accident or event in question are not covered by Rule 407.

- Rule 407 covers remedial measures taken in product liability cases.

- Such evidence is not excluded when offered to show another purpose such as:

  o   Impeachment; or

  o   Ownership, control, or feasibility of preventative measures, if controverted.

- Such other purposes are subject to a Rule 403 balance, where the evidence will be excluded if the unfair prejudice of the prohibited purpose substantially outweighs the probative value of the permitted purpose.

Offers to Compromise (Settlement Negotiations and Agreements) [Fed. R. Evid. 408]

- Settlement offers, agreements, and negotiations relating to a settlement offer are generally inadmissible to prove the validity of a claim, Fed. R. Evid. 408.

- Rule 408 applies to settlements or attempted settlements between the parties as well as to settlements between parties and nonparties.

- Rule 408 excludes evidence of the compromise offer as well as surrounding remarks in negotiation.

- Evidence of statements made during negotiations is not admissible as impeachment.

- Rule 408 does not apply to conduct or statements made by the accused to a public office or agency in the exercise of its regulatory, investigative, or enforcement authority when the prosecutor offers such conduct or statements in a subsequent criminal case, Fed. R. Evid. 408(a)(2).

- Such evidence is not excluded when offered to show another purpose such as:

  o Demonstrating witness bias;

  o Negating a claim of undue delay; or

  o Proving an effort to obstruct justice.

- Such other purposes are subject to a Rule 403 balance, where the evidence will be excluded if the unfair prejudice of the prohibited purpose substantially outweighs the probative value of the permitted purpose.

Payment of Medical and Similar Expenses [Fed. R. Evid. 409]

- Evidence of payment or offering to pay medical expenses is not admissible to prove liability for injury, Fed. R. Evid. 409. This rule applies mostly to payments by insurance companies, and does not shield surrounding statements, but only the payment itself.

Plea Bargains/Nolo Contendere and Statements Made in Plea Bargaining [Fed. R. Evid. 410]

- Fed. R. Evid. 410 excludes from evidence in both civil and criminal suits:

  o A withdrawn guilty plea;

  o A plea of nolo contendere;

- o   Statements surrounding a withdrawn guilty plea or a plea of nolo contendere; and

- o   Statements made during plea bargaining with a prosecuting attorney.

- To fall within Rule 410's exclusion, negotiation has to be with the prosecutor or the prosecutor's agent, not the police.

- Rule 410 does not allow the use of statements made during plea negotiations to impeach the accused. However, many prosecutors require the accused to waive certain rights under Rule 410 before they will engage in plea negotiations.

Evidence of Liability Insurance [Fed. R. Evid. 411]

- Fed. R. Evid. 411 excludes evidence concerning liability insurance when offered on the issue of whether the insured party acted negligently or wrongfully.

- Evidence of insurance may be received for other purposes, such as proving:

- o   Agency;

- o   Ownership;

- o   Control; or

- o   Bias or prejudice of a witness.

- In deciding whether evidence of insurance should be admitted for another purpose other than negligence or wrongful conduct, the trial judge must use Rule 403 to weigh the danger of prejudice against the probative value of the evidence.

CHAPTER 4

Impeachment and Rehabilitation of Witnesses

§ 4.1 *Introduction to Impeachment of Witnesses*

[Fed. R. Evid. 607]

Impeaching a witness means discrediting that witness's testimony by presenting flaws, whether they are flaws in the person, such as the witness's ability to perceive and relate events, or flaws in the content of her testimony. Such flaws can be demonstrated on cross-examination and sometimes by extrinsic evidence. Trial courts have the authority to limit impeachment that is unrelated to the original testimony or risks exposing the jury to potentially unfair prejudice. Additionally, counsel must possess a good-faith belief in the grounds for impeachment.

What Is Extrinsic Evidence?

Impeachment by extrinsic evidence refers to impeachment by any evidence other than questions on cross-examination. A separate witness who contradicts the witness being impeached presents extrinsic evidence. For example, a witness who offers reputation or opinion evidence of another witness's character provides extrinsic evidence impeaching that witness. A piece of paper such as a business or public record can also constitute extrinsic evidence.

When May a Witness Be Impeached?

Generally, a witness must actually testify to be impeached. An accused who invokes her Fifth-Amendment right against self-incrimination and declines to testify cannot be impeached with prior statements or actions because there is no testimony to impeach. Some of the accused's prior statements or actions may be admissible, but not on an impeachment theory.

When an out-of-court statement is admitted via an exemption under Fed. R. Evid. 801(d)(2) or via a hearsay exception, the declarant's credibility may be attacked by impeachment evidence in the same manner as if the declarant had testified as a witness, Fed. R. Evid. 806.

Who May Do the Impeachment?

Fed. R. Evid. 607 provides that the credibility of a witness may be impeached by any party, including the party who called the witness. This is a departure from the common law that prohibited impeaching one's own witness except in very limited circumstances.

Forms of Impeachment

Some forms of impeachment are delineated in the Federal Rules of Evidence. Others are not, but these forms of common-law impeachment have clearly been preserved.

TYPE OF IMPEACHMENT	IS THERE A FEDERAL RULE ASSOCIATED WITH THIS FORM OF IMPEACHMENT?	IS EXTRINSIC EVIDENCE ALLOWED?
Bias or interest	No, though it is mentioned in Rules 408 and 611 and in the advisory committee notes; Subject of *United States v. Abel*, 469 U.S. 45 (1984)	Yes (*Abel*)
Impairment in ability to perceive: defects in the witness's perception or cognition	No	Yes, based on common law
Prior crime, used to demonstrate lack of credibility	Fed. R. Evid. 609	Yes, evidence of the conviction record is admissible if the prior crime is the

		type that may be used to impeach
Reputation or opinion evidence concerning witness's character for truthfulness	Fed. R. Evid. 608(a)	Yes, the witness offering reputation or opinion evidence is offering extrinsic evidence
Contradiction through another witness		Yes, but not for collateral matters; must pass Fed. R. Evid. 403 and will be excluded if the waste of time substantially outweighs the probative value
Self-contradiction through prior statement by a witness	Fed. R. Evid. 613; Sometimes this type of impeachment will fit under Fed. R. Evid. 801(d)(1)(A) and can be used as substantive evidence as well as impeachment	Yes, but not for collateral matters; must pass Fed. R. Evid. 403 and will be excluded if the waste of time substantially outweighs the probative value

§ 4.2   *Impeachment for Bias*

The credibility of a witness may be impeached with evidence of bias. For example, a witness may be found biased if she:

- Is a friend or relative of a party;

- Bears a grudge against a party;

- Has a business relationship with a party;

- Testifies for the government and hopes to receive leniency in a pending criminal case;

- Is being paid by a party to testify as an expert;

- Is a member of an organization that is interested in the lawsuit; or

- Has a financial interest in the outcome of the case.

Evidence of bias may be proved by extrinsic evidence, that is, evidence outside the cross-examination of the witness. Because extrinsic evidence is permitted to demonstrate bias, the cross-examiner is not obliged to "take the answer" of the witness. *See United States v. Abel,* 469 U.S. 45, 52 (1984) (holding that even though not mentioned in the Federal Rules, impeachment for bias exists and may be demonstrated by extrinsic evidence).

EXAMPLE

Wendy the witness testifies that the light was red when the Defendant entered the intersection. On cross-examination, based on Plaintiff's good-faith belief, Plaintiff asks Wendy whether she harbors negative feelings against the Defendant. That question is proper impeachment. If Wendy denies having negative feelings about the Defendant, counsel for the Defendant may call a witness who observed a fight between Wendy and the Defendant. The extrinsic evidence of the fight offered by another witness is permissible to demonstrate bias, so long as it is not deemed unfairly prejudicial or a waste of time that substantially outweighs the impeachment value under Rule 403.

§ 4.3 *Impeachment with Evidence of Impairment: Defects in Perception or Cognition*

Impeachment for impairment includes impeaching the witness's capacity to:

- See;

- Hear;

- Remember; or

- Understand, including evidence of dementia, mental illness, mental handicap, or the effects of a stroke.

Alcohol or drug use on the occasion in question may be used to show the witness's impairment. Defects in the witness's capacity may be shown on cross-examination or by extrinsic testimony.

EXAMPLE

Ron testifies that he saw Hermione steal a book from the library. Evidence that the library was poorly lit at the time of the alleged theft and that Ron's vision is impaired may be used to impeach Ron. If Ron denies that he has vision problems, Hermione's attorney may introduce extrinsic evidence, such as Ron's driver's license that requires Ron to wear glasses, or, subject to Rule 403 waste of time, Ron's ophthalmologist's testimony about Ron's vision.

§ 4.4   *Impeachment Showing the Untruthful Character of a Witness*

[Fed. R. Evid. 608]

As an exception to the general prohibition on character evidence,[1] a witness may be impeached by showing that the witness is generally an untruthful person, Fed. R. Evid. 608. This type of character evidence focuses on the witness's character for *truthfulness*. Thus, a witness may be questioned on cross-examination about the witness's dishonesty in falsifying her résumé or lying on a marriage license application, but not about a bar fight, tortious conduct, or cruelty to animals. Not all bad conduct is dishonest conduct.

Fed. R. Evid. 608 applies to all witnesses in both civil and criminal cases. Under Fed. R. Evid. 608(a), the impeaching party may present opinion and reputation evidence concerning the witness's general character for truthfulness. Such testimony cannot include evidence of specific incidents.

Once a witness's character for truthfulness has been attacked, the opponent may rebut such evidence with reputation and opinion evidence supporting the witness's *good* character for truthfulness, Fed. R. Evid. 608(a). Such good-character testimony cannot be triggered unless the witness's character for honesty has been impugned. Character evidence admitted under Rule 608(a), whether positive or negative, is limited to reputation and opinion evidence.

Fed. R. Evid. 608(b) allows the opposing party to inquire on cross-examination into specific incidents regarding truthfulness of a witness. Subject to a Rule 403 balance, the impeaching party may cross-examine the witness regarding the witness's own specific misconduct reflecting on truthfulness. Also, subject to a Rule 403 balance, the impeaching party may cross-examine the witness about specific conduct regarding truthfulness of another witness about whose character the current witness is testifying.

---

[1]   *See* Fed. R. Evid. 404(a)(3) (exception for witnesses).

Fed. R. Evid. 608(b) does not apply to convicted conduct (to which Rule 609 applies). However, Rule 608(b) does apply to dishonest conduct that, though potentially criminal, was never subject to conviction.

EXAMPLE

Wendy, a key witness in Angela's criminal trial, testifies against Angela. On cross-examination, Angela's attorney may question Wendy about her embezzlement of funds from an employer, for which Wendy was never convicted. Such conduct reflects on Wendy's character for honesty.

The trial court may exclude questions pertaining to specific instances on cross-examination if it finds that its value for impeachment purposes is substantially outweighed by any of the dangers listed in Fed. R. Evid. 403.

If, on cross-examination, the witness denies the misconduct, the cross-examiner must simply accept the witness's answer. No extrinsic evidence concerning the specific instances posed on cross-examination is allowed, Fed. R. Evid. 608(b). The main purpose of this ban on extrinsic evidence is to prevent the waste of time and confusion that would occur if "mini-trials" were held on blemishes in each witness's past.

EXAMPLE

Winifred is called by the Plaintiff to testify about a financial matter. The Defendant wishes to discredit Winifred's testimony. The Defendant may call Claudia to testify that Winifred has a reputation as a liar. The Defendant may also cross-examine Winifred about whether she ever used a fake ID, something for which she was arrested but never convicted. The Plaintiff may then call Sam in rebuttal to testify that in his opinion, Winifred is honest. The Defendant may cross-examine Sam about whether he knows that Winifred used a fake ID. The Defendant is stuck with Sam and Winifred's answers and may not use extrinsic evidence to prove that Winifred did indeed use a fake ID.

§ 4.5   *Impeachment of a Witness with Evidence of Prior Convictions*

[Fed. R. Evid. 609]

Fed. R. Evid. 609 allows parties to impeach witnesses with their prior crimes. The theory is that someone who is antisocial enough to violate social norms and commit a crime might also lie on the witness stand. The witness must have been convicted of a crime for Fed. R. Evid. 609 to apply. A guilty plea counts as a conviction. Rule 609 applies to all witnesses—both in civil and criminal cases—but generally excludes crimes that were pardoned or committed by juveniles.

Extrinsic Evidence of Prior Convictions

When prior convictions qualify for admission under Fed. R. Evid. 609, the proponent of the evidence may prove them with extrinsic evidence, most often by public record. It is quick and easy to introduce conviction records, so there is no waste of time or danger of a mini-trial.

Ten-Year Time Limit [Fed. R. Evid. 609 (b)]

Fed. R. Evid. 609(b) provides a time limit on the use of all types of convictions to impeach witnesses. If more than ten years have passed since the witness's conviction or release from confinement (whichever is later), and the impeachment would be otherwise admissible under Rule 609(a), the Rule requires an extremely strong showing of probative value to admit the conviction. A conviction after the ten-year limit will be admitted only if its probative value, supported by specific facts and circumstances, substantially outweighs its prejudicial effect. Although this rule sounds a lot like Rule 403, it is meaningfully different. In fact, the standard of proof is the mirror opposite of that found in Fed. R. Evid. 403 and highly favors *exclusion* of the evidence. Fed. R. Evid. 609(b) also requires that the proponent provide advance written notice of an intention to introduce a conviction of any type beyond the ten-year limit.

Crimes Involving Dishonesty or False Statement [Fed. R. Evid. 609(a)(2)]

Under Fed. R. Evid. 609(a)(2), crimes of dishonesty or false statement within the ten-year limit *must* be received for impeachment if the witness admitted a dishonest act or false statement or the requisite elements of such a crime were proved. The judge has no discretion under this part of the Rule to admit or reject the evidence under Rule 403 or a variation thereof.[2] Courts may exclude such convictions only if they fall within Fed. R. Evid. 609's limitations regarding timing (Fed. R. Evid. 609(b)), pardon, or juvenile adjudication.

---

[2]   For a critical view of the absence of balancing see Aviva Orenstein, *Honoring Margaret Berger with a Sensible Idea: Insisting that Judges Employ a Balancing Test before Admitting the Accused's Convictions under Federal Rule of Evidence 609(a)(2)*, 74 BROOK. L. REV. 1291 (2010).

For crimes of dishonesty or false statement (*crimen falsi*), the rule does not distinguish between felonies and misdemeanors.

Some crimes are clearly crimes of dishonesty or false statement and indisputably fall under Fed. R. Evid. 609(a)(2), such as:

- Perjury;

- Fraud;

- Tax evasion;

- Embezzlement; and

- Forgery.

The standard requires that the elements of the crime proved (or admitted) establish a dishonest act or false statement. The mere fact that, in retrospect, it appears that the witness lied about committing the crime or that the crime involves a tendency to deny such activity (such as drug abuse or child molestation) does not render it a crime involving false statement or dishonesty.

§ 4.6   *Crimes Punishable for More than One Year That Do Not Involve False Statement or Dishonesty*

[Fed. R. Evid. 609(a)(1)]

Fed. R. Evid. 609(a)(1) admits evidence of the witness's commission of certain serious crimes even if they are not crimes of dishonesty or false statement. Crimes punishable for more than one year may be admitted subject to balancing tests. The witness need not have actually served any time in jail. The rule has two separate standards: one for the accused in a criminal case, and one for all other witnesses.

Prior Felonies by the Accused [Fed. R. Evid. 609(a)(1)(B)]

- An accused may be impeached with a conviction punishable for more than one year if the probative value of the evidence outweighs its prejudicial effect to the accused.

- This test provides greater protection for the accused than the normal Fed. R. Evid. 403 balancing test. It places the burden on the prosecutor to show probative value. For the accused to exclude her conviction for a felony, the prejudice need not "substantially outweigh" probative value but merely outweigh the probative value.

In performing this balance, courts include the following factors:

Favoring Admission of the Prior Crime

o The degree to which the crime reflects on credibility; and

o Whether the accused's credibility is central to the case—the more central, the more probative it is, and the more likely it will be admitted.

Mitigating Against Admission of the Prior Crime

o The remoteness of the prior conviction—the older the conviction, the less probative it is and the less likely it will be admitted;

o The similarity of the prior offense to the offense charged—the more similar the prior conviction is to the current charge, the greater the potential unfair prejudice, and the less likely the court is to admit it. The fear is that instead of using the evidence for its bearing upon the credibility of the accused who is testifying (a legitimate use), the jury will use it for a different, forbidden, propensity inference, reasoning that "because she did it before she probably did it again" (a prohibited use). Even worse, the jury may decide to further punish the accused for the prior crime, disregarding whether the accused actually committed the current crime;

o The extent to which the prior crime will inspire jury disgust or hatred against the accused;

o The extent to which the accused will make the strategic choice not to take the witness stand in order to avoid impeachment with her prior crime. The more the evidence discourages the accused from testifying, the less it should be admitted; and

o Whether the witness's credibility can be explored adequately another way, without using evidence of the witness's prior conviction. If the witness can be impeached convincingly using other means (for example, bias, prior inconsistent statement), the existence of such alternative impeachment methods is a factor weighing against allowing use of the prior conviction.

For All Other Witnesses in both Criminal and Civil Cases [Fed. R. Evid. 609(a)(1)(A)]

- All other witnesses may be impeached with a conviction punishable for more than one year, subject to a Fed. R. Evid. 403 balancing test.

- This places the burden on the party objecting to the impeachment to demonstrate that the probative value of the evidence for impeachment purposes is substantially outweighed by the unfair prejudicial effect (or other dangers listed in Fed. R. Evid. 403). This showing will be difficult to make in most cases.

EXAMPLES

David is charged with assault with a deadly weapon. He takes the stand in his own defense.

Under Fed. R. Evid. 609(a)(2), the Prosecutor may impeach David with his conviction three years ago for making a false statement on a federal application for a pilot's license. This is a crime of dishonesty and will be automatically admitted because it is within the ten-year limit of Fed. R. 609(b).

Under Fed. R. Evid. 609(a)(1)(B), David's conviction five years ago for possession of stolen iPads, a crime punishable for two years, would be subject to the special balancing test for the accused. Reasonable minds could differ about how the special balancing test for the accused should come out in this case. The five-year-old crime is not very recent, but well within the ten-year limit. The prior crime has nothing to do with the current charge, so there is less chance of the jury engaging in the impermissible propensity argument that David tends to commit a certain specific crime. The decision would rest with the trial judge's discretion and would reflect the importance of the Accused's credibility to the case, as well as how much the possession of stolen iPads would reflect on credibility.

Under Fed. R. Evid. 609(a)(1)(A), David's conviction nine years ago for assault with a deadly weapon should probably be excluded. The crime is older—close to the ten-year limit—and the activity is identical to the current crime charged. The jury is likely to make the wrong propensity argument, concluding that David tends to assault people with weapons, instead of the correct propensity argument that David is someone who once broke the law, so he may now be lying. Given the seductiveness of the inappropriate notion that David keeps on committing the same crime and has a propensity to attack others with weapons, it is unlikely that the jury will be able to focus on the correct propensity argument: that David is a felon and hence may also tend to lie.

Pardons; Juvenile Adjudications [Fed. R. Evid. 609(c)–(d)]

Juvenile adjudications and crimes that have been pardoned are generally not admissible. Juvenile convictions may be received, however, if the convicted witness is someone other than the accused and the judge decides that justice requires the impeachment, Fed. R. Evid. 609(d). Evidence of pardoned offenses may be received for impeachment if the witness was convicted of a crime committed after the pardoned crime and the pardon was granted for a reason other than a finding that the witness was innocent, Fed. R. Evid. 609(c).

§ 4.7 *Impeachment by Contradiction*

Impeachment by contradiction occurs when one side uses contradictory evidence to challenge a witness about the underlying facts of her testimony. When proven by extrinsic evidence, impeachment by contradiction must be independently admissible, that is to say, relevant and admissible for the light it sheds on the case, and not just for impeachment.

For example, if Anna testifies that the light was red and witness Vronsky then testifies that it was green, Vronsky has not only offered independent substantive evidence in the case but has also impeached Anna by contradiction. The common law prohibited the use of extrinsic evidence for impeachment by contradiction on collateral matters. The modern approach abandons the "collaterality" framework but, by using a 403 balance, it accomplishes the same goal of forbidding extrinsic evidence to prove impeachment by contraction if such evidence confuses, distracts, or wastes time.

EXAMPLES

Evidence is presented that Wanda observed the accident in question. Wanda testifies that she saw the accident on the way home. In fact, Wanda was on her way to a bar. Extrinsic evidence that Wanda lied when she said that she was on her way home will probably be excluded under Fed. R. Evid. 403 as distracting and a waste of time, because the evidence has no relevance to the substance of the case; it is only relevant to impeach the witness by contradiction. If Wanda had been returning from the bar, rather than heading toward it, her time at the bar might be significant to show impairment and extrinsic evidence would be admissible to impeach her for impairment.

* * *

A witness for the Plaintiff testifies that he had never met the Plaintiff before the litigation. Actually, the witness was closely involved with the Plaintiff in creating a non-profit charity. Extrinsic evidence of the prior relationship is admissible not only because it impeaches the witness by contradiction and makes that witness look mistaken or mendacious, but also because it is relevant to the witness's bias. The relationship between the Plaintiff and the witness may bias the witness in the Plaintiff's favor.

§ 4.8   *Impeachment by Prior Inconsistent Statement*

[Fed. R. Evid. 613]

Witnesses are often impeached with their own out-of-court statements that are inconsistent with their testimony at trial. (This is a form of impeachment by contradiction.) Evidence that the witness said different things at different times casts doubt upon the witness's overall credibility, independent of which statement the finder-of-fact ultimately believes.

Fed. R. Evid. 613(a) provides that, when examining a witness about the witness's prior statement (whether that statement is written or oral), the statement need not be disclosed to the witness but must be disclosed to an adverse party's attorney.

The prior statement by the witness must actually be inconsistent with the witness's current testimony. Under Fed. R. Evid. 613(b), to admit extrinsic evidence of a prior inconsistent statement either (1) the witness must be provided an opportunity to "explain or deny" the statement and the opposing party must be given an opportunity to question the witness; or (2) the interests of justice must require admission of the extrinsic evidence. This rule does not apply to statements of a party-opponent, which require no such foundation.

A prior inconsistent statement may not be proved with extrinsic evidence when the statement is being offered solely for collateral impeachment.

EXAMPLE

Joanne testifies that as she was eating a tuna sandwich, she witnessed Annie reach into the cash register at a restaurant and take a fistful of cash. At trial she described Annie as tall with red hair. Joanne can be impeached with her prior statement (which would be extrinsic evidence) if, in her prior statement, Joanne described Annie as short and blonde. However, Joanne cannot be impeached by her prior statement if it is being used to contradict her statement regarding eating a cheeseburger (instead of a tuna sandwich). The inconsistency about Joanne's description of Annie is independently relevant and central to the case. The inconsistency about the sandwich is collateral and relevant only to contradicting Joanne.

§ 4.9   *Improper Witness Rehabilitation*

No witness can be rehabilitated unless her credibility has been attacked.

One specific application of this rule is that rehabilitation with evidence of good character for truthfulness is not permitted unless the witness's character for truthfulness has been attacked, Fed. R. Evid. 608(a). When character for truthfulness has been attacked in any fashion, the witness can be rehabilitated with reputation or opinion testimony about character for truthfulness. Impeachment for bias is not normally a character attack; therefore, the witness who is impeached with evidence of bias cannot be rehabilitated with testimony about character for truthfulness, but she could be rehabilitated to show absence of bias. The witness can, however, deny bias and offer extrinsic evidence that she is not biased.

Rehabilitation with evidence of prior consistent statements has always been permitted in response to an attack based on fabrication or other improper influence. In 2015, the Federal Rules of Evidence were amended to allow more substantive use of prior consistent statements.[3]

            IMPEACHMENT CHECKLIST

1.   Is there testimony from a witness (either a live witness on the witness stand or an absent declarant's out-of-court statement being used to prove the truth of the matter asserted)?[4]

If yes: Go to Step 2.

---

[3]   *See* § 6.4.

[4]   For the rest of the checklist, I will refer to the live witness only, even though under Fed. R. Evid. 806 impeachment includes impeachment of absent declarants.

If no: There is nothing to impeach.

Impeaching for Bias

2.   Does the witness possess a bias such as:

*   Familial relationship or emotional involvement with a party;

*   Business or financial relationship with a party or interest in the case;

*   A deal with the government to testify and receive leniency in a pending criminal case; or

*   Membership in an organization that is interested in the lawsuit?

If yes: The witness can be impeached for bias. Extrinsic evidence of bias is admissible. Go to Step 3 to see if other forms of impeachment are also appropriate.

If no: Go to Step 3.

Impeaching for Impairment

3.   Is there a potential problem with the witness's ability to perceive, such as:

*   A physical impairment to sight or hearing;

*   A mental defect affecting perception, memory, or understanding; or

*   Substance abuse that interferes with the ability to process information or remember the incident in question?

If yes: The witness can be impeached for sensory perception, and extrinsic evidence of impairment is probably admissible. Go to Step 4 to see if other forms of impeachment are also appropriate.

If no: Go to Step 4.

Impeaching for Character for Truthfulness [Fed. R. Evid. 608]

4.   Does a party believe that a witness has a general characterological problem with truthfulness?

If yes:

*   Opinion and reputation evidence about the witness's character for lack of truthfulness may be presented. Extrinsic evidence in the form of character witnesses may be used to prove the opinion and reputation evidence, Fed. R. Evid. 608(a);

- Additionally, the witness may be cross-examined regarding her own specific instances of lack of truthfulness, but this rule does not apply to convictions, the questioner must take the answer, and extrinsic evidence disputing the witness's answer is not permitted, Fed. R. Evid. 608(b). Go to Step 5.

If no: Go to Step 6.

5. Has the witness's character for truthfulness been attacked? (This mostly concerns a direct attack but can include a line of argument where the only possible conclusion is that the witness is lying.)

If yes:

- Opinion and reputation evidence about a witness's character for truthfulness may be presented to rehabilitate the witness. Extrinsic evidence is allowed to prove the opinion and reputation testimony that the witness is truthful, Fed. R. Evid. 608(a);

- Additionally, a negative character witness may be cross-examined regarding the specific instances of truthfulness, but the questioner must take the answer, and extrinsic evidence disputing the witness's answer is not permitted. Go to Step 6.

If no: Evidence of a witness's character as truthful and honest is not admissible. Go to Step 6.

6. Has a witness, as a character witness, offered reputation or opinion testimony concerning the lack of truthfulness of another witness?

If yes:

- As indicated in Step 5, that witness can be impeached concerning her own character for truthfulness by reputation and opinion evidence and by specific instances on cross-examination;

- That witness's testimony can trigger other witnesses to contradict her, rehabilitating the witness about whom the character witness offered a negative portrayal. These new witnesses could offer opinion and reputation evidence;

- That witness can be asked about specific instances of conduct relating to truthfulness of the witness about whom she provided character evidence. The cross-examiner must take the answer and no extrinsic evidence is permitted. Go to Step 7.

If no: Go to Step 7.

Impeaching with Prior Crimes [Fed. R. Evid. 609]

7. Was a witness the subject of a criminal conviction? (Guilty pleas are convictions; pleas of nolo contendere are not.)

    If yes: Go to Step 8.

    If no: Go to Step 15.

*   Was the crime subject to a pardon or juvenile adjudication?

    If yes: The impeachment is generally inadmissible.

    If no: Go to Step 9.

*   Did the witness's crime involve dishonesty or false statement?

    If yes: Go to Step 10.

    If no: Go to Step 11.

*   Have fewer than ten years passed since the conviction or release from confinement (whichever is later)?

    If yes: Evidence of that crime is admissible against any witness, whether the crime was a felony or a misdemeanor. The trial judge must admit the evidence, and no Rule 403 balancing is allowed. Go to Step 15 to examine whether any other forms of impeachment are also available.

    If no: Go to Step 14.

8. Was the witness convicted of a crime punishable by a year or more in prison? (Note: the rule does not require that time was actually served.)

    If yes: Go to Step 12.

    If no: The witness cannot be impeached with her prior crime. Go to Step 15 to examine whether any other forms of impeachment are available.

9. Have fewer than ten years passed since the conviction or the release from confinement (whichever is later)?

    If yes: Go to Step 13.

    If no: Go to Step 14.

10. Is the witness also the accused in a criminal case?

    If yes: The prior crime is admissible only if the prosecution can demonstrate that the probative value of the impeachment outweighs the unfair prejudice to the accused, Fed. R. Evid.

609(a)(1)(b). Go to Step 15 to explore whether other types of impeachment are available.

If no: Unless the impeachment value fails Rule 403, the prior crime is admissible under Fed. R. Evid. 609(a)(1)(A). The party resisting the impeachment evidence bears the burden of proving that the unfair prejudice of the impeachment substantially outweighs its probative value and should therefore be excluded. Go to Step 15 to examine whether any other forms of impeachment are available.

11. Does the probative value of the impeachment with the conviction that took place after the ten-year limit, supported by specific facts and circumstances, substantially outweigh its prejudicial effect, Fed. R. Evid. 609(b)(1)? (This is a very high threshold for admitting the evidence.)

    If yes: The impeachment evidence is admissible if appropriate notice was given.

    If no: The impeachment evidence is inadmissible under Rule 609. Go to Step 15.

Impeachment by Contradiction

12. Is the proposed impeachment independently admissible extrinsic evidence that contradicts a witness's testimony?

    If yes: The impeachment by contradiction is admissible so long as it is not so tangential that it fails the Rule 403 balance for waste of time. Go to Step 16 to examine whether the witness could be impeached by her own prior inconsistent statement.

    If no: It is not admissible. Go to Step 16 to examine whether the witness could be impeached by her own prior inconsistent statement.

13. Does the proposed impeachment involve a prior inconsistent statement by the witness?

    If yes: The witness may be questioned about her prior statement. Go to Step 17.

    If no: Impeachment for prior statement is not available.

14. Does a party wish to prove the witness's prior inconsistent statement via extrinsic evidence?

    If yes: To admit extrinsic evidence of a prior inconsistent statement, either (1) the witness must be provided an opportunity to "explain or deny" the statement and the opposing party must be given an opportunity to question the witness, or

(2) the interests of justice require admission of the extrinsic evidence.

If no: The witness may be questioned about the statement on cross-examination as Step 16 provides.

ILLUSTRATIVE PROBLEMS

■ PROBLEM 4.1 ■

Q: Audrey is accused of mail fraud. Will the following evidence offered by the prosecution be admissible to impeach Audrey?

(1) Audrey's neighbor's testimony that Audrey has a reputation for being dishonest.

(2) Audrey's boss's testimony that, in his opinion, Audrey is belligerent.

(3) Testimony from a fellow parishioner that Audrey embezzled funds from the church's fund for the homeless.

(4) Audrey's arrest record for mail fraud five years previously.

(5) Evidence that Audrey was convicted for felony elder abuse two years previously.

A: First, we must ascertain whether Audrey will take the stand. If she does not testify, then none of the evidence above can be used for impeachment. Perhaps her arrest for mail fraud (4) might be admissible under a theory of intent or absence of mistake, under Fed. R. Evid. 404(b)(2).[5] If it is, evidence of her prior bad act may be admissible regardless of whether Audrey takes the stand.

If, however, Audrey does testify, the testimony of Audrey's neighbor that Audrey has a reputation for being dishonest (1) is permissible under Fed. R. Evid. 608(a) to demonstrate Audrey's character for lack of truthfulness. Once that evidence is admitted, Audrey may rebut the same with reputation or opinion evidence that she is truthful. The neighbor may also be cross-examined about the neighbor's knowledge of Audrey and about whether she is aware of certain specific instances that demonstrate Audrey's truthfulness.

Audrey's boss's opinion testimony that Audrey is belligerent (2) is not admissible as impeachment evidence. Under Rule 608, witnesses may be impeached for their general credibility and character for truthfulness, but not other character traits. It is unclear how belligerence would even be pertinent to mail fraud, but if it were,

---

[5]   *See* § 2.11 (discussing Fed. R. Evid. 404(b)(2)).

under Fed. R. Evid. 404(a)(2)(A) it could only be introduced to rebut a character claim of non-belligerence initiated by Audrey.

Testimony from a fellow parishioner that Audrey embezzled funds from the church's fund for the homeless (3) is impermissible impeachment. Even though it relates to honesty, the impeachment comes in the form of a specific instance, which may be inquired into only on cross-examination and may not be introduced via extrinsic evidence, Fed. R. Evid. 608. The parishioner could testify as to her opinion of Audrey's truthfulness or as to Audrey's reputation for truthfulness, but could not discuss the specific act unless, in a stunning case of ineptitude, the attorney for the Accused questions the witness about why the witness believes Audrey is untruthful. The policy of this rule is to allow testing of a witness's credibility with specific instances, while avoiding a time-wasting mini-trial regarding evidence that has no direct relationship to the substance of the case. If Audrey takes the stand, she could be asked about the embezzlement on cross-examination, but the Prosecutor would have to accept Audrey's answer, and could not introduce extrinsic evidence.

Audrey's arrest record for mail fraud five years previously (4) is not admissible as impeachment under Fed. R. Evid. 609 because the evidence is of an arrest, not of a conviction. Had Audrey been convicted of mail fraud within the Rule 609(b) ten-year limit, her conviction would have been admitted with no balancing under Rule 609(a)(2). The Judge may permit Audrey to be asked about the underling conduct on cross-examination under Rule 608(b). To admit the evidence, the judge must conduct a Rule 403 balance. Because the crime currently charged and the behavior involved in the arrest are the same (fraud), the unfair prejudice will be very high. Nevertheless, the judge could believe that the question elicits significantly probative evidence about whether Audrey should be believed, and the judge may admit the evidence under Fed. R. Evid. 403 despite the substantial unfair prejudice. It would be wise for Audrey's defense counsel to make a motion in limine to resolve this question in advance. It might even influence whether Audrey takes the stand. However, the arrest record itself is not admissible as impeachment because it is extrinsic evidence of a specific instance forbidden by Rule 608(b).

Finally, evidence that Audrey was convicted for elder abuse two years previously (5) could possibly be admitted as impeachment under Fed. R. 609(a)(1)(B), which has a special test for felony convictions of the accused. Under Rule 609(a)(1)(B), in order for the prior crime of the accused to be admitted, the Prosecutor must demonstrate that the probative value outweighs the unfair prejudice to the accused. The conviction falls within the 609(b) time limit, and it is fairly recent, which raises the probative value for impeachment. Credibility may be central to the mail fraud case, but based on the facts, there are apparently other ways to investigate Audrey's truthfulness and credibility. Furthermore, the probative value of elder abuse to credibility is questionable. Certainly, the unfair prejudice is very high and may lead the jury to dislike Audrey and behave irrationally. In my opinion, this evidence should fail that special test. However, the trial court would not abuse its wide discretion if it permitted the impeachment. This is another case in which it would be wise for Audrey's defense counsel to make a motion in limine to resolve this question in advance. It might even influence whether Audrey takes the stand, which should be another important factor in the judge's consideration.

■ PROBLEM 4.2 ■

Q: Erica is called as an expert witness for the defense in a products liability case. After testifying about the safety of the vehicle's design, she is cross-examined, including the following exchange:

Plaintiff's attorney: Isn't it true that you accepted a lucrative consulting position with the Defendant automaker before making your report?

Erica: No, that is not true. The Defendant was happy with my thorough report and hired me *after* I rendered my expert opinion in this case. My new position in no way influenced my expert opinion.

Was the question proper? May the Plaintiff's attorney contradict Erica with an email demonstrating that she accepted the consulting position with the Defendant before her expert report was complete?

A: The question was proper on cross-examination and the Plaintiff's attorney may impeach Erica with extrinsic evidence concerning when she accepted the position. The type of impeachment involved in the question is impeachment for bias, which permits extrinsic evidence. We know from the Supreme Court case *United States v. Abel* that impeachment for bias is allowed (even though it is not explicitly stated in the rules) and that a party may prove bias with extrinsic evidence. In this example, the attorney is not impeaching Erica with Rule 608 character impeachment for lack of truthfulness, which does not allow extrinsic evidence. That is, the attorney is not saying that Erica has the character trait of someone who lies (as would be the argument under Rule 608) but instead is saying that her testimony may have been influenced by the new position she accepted before she rendered her expert opinion.

POINTS TO REMEMBER

- Impeaching a witness means discrediting that witness's testimony by presenting flaws in either the witness or her testimony.

- Only a witness who actually testifies or a declarant whose out-of-court hearsay statement is offered for its truth can be impeached. An accused who exercises her Fifth Amendment right not to testify cannot be impeached with prior crimes or dishonest propensities.

- The credibility of a witness may be impeached by *any* party, including the party who called the witness, Fed. R. Evid. 607.

- Types of impeachment include:

  o Bias;

  o Sensory Perception;

  o Character for Truthfulness;

  o Prior Convicted Crimes; and

  o Impeachment by Contradiction, including impeachment by prior statement by the witness.

- All types of the above impeachment may be performed on cross-examination. Some types of impeachment limit the use of extrinsic testimony.

Bias [no rule in the Federal Rules]

- Impeachment for bias does not necessarily mean that the witness is dishonest or unfair. It is used to show that the witness, knowingly or not, might be influenced because of her beliefs, personal interests, or relationship with a party.

- Federal Rules of Evidence do not have a specific rule for impeachment for bias, but the United States Supreme Court has recognized it and allows extrinsic evidence to show bias, *United States v. Abel,* 469 U.S. 45 (1984).

Sensory Perception [no rule in the Federal Rules]

- Witnesses can be impeached for their sensory perception, such as poor eyesight, limited hearing, or cognitive impairment.

- To impeach a witness for addiction to or use of mind-altering substances, courts generally require that the impeaching party demonstrate that the witness was under the influence of the mind-altering substance at the time the witness made her observations.

- Although the Supreme Court has not spoken on the subject, extrinsic evidence of sensory perception is probably allowed.

Impeachment for Character of Lack of Truthfulness and Rehabilitation for Truthfulness [Fed. R. Evid. 608]

- A witness, in both civil and criminal cases, may be impeached by reputation or opinion evidence regarding her truthfulness.

- If, and only if, a witness's character for truthfulness has been attacked, such impeachment can be rebutted with reputation and opinion evidence supporting the witness's good character for truthfulness.

- Impeachment based on specific instances of dishonesty is limited under Fed. R. Evid. 608(b) to cross-examination. The questioner must accept the witness's answer, and extrinsic evidence is not permitted. Questions on cross-examination as to specific instances of dishonesty may be excluded by the trial court if their impeachment value is substantially outweighed by any of the dangers listed in Fed. R. Evid. 403.

Impeachment with Prior Convictions [Fed. R. Evid. 609]

- Any witness in a civil or criminal case may be impeached with certain prior crimes for which she was convicted or pleaded guilty.

- Such prior crimes may be demonstrated using extrinsic evidence.

- Under Fed. R. Evid. 609(a)(2), any crime of dishonesty or false statement (felony or misdemeanor) that falls within the ten-year limit must be received for impeachment. Some crimes that fall in this category are perjury, fraud, tax evasion, embezzlement, and forgery.

- Fed. R. Evid. 609(a)(1) admits crimes punishable for more than one year. The witness need not have actually served any time in prison. Impeachment for these crimes is subject to one of two balancing tests:

  o *Balancing test for the accused in a criminal case:* The prosecution must demonstrate that the probative value of the impeachment outweighs its prejudicial effect to the accused, Fed. R. Evid. 609(a)(1)(B).

  o *Balancing test for all other witnesses:* The party opposing the impeachment must demonstrate that it fails the traditional Rule 403 balancing test, Fed. R. Evid. 609(a)(1)(A).

- If more than ten years have passed since the witness's conviction or release from confinement (whichever is later), the Rule requires an extremely strong showing of probative value, admitting such impeachment only if its probative value, supported by specific facts and circumstances, substantially outweighs its prejudicial effect. In addition, the proponent of the impeachment must give the adverse party advance written notice of an intention to introduce a conviction of any type beyond the ten-year limit.

Impeachment by Contradiction

- Impeachment by contradiction uses contradictory evidence to challenge a witness about the substance of her testimony.

- When offered via extrinsic evidence, the contradictory evidence must be independently admissible; in other words, it must be relevant to the overall case, not just to the contradiction of this particular witness, and it must pass hearsay and other rules of exclusion.

- Impeachment by contradiction must pass the Rule 403 balancing test. If the impeachment is too tangential or collateral, the waste of time it engenders may substantially outweigh the probative value of the impeachment.

Prior Inconsistent Statements [Fed. R. Evid. 613]

- When examining a witness about the witness's prior inconsistent statement (whether that statement is written or oral), the examiner need not disclose the statement to the witness but must upon request disclose it to an adverse party's attorney.

- To admit extrinsic evidence of a prior inconsistent statement other than a statement by a party-opponent, either:

  (1) The witness must be provided an opportunity to "explain or deny" the statement, and the opposing party must be given an opportunity to question the witness; or

  (2) The interest of justice must require admission of the extrinsic evidence.

CHAPTER 5

Definition of Hearsay

§ 5.1 What Qualifies as a Statement?

Under the Federal Rules, a statement is an assertion—oral, written, or nonverbal—by which the declarant intends to communicate, Fed. R. Evid. 801(a). People make statements when they talk and write, but they can also make statements nonverbally, such as when they nod or make a rude gesture to a fellow driver. Although there is some debate, animals and machines do not make statements for hearsay purposes.

§ 5.2 When Is a Statement Hearsay?

A statement is hearsay if it is made outside of court and is being offered to show the truth of the matter asserted in the statement, Fed. R. Evid. 801(c). For evidence to be considered hearsay, it must: (1) be a statement, (2) have been made out-of-court, and (3) be used by the party offering the statement to show that the matter asserted by the statement is actually true.

EXAMPLES

In response to a question about who saw the accident, Darlene raises her hand. The hand-raising gesture is assertive conduct, and, if offered by a witness to show that Darlene saw the accident, would be hearsay.

* * *

To prove that it was raining, the proponent offers into evidence the fact that the witness saw pedestrians walking outside with open umbrellas. Because the pedestrians did not intend to make a statement by opening the umbrellas, the evidence is not hearsay.

§ 5.3 Who Is the Declarant?

The declarant is the person making the statement. Sometimes the declarant and the witness are the same person (and the witness is just repeating her own out-of-court statement). More often, the declarant is not the same person as the witness and the witness repeats the out-of-court statement of the declarant. The declarant may not be in court at all, may testify in court, or may be in court but otherwise unavailable because of an asserted privilege or refusal to testify.

§ 5.4   *What Does "Out-of-Court" Mean?*

By "out-of-court," the hearsay rule means outside of the very court proceeding in which the evidence is being offered. A statement in a different court is still considered an "out-of-court" statement. A deposition taken in the case is an out-of-court statement. Testimony from another case or even the same case on retrial is also considered an out-of-court statement.

§ 5.5   *When Is a Statement Being Used for the Truth of the Matter Asserted?*

A statement is being used for the truth of the matter asserted when the finder-of-fact (judge or jury) is being asked to believe that the statement itself is actually true. Focus on the statement itself, not on the broader theory of the case or on the larger principle that the piece of evidence would help prove.

EXAMPLE

Wanda heard an out-of-court statement from the Declarant, Donald, who said, "Abigail robbed the bank." If Wanda testifies and repeats Donald's out-of-court statement to prove its truth—that is to say, that Abigail did indeed rob the bank—then the statement is hearsay. Wanda has no personal knowledge of what Abigail has done; all she knows is what Donald told her. The proponent of the evidence is asking the finder-of-fact to believe that the statement is actually true, and therefore Wanda's testimony is hearsay.

Under the Federal Rules of Evidence, nonverbal conduct is hearsay if it was intended as an assertion and is being offered to prove the truth of the matter asserted.

§ 5.6   *What Are the Reasons for the Hearsay Rule?*

Traditionally, hearsay has been excluded because it is considered inferior evidence, often lacking assurances of reliability, such as:

- An in-court oath;

- The ability of the fact-finder to observe the witness's demeanor;

- The possible prosecution of the declarant for perjury; and

- The opportunity for cross-examination, which can illuminate problems in the witness's testimony that cannot be addressed adequately if the information is second-hand.

Although not identical, the purposes of hearsay and the Confrontation Clause of the Sixth Amendment are closely connected.[1] The opportunity to confront and cross-examine the witness presents the best protection against faulty memory and coerced or manufactured testimony. Also, the use of hearsay against an accused could lead to abuse whereby a party manufactures evidence or pressures a declarant who is not available to be questioned in court.

§ 5.7   *Out-of-Court Statements That Do Not Fit the Hearsay Definition*

Not all out-of-court statements qualify as hearsay because not all out-of-court statements are being offered for their truth. The number of ways an out-of-court statement can be used for something other than its truth is infinite.

The common law developed classic categories that assist in identifying statements that look like hearsay but do not fit the definition. These categories of out-of-court statements that are *not* being used for the truth of the matter asserted are still useful today.

Circumstantial Evidence of State of Mind of the Declarant

Within this category are utterances that are not hearsay because they can be used to show the declarant's state of mind circumstantially, without the finder-of-fact needing to accept the declarant's assertion in the statement as true.

EXAMPLE

In class, your evidence professor—who is not Lady Gaga, though she is wearing a suit made of meat—announces: "My name is Lady Gaga." At your professor's commitment hearing, the Dean, who wishes to have your evidence professor committed to a mental institution, offers the statement to demonstrate mental incompetence. The Dean

---

[1]   The Confrontation Clause of the Sixth Amendment to the United States Constitution provides that "in all criminal prosecutions, the Accused shall enjoy the right . . . to be confronted with the witnesses against him." *See* Chapter 8 (discussing confrontation).

may testify about the statement because although it was out-of-court, it is not being offered for its truth, and therefore it is not hearsay. When offering the evidence to prove incompetence, the Dean is not asking the finder-of-fact to believe the statement is actually true—that your evidence professor is Lady Gaga—just that your evidence professor said it.

Observe that the "truth of the matter asserted" is judged by analyzing the statement itself. Is the finder-of-fact being asked to believe that your evidence professor is Lady Gaga? If so, that is a hearsay use. If not, the evidence is being offered for another purpose: to demonstrate circumstantial (or indirect) evidence of state of mind. The finder-of-fact is being asked in this case to infer that your professor is crazy. That is *not,* however, the truth of the matter asserted by the Declarant in making the statement (even though that is what the statement implies, and the statement supports the theory of the case). Had your professor simply announced, "I'm having mental health issues," then her statement used to prove that she is mentally incapacitated would be a hearsay use.

One mistake students sometimes make with hearsay is to think too broadly about the nature of the matter asserted. Sloppy thinking can lead to the following mistaken analysis: "The Professor's statement is being used to assert the Professor's incompetence, therefore it is hearsay to prove incompetence." The mistake arises because the student thought about the theory of the case and decided that because the out-of-court statement supports the Dean's argument, it must be hearsay. The mistake arises from the failure to focus on the statement itself. The student is confusing relevance (and of course the statement has to relate to the theory of the case) with hearsay. To make the hearsay determination, focus on what the statement actually asserts. Next, determine whether the finder-of-fact is being asked to believe that that assertion is actually true.

Effect on the Listener

If a statement is not offered for the truth of what it asserts, but to show its effect upon the hearer or reader of the statement, then it is not hearsay. In other words, the out-of-court statement is being offered not to prove that the assertion is actually true but to demonstrate the effect on the person who heard it, such as displaying the listener's knowledge or elucidating the listener's intent. Be careful: you must be able to articulate a theory of relevance concerning why anyone would care about the effect on the listener.

EXAMPLE

In a lawsuit where a Plaintiff sues a homeowner after tripping on some allegedly rotted boards, the Plaintiff wishes to provide evidence that a neighbor had said to the homeowner a week before the accident: "The floorboards on your front porch have rotted." This out-of-court statement would be hearsay to prove that the floor was actually rotted. It is not hearsay to show that the homeowner, upon hearing this statement, was put on notice of the condition of the boards. Such notice is an example of effect on the listener, a non-hearsay use of the statement.

Impeachment

Sometimes an out-of-court statement is offered not for its truth but merely to impeach a witness on the stand with her own prior statement. The out-of-court statement is not being offered to show that the out-of-court statement was true, but just to show that it was made and that the witness has been inconsistent and arguably unreliable.

EXAMPLE

A witness may testify that the light was green. This is clearly not hearsay because it is an in-court statement. At the scene of the accident, however, that same witness stated that the light was red. The party impeaching the witness cannot use the out-of-court statement to prove that the light was red (even though one might suppose it more reliable because of its proximity in time to the accident). The statement can be introduced for another purpose, however: to show the uncertainty, capriciousness, and perhaps even mendacity of the witness. Green? Red? Which is it? The impeachment shows that the witness is unreliable. Although the finder-of-fact cannot use the prior out-of-court statement made at the scene of the accident as proof that the light was red (that would be an impermissible hearsay use of the statement), the finder-of-fact can use the statement to discredit the witness's in-court assertion that the light was green.

Verbal Acts

Verbal acts are actions with words. They fall into two categories:

(1) The words themselves do not matter, just the fact of speech. For instance, a mother knocks on a teenager's door at 3:00 p.m. on a Saturday afternoon and asks, "Are you alive?" The surly answer, "No, I'm dead," conveys just as much information regarding the vitality of the child as the more polite, "Yes, thanks, Mom. I'm OK. I'm just doing my Advanced Placement U.S. History homework." The fact of speech, not its content, conveys that the teenager is alive.

(2) Legally operative language whereby the words themselves have legal consequences. In essence, the speaker is acting with words, creating a legal right, duty, or status. This second category includes verbal parts of acts, or speech that is necessary to explain the legal consequences of the action.

EXAMPLE

In an action for defamation, Peter introduces Don's statement that "Peter is a slimeball and a plagiarist" to prove that Don defamed him. The statement is not hearsay, but rather a verbal act. The only way to defame someone is with words. The act of defamation is performed by Don's statement. This example does not qualify as hearsay under hearsay's classic definition: When Peter introduces Don's defamatory statement, Peter is not asking the finder-of-fact to believe that the statement is true (in fact, Peter strenuously argues that it is false). Peter just wants to prove that Don made the statement.

Sometimes legally operative language looks a lot like hearsay. You could be forgiven for finding this confusing. In deciding whether a statement is a verbal act, ask yourself whether the words are *necessary* to effect a change in legal status. For instance, stating the response "I do," in a legal marriage ceremony transforms a single person to a spouse. The statement "I got married yesterday" has no similar effect on legal status. Similarly, "Here is the rent money for August" is a verbal part of an act (without the verbiage it would be unclear what the purpose of the check was) and is not hearsay if introduced to prove payment. "Yesterday, I paid my rent for August" is an out-of-court statement describing a past event, not creating a legal status via a verbal act. This latter statement is not part of a legal event; it is hearsay to prove the payment of the rent.

Be on the lookout for statements that have independent legal significance. Some examples include:

- "I accept your offer." (Language of contract formation)

- "Sold to the gentlemen in the third row." (Auction)

- "Please accept this $100 as my gift." (Clarifying that the transfer of money is not a loan, bribe, or repayment)

- "If you do not steal the exam key, I will kill your cat." (Extortion)

- "Hand over your wallet." (Theft)

- "Sure, you can borrow the car." (Entrustment)

- "Please join our merry band of bank robbers. You could drive the getaway car." (Formation of a conspiracy)

 HEARSAY DEFINITION CHECKLIST

1. Is there an out-of-court statement, such as a written or oral statement or a non-verbal gesture?

    If yes: Go to Step 2.

    If no: There is no hearsay problem. For instance, a photograph is not covered by the hearsay rule.

2. Did the declarant intend to make an assertion?

    If yes: Go to Step 3.

    If no: There is no hearsay problem under the Federal Rules.

3. Is the out-of-court statement being offered to prove the truth of the matter asserted? In other words, looking at the statement and the statement alone, is the finder-of-fact being asked to believe that the statement is actually true?

    If yes: The statement is hearsay. You have to look to exceptions and exemptions in order to admit the statement. Go to Step 4.

    If no: The finder-of-fact is not being asked to believe that the statement itself is actually true, and the statement is not being offered for its hearsay use.

4. Before you determine that a statement is hearsay (Step 3 above), double check whether it falls under one of these classic categories:

    - Circumstantial evidence of the state of mind of the speaker;

    - Effect on listener;

- Impeachment of a witness with an inconsistent prior statement; or

- Verbal acts.

If yes: It is not within the hearsay definition.

If no: It is within the hearsay definition.

ILLUSTRATIVE PROBLEMS

■ PROBLEM 5.1 ■

Q: Wolf Blitzer, the CNN newscaster, is called to testify about a physical fight between Bill O'Reilly and Al Franken. Wolf testifies as follows at trial:

> *Question*: Mr. Blitzer, you've testified that Al stomped on Bill's cigar. What happened next?
>
> *Blitzer*: Al picked up a volume of the *U.S. Reporter* and threw it at Bill O'Reilly.
>
> *Question*: Did Bill O'Reilly commit any violence against Al to precipitate the throwing?
>
> *Blitzer*: No, sir, he did not.

On cross-examination, the attorney for Al Franken wishes to introduce the following statement made by Wolf Blitzer on CNN:

> This is Wolf Blitzer from the Capital Grill & Library reporting to you about the ongoing conflict between Al Franken and Bill O'Reilly. You can see the police are on the scene. Moments ago, Al Franken extinguished Bill O'Reilly's cigar with his bare hands. Bill O'Reilly appeared furious. Bill O'Reilly then picked up a statue of Moses bearing the Ten Commandments. He flung it at Al. He made a direct hit! Al staggered. Al approached the bookshelf, grabbed a volume of the *U.S. Reporter*, and hurled it at Bill O'Reilly. Back to you, Greta.

Bill O'Reilly's attorney objects that the CNN report is hearsay. How should the court rule?

A: The court should overrule the objection. The statement on CNN would be hearsay to prove that Bill hurled the statue, because that would be offering it for the truth of the matter asserted. The CNN segment could be offered, however, for the non-hearsay purpose of impeachment. That is, the statement indicates that Wolf Blitzer's account of events has changed, which demonstrates his unreliability as a witness. Upon request, the court should provide a limiting instruction, telling the jury to use the out-of-court statement for impeachment and not for its truth. Per Fed. R. Evid. 613,[2] Wolf must have the opportunity to explain the contradiction, but Wolf need not be presented with his out-of-court statement in advance.

■ PROBLEM 5.2 ■

Q: The police, pursuant to warrant, raid Donald's apartment and find a pair of diamond and opal earrings worth $52,000 that were reported stolen. Donald is charged with harboring stolen goods. At trial, Donald claims that he did not know the earrings were stolen, and hence did not possess the appropriate mens rea for the crime. Donald proposes to testify that his friend, Sam, had given him the earrings and that Sam said, "Please hold onto these earrings—I bought them at Tiffany's, and I'm saving them as an anniversary surprise for my darling wife." The prosecution objects to the testimony of what Sam said on hearsay grounds. How should the judge rule?

A: Sam's statement is certainly out-of-court and would be hearsay to prove that he bought the earrings at Tiffany's (or for that matter that Sam's wife is darling). It would not be hearsay if offered to show the effect on the listener. Donald may offer the statement not to prove that it is true (by now, he probably realizes that the earrings were stolen and that he was an idiot for holding onto them). Instead, Donald offers it to show that the statement was made and that the statement—whether true or not—had an effect on Donald, who innocently believed that the earrings were honestly purchased.

■ PROBLEM 5.3 ■

Q: Vincent and Zenobia are looking to buy marijuana. Vincent says that he'll go to Alfred, a local marijuana dealer, to buy some. Zenobia warns Vincent, "I'd be careful—Alfred has a reputation for beating up customers and taking their money without giving them the pot." Vincent ignores Zenobia's warnings. Four hours later Vincent is found badly beaten near Alfred's apartment complex. May the Prosecutor introduce Zenobia's statement?

A: Zenobia's statement is hearsay to prove that Alfred tends to beat up customers. (It is also probably inadmissible character evidence.) Zenobia's out-of-court statement cannot be reasonably offered to show the effect on the listener. It is hard to see how the effect on Vincent would be relevant. There is no such defense to assault and battery that the Victim should have known that the Accused was dangerous or that the Victim was incautious. Therefore, the only

---

[2] *See* § 4.8.

relevant use is the impermissible hearsay use, so it will not be admissible.

POINTS TO REMEMBER

- Hearsay is an out-of-court statement used to prove that the statement itself is actually true.

- Statements can be written, oral, or non-verbal.

- The person making the out-of-court statement is called the declarant.

- To make a statement, the declarant must *intend* to communicate.

- A statement is "out-of-court" unless it is made under oath at the very trial in which the statement is offered. An out-of-court statement includes statements made in depositions, testimony in other cases, and testimony in previous proceedings in the same case.

- Not all out-of-court statements are hearsay. Some out-of-court statements are not offered for their truth but for another purpose and are therefore not hearsay. Examples of out-of-court statements *not* offered for their truth include:

  o Circumstantial (indirect) evidence of a declarant's state of mind;

  o Statements offered to show their effect on the listener;

  o Impeachment; and

  o Verbal acts.

CHAPTER 6

Prior Statements by Witnesses; Statements by Party-Opponents

§ 6.1 *Introduction to the Doublespeak of Rule 801(d) "Not Hearsay" Exemptions*

Fed. R. Evid. 801(d) addresses two types of out-of-court statements:

- Prior statements by witnesses, Fed. R. Evid. 801(d)(1); and

- Prior statements by a party, offered by an opposing party, Fed. R. Evid. 801(d)(2).

When offered for their truth, both types of statements fit squarely within the traditional definition of hearsay. Nevertheless, the rule confusingly designates all of the out-of-court statements in Rule 801(d) as "not hearsay." Classic examples of statements that do not fit the hearsay definition (circumstantial evidence of the speaker's state of mind, effect on the listener, impeachment, and verbal acts) are not hearsay at all because they are not being offered for the truth of the matter asserted.[1] By contrast, Rule 801(d) statements are offered for their truth and fit the common-law definition of hearsay. They are "not hearsay" by Congressional fiat, and the rules functionally operate as exceptions.

For statements falling within Rule 801(d), we use the term "exemption" or refer to them as "not hearsay under Rule 801(d)" to distinguish them from the exceptions under Rules 803, 804, and 807.

---

[1] *See* § 5.7 (discussing statements offered not for the truth of the matter asserted).

§ 6.2   *Prior Statements of Witnesses Generally*

[Fed. R. Evid. 801(d)(1)]

Generally, the hearsay rule applies to out-of-court statements even when the witness and the declarant are the same person. Yet there are many ways that a witness's prior statement, though hearsay under the common-law definition, may nevertheless be admissible. The witness's prior statement may not be hearsay at all if it is offered just for its impeachment value and not to prove the truth of the matter asserted.[2] Alternatively, even if offered for its truth, it may fall under one of the many traditional hearsay exceptions of Fed. R. Evid. 803 or 804, or under the Rule 807 residual exception. Finally, it may also fall under one of the special exemptions created by Fed. R. Evid. 801(d)(1), detailed below. The Rule 801(d)(1) exemption applies to some out-of-court statements by a witness and only if the declarant is currently available as a witness and is subject to cross-examination. If the declarant is unavailable, or is not subject to cross-examination, Rule 801(d)(1) does not apply.

§ 6.3   *Prior Inconsistent Statements*

[Fed. R. Evid. 801(d)(1)(A)]

What if a live witness testifying under oath contradicts her prior out-of-court statement? There are two separate bases for receiving the prior inconsistent statement of a witness: (1) Rule 801(d)(1)(A) and (2) common-law impeachment. Common-law impeachment can only be offered to contradict the witness and show that the witness is unreliable; it cannot be used to prove the truth of the out-of-court statement. If the prior inconsistent statement falls under Rule 801(d)(1)(A), however, then it is admissible both as impeachment *and* as substantive evidence; that is to say, the finder-of-fact may choose to believe and rely on the witness's out-of-court statement instead of her in-court testimony.

Rule 801(d)(1)(A) limits the type of a witness's prior out-of-court statement that can be used for its truth. It designates the prior out-of-court statement by a witness as "not hearsay" (and hence able to be used for its truth) only if:

- The declarant testifies at the current trial or hearing;

- The declarant is subject to cross-examination concerning the prior statement at the current trial or hearing;

---

[2]   *See* § 5.5 (When is a Statement Being Used for the Truth of the Matter Asserted?).

- The prior out-of-court statement is *inconsistent* with the declarant's current testimony;

- The prior out-of-court statement was given under oath subject to the penalty of perjury; and

- The out-of-court prior statement was made at a trial, hearing, or other proceeding, or in a deposition.

Congress vigorously debated the scope of Rule 801(d)(1)(A). The current rule requires significant formality in order for the prior out-of-court statements covered by the rule: they must be under oath, subject to penalty of perjury, and made at some sort of formal hearing or deposition. However, the prior out-of-court statement did not have to be subject to cross-examination at the time it was made. Therefore, grand-jury testimony, which is made under oath and subject to penalty for perjury at a prior proceeding, but is not cross-examined, falls within Rule 801(d)(1)(A) if it is inconsistent with the current in-court testimony. One benefit of these formal requirements is that the prior statement is part of an official record and there will be little debate about its content.

If an inconsistent prior statement does not meet all of the 801(d)(1)(A) criteria, then it can be used for common-law impeachment only. For impeachment purposes, the inconsistent statement is offered only to demonstrate the unreliability of the witness. The fact that the witness said different things at different times reflects poorly on the witness's credibility, whether or not the out-of-court statement was true.

EXAMPLE

In 2012, on a street corner in Bloomington, Indiana, a van hit a car, killing the driver of the car. David, a bystander who witnessed the accident, made two statements:

(1) At the scene of the accident, after he had calmed down, David said to Wynona: "The van ran through the red light." Wynona is prepared to testify to David's statement.

(2) In 2013, at the criminal trial for the van driver's drunk driving, David testified (consistent with his on-the-scene statement) that the van failed to stop at the red light. The transcript of that previous trial is available.

Imagine that in a 2014 civil trial for the wrongful death of the driver of the car, David surprises everyone and testifies that the light was green for the van.

David's two prior inconsistent statements could be used in the wrongful death suit. The first statement, made at the scene, would not qualify for admission under Rule 801(d)(1)(A) and would not be admissible for its truth (that the van actually ran through a red light). The statement made at the scene was not made under oath or at a "proceeding" and hence does not qualify for admission under Rule 801(d)(1)(A). That first statement could, however, be admitted for the limited, non-hearsay purpose of impeachment: to demonstrate that David is an inconsistent and unreliable witness. Such a prior inconsistent statement is offered *solely to impeach*—not to prove the truth of the matter asserted.

The second statement, made at the criminal trial under oath and subject to penalty of perjury at a previous trial, fits within Rule 801(d)(1)(A). It is therefore admissible as substantive evidence and may be offered for its truth. The jury is free to disbelieve David's current testimony and instead believe his former statement at the criminal trial for drunk driving.

If only the first statement were available at the 2014 wrongful-death trial, and that statement constituted the only evidence of the van's negligence, then the judge would have to grant a judgment as a matter of law in favor of the Defendant. The Plaintiff would have no affirmative evidence to offer. The first out-of-court statement presents no substantive evidence in the Plaintiff's case; it can only be used to impeach the witness.

§ 6.4   *Prior Consistent Statements*

[Fed. R. Evid. 801(d)(1)(B)]

Prior consistent statements by an available witness are admissible as both common-law rehabilitation and substantive evidence. Under Fed. R. Evid. 801(d)(1)(B)(i), the prior consistent statement made by the witness can be admitted "to rebut an express or implied charge that the declarant recently fabricated it or acted from improper influence or motive." Questions of timing arise regarding rebutting charges of improper influence or motive. A prior consistent statement is not useful to rebut a claim of fabrication, undue influence, or improper motive if the statement was made *after* the alleged motive or influence arose.

EXAMPLE

Charlene testifies against her alleged co-conspirator Andrea. Andrea may attack Charlene's credibility at trial on the grounds that the witness Charlene is shading her testimony in exchange for the recommendation of a reduced prison sentence from the prosecution. Any prior consistent statement that Charlene made *after* she had acquired hope for leniency has little probative weight and will not be permitted for rehabilitative purposes or as substantive evidence under Fed. R. Evid. 801(d)(1)(B)(i).

The Supreme Court addressed this timing issue in *Tome v. United States*, 513 U.S. 150 (1995), holding that prior consistent statements rebutting charges or improper influence or motive are only admissible under Rule 801(d)(1)(B) if they were made *before* the alleged recent fabrication or improper influence or motive arose.

The rule was recently revised to include other rehabilitative uses, such as to explain a prior inconsistency or to rebut a charge of faulty recollection. Fed. R. Evid. 801(d)(1)(B)(ii). This revision has no effect on the timing requirement.

You would be forgiven for wondering what the big deal is about prior consistent statements. Most of the time, such out-of-court statements are repetitive of the in-court testimony, innocuous, and only objectionable as a waste of time. The witness is testifying now and she said the same thing before—big yawn. However, in some types of cases, especially those involving child victims, repetition of out-of-court statements can be very powerful. For instance, in *Tome*, the child made a poor witness, but all the adults (the mother, the police, the investigator, the babysitter, etc.) who repeated the child's consistent out-of-court statements made compelling witnesses and deeply influenced the jury by recounting the witness's prior consistent out-of-court statements.

§ 6.5 *Prior Statements of Identification*

[Fed. R. Evid. 801(d)(1)(C)]

A witness's prior statement of identification (which can be reported by others, such as police officers, who witnessed the identification) is "not hearsay" and is admissible under Rule 801(d)(1)(C). A prior identification is often more reliable than the identification made later at trial because it was made closer in time and because subsequent information may have infected a later identification.

As with other prior witness statements governed by Rule 801(d)(1), prior identification statements are admissible only if the declarant testifies in court and is subject to cross-examination concerning the prior identification. A witness's out-of-court identification can be admitted at trial either through that witness's own testimony or through the testimony of another witness who observed the out-of-court identification.

EXAMPLE

A witness who identified the Accused from a photo array can testify to that fact, and the testimony can be corroborated by the police officer who observed the identification. The testimony about the prior identification will be admissible even if the witness, because of a lack of current memory, could not make an identification in court. Furthermore, if the witness cannot remember, or perhaps even denies, having made the out-of-court identification, another witness can testify to the prior identification. The original Declarant need not remember or support her out-of-court statement, but must be available to be cross-examined about it, including about the conditions under which it was a made.

§ 6.6   *Statements of a Party-Opponent*

[Fed. R. Evid. 801(d)(2)(A)–(E)]

Essentially, anything a party says or does is admissible if offered by the party's opponent. Exceptions arise in criminal cases where the accused did not receive *Miranda* warnings about her right to remain silent. Additionally, some statements by party-opponents are banned by other evidence rules such as Fed. R. Evid. 408 (compromise) or 407 (remedial repair).

A party's personal statement falls under Rule 801(d)(2)(A); others can also make a statement on the party's behalf. Such party-statements may only be offered by an opposing party. When so offered, parties' statements, following the organization of Rule 801(d), are "not hearsay" and are therefore admissible for their truth. They include:

(1)   The opposing party's own statement, Fed. R. Evid. 801(d)(2)(A);

(2)   A statement that the opposing party appears to adopt or believe is true, Fed. R. Evid. 801(d)(2)(B);

(3) A statement by a person authorized by the opposing party to make a statement concerning the subject, Fed. R. Evid. 801(d)(2)(C);

(4) A statement by the opposing party's agent or servant concerning a matter within the scope of the agency or employment, made during the existence of the relationship, Fed. R. Evid. 801(d)(2)(D); and

(5) A statement by a co-conspirator of an opposing party during the course and in furtherance of the conspiracy, Fed. R. Evid. 801(d)(2)(E).

To qualify under Rule 801(d)(2), the statement does not have to be against the party's self-interest when made. Nor does the statement have to be based upon personal knowledge. This rule applies to party statements only and not to statements by victims in criminal cases, who are not parties. The opposing party, not the party who made the statement, may introduce it.

EXAMPLES

In a suit over a head injury that occurred in a private swimming pool, the Defendant says, "It wasn't my fault—I told the Plaintiff not to dive." Although not against interest when made, the out-of-court statement is admissible if offered by the opposing party for any purpose, such as to show that the Plaintiff was an invited guest, swimming with the Defendant's knowledge.

* * *

A pedestrian is hit by a truck. The truck owner calls the pedestrian in the hospital and says, "It was all my driver's fault." That statement is exempted from the hearsay rule and admissible if offered by a party-opponent—even if the owner had no personal knowledge regarding the accident. There is no reliability or trustworthiness requirement for statements offered by party-opponents.

§ 6.7 *Silence as a Statement*

A party can adopt a statement by remaining silent in circumstances in which one would expect a person to make a denial if the statement were untrue.

EXAMPLE

Veronica suffers a terrible case of hepatitis A after eating in Chef Alfredo's swanky Balkan-fusion restaurant. In front of a large group of restaurant reviewers, Veronica accuses Chief Alfredo of poor kitchen hygiene and giving her hepatitis. Chef Alfredo hangs his head and says nothing. Unless special circumstances can explain Chef Alfredo's silence (such as that he was afraid to contradict Veronica lest she become violent, or he did not understand sufficient English to comprehend her accusation), Chef Alfredo has adopted Veronica's statement as his own statement.

Sometimes an accused in a criminal case remains silent because she has invoked her Fifth Amendment right to remain silent. The fact of her silence is not admissible, though pre-arrest silence may be admitted if a reasonable person would have spoken had she been innocent.

§ 6.8   *Statements of Agents and Employees*

[Fed. R. Evid. 801(d)(2)(C)–(D)]

Under the Federal Rules of Evidence, a statement is admissible if it was made by:

- An agent authorized to speak for the party, Fed. R. Evid. 801(d)(2)(C); or

- An employee speaking about a matter within the scope of her employment during the time of her employment by the party, Fed. R. Evid. 801(d)(2)(D).

Agency and employment are determined by the substantive law of agency. Statements by independent contractors do not fall within Rule 801(d)(2)(D).

EXAMPLES

A taxi driver says to the other driver at the scene of a rear-end collision: "Sorry, I was texting and did not see that you were stopped." That out-of-court statement is a personal admission of fault under Rule 801(d)(2)(A) as well as an employee's admission on behalf of the taxi company under Rule 801(d)(2)(D), assuming the driver is an employee and not an independent contractor. It falls under a statement by a party's employee because driving was within the scope of her employment. The driver's statement about something outside her job responsibilities, however, such as a statement about the safety of elevators at the company's office, would not be admissible against the company.

* * *

A drug company discovers that its baldness cream, "Balderdash," promotes the permanent growth of dense ear hair. The drug company fires Edna, the chief chemical engineer responsible for Balderdash. The next day, Edna makes a public statement: "The company pressured my colleagues and me to take Balderdash to the market before all testing was complete. I apologize to all those consumers who will suffer lifelong unsightly ear hair. This whole debacle is the fault of upper management." Edna's statement is not admissible by a Plaintiff in a lawsuit against the drug company as a statement by a party-opponent because although the statement was within the scope of her employment, she was not an employee at the time the statement was made and she was not authorized to make a statement on the company's behalf.

§ 6.9   *Co-Conspirator Statements*

[Fed. R. Evid. 801(d)(2)(E)]

Under Fed. R. Evid. 801(d)(2)(E), some statements by a member of a conspiracy are admissible as the party-statements of fellow co-conspirators.

To satisfy the requirements of Fed. R. Evid. 801(d)(2)(E), the statements must have been made:

- As part of a *conspiracy*. Conspiracy need not be one of the charged offenses or claims, but the opposing party must prove to the judge by a preponderance of the evidence that a conspiracy existed.

- In *furtherance of* the conspiracy, advancing the main objectives of the conspiracy. Statements of idle chatter or bragging about the conspiracy do not count as furthering the conspiracy.

- *During the course of* the conspiracy. The statement must have been made before the conspiracy ended. It is usually safe to say that the conspiracy is over when the co-conspirators are in custody.

Although it applies in both civil and criminal cases, the co-conspirator rule is primarily a powerful tool for prosecutors. Even if the accused invokes her Fifth Amendment privilege and remains silent, the statements of a co-conspirator are admissible to the same extent as if the accused uttered them herself. Many prosecutions involve testimony of witnesses who made deals with the government for lesser punishment in exchange for their testimony. Such witnesses are often in a good position to repeat co-conspirator statements.

§ 6.10 *"Bootstrapping"*

Rule 801(d)(2) requires that the prosecution show the judge, by a preponderance of the evidence, that the foundational requirements for agency, employment, or conspiracy have been met. To meet this burden, the prosecutor may rely on the statement itself as partial evidence of agency, employment, or conspiracy. "Bootstrapping" is where hearsay picks itself up by its own bootstraps—that is to say, where the statement itself is used to prove a necessary preliminary fact controlling the admissibility of the statement. In the context of Fed. R. Evid. 801(d)(2)(C)–(E), this means that the judge may use the very statements that are sought to be admitted to decide whether the preliminary requirements of the exemption have been met. For instance, to apply 801(d)(2)(E), the court must first determine whether a conspiracy exists. The out-of-court statement itself may be used to determine the preliminary question of conspiracy. Fed. R. Evid. 801(d)(2)(C)–(E) require, however, that *some* independent evidence of agency, employment, or conspiracy exist.

 PRIOR STATEMENTS CHECKLIST

1. Is the out-of-court statement being used to prove the truth of the matter asserted?

    If yes: Go to Step 2.

    If no: It is not a hearsay use of the statement, and there is no need for a Rule 801(d) exemption. If it is a close question on whether the statement is hearsay, continue with the analysis for an alternate theory for admission.

Statements by Party-Opponents

2. Is the out-of-court statement made by a party herself (either directly or adopted)? Note: a victim is not a party in a criminal case.

    If yes: Go to Step 5.

    If no: Go to Step 3.

3.   Is the out-of-court statement made by:

- A party's agent during the course of the agency relationship;

- A party's employee during the course of the employment; or

- A party's co-conspirator during and in furtherance of the conspiracy?

If yes: Go to Step 4.

If no: The statement does not fall under 801(d)(2). Try to get it in another way. Go to Step 6.

4.   Was there independent evidence (besides the statement itself) to prove that the declarant was an agent, employee, or co-conspirator?

If yes: Go to Step 5.

If no: The out-of-court statement cannot qualify as a statement made by a party. Check for other ways the statement may be exempted or excepted from the hearsay rule. Go to Step 6.

5.   Did the *opposing* party offer the statement by a party, agent, employee, or co-conspirator?

If yes: It is exempted from the hearsay rule and can be offered for its truth under 801(d)(2). It may also be admissible under 801(d)(1) and other hearsay exceptions. Go to Step 6.

If no: It is not admissible under Rule 801(d)(2). Parties cannot simply offer their own statements. Go to Step 6 to see if it is admissible as a prior statement by a witness.

Prior Statements by a Witness

6.   Is the declarant testifying at the current trial and is the declarant available for cross-examination?

If yes: Go to Step 7.

If no: The declaration cannot be admitted under any part of Rule 801(d)(1). Check hearsay exceptions under Rules 803, 804, and 807.

7.   Does the declarant's prior statement concern a prior identification of someone?

If yes: The prior identification is admissible under Fed. R. Evid. 801(d)(1)(C).

If no: Go to Step 8.

8. Is the declarant's prior statement consistent with the witness's current testimony?

If yes: Go to Step 9.

If no: Go to Step 12.

9. Is the prior consistent statement offered to rebut "an express or implied charge that the declarant recently fabricated" the current in-court testimony, or "acted from a recent improper influence or motive"?

If yes: Go to Step 10.

If no: Go to Step 11.

10. Was the prior consistent statement made *after* the improper influence or motive to fabricate arose?

If yes: The statement is not admissible under Fed. R. Evid. 801(d)(1)(B)(i). Check hearsay exceptions under Rules 803, 804, and 807.

If no: The prior consistent statement is admissible both as common-law rehabilitation and for its truth under 801(d)(1)(B)(i).

11. Is the prior consistent statement offered to rehabilitate a witness whose credibility has been attacked for any reason?

If yes: The statement may be admitted under Rule 801(d)(1)(B)(ii).

If no: Try to get it in another way. Check hearsay exceptions under Rules 803, 804, and 807.

12. Was the prior statement by the witness inconsistent with her current testimony in court?

If yes: The statement can be used for common-law impeachment. Go to Step 13 to see if the statement can also be used for its truth under Fed. R. Evid. 801(d)(1)(A).

If no: The hearsay statement is not admissible under 801(d), but may be admissible under exceptions found in Rules 803, 804, and 807.

13. Was the prior statement made under oath and subject to penalty of perjury at a prior trial, proceeding, hearing, or deposition (including a grand jury)?

If yes: The statement can be used for common-law impeachment and for the truth of the matter asserted under Rule 801(d)(1)(A).

If no: The statement is not admissible under 801(d), but it may be admissible under exceptions found in Rules 803, 804, and 807.

ILLUSTRATIVE PROBLEMS

■ PROBLEM 6.1 ■

Q: Andrew is charged with raping Viola. At the police station, Viola tells an officer that the rapist, whom she had never seen before, followed her home and pushed his way into her apartment. At trial, she tells a slightly different story, stating that she met Andrew at a bar, invited him into her apartment for a drink, and then he raped her. Andrew is claiming consent. Earlier on the night in question, Andrew said to his roommate George, "I'm going to have sex tonight no matter what! I am going to the bar to find someone to sleep with. See you tomorrow." Is either Viola's or Andrew's prior out-of-court statement admissible?

A: Andrew's prior statement to his roommate is admissible under Fed. R. Evid. 801(d)(2)(A) because it is a statement by a party that will be offered by the opposing party (the prosecution). It does not matter that it was not against Andrew's interest when it was made or that the statement may not be proof of intent to rape. It is relevant and the prosecution will be able to admit the statement as substantive evidence.

Additionally, Andrew's statement might be admissible as impeachment if Andrew testifies. If Andrew does testify and he contradicts his prior statement to George, his statement to George could serve as common-law impeachment but the jury would not be allowed to consider it for its truth. Andrew's statement would not be admissible under Fed. R. Evid. 801(d)(1)(A) for its truth because it was not made under oath, subject to penalty of perjury at a formal proceeding such as trial grand jury or deposition. However, as noted above, the statement would be admissible for its truth as a statement by a party, whether or not Andrew takes the stand.

Viola's statement is not admissible under Rule 801(d)(2)(A) because she, as a victim, is not a party. Her statement at the police station is not admissible as a prior inconsistent statement by a witness under Rule 801(d)(1)(A). Even though Viola is available for cross-examination and her prior statement is inconsistent with her current testimony, the exemption under Rule 801(d)(1)(A) does not apply because Viola made her statement to an officer, not under oath, and not in a prior proceeding, hearing, or deposition. Her prior statement could be used by Andrew to impeach Viola's credibility as common-law impeachment, but the prior statement cannot be offered for its truth.

■ PROBLEM 6.2 ■

Q: Bob, Carol, Ted, and Alice are charged with conspiracy to rob a federal bank. Their plans are discovered by the police and the four are awaiting trial in jail because bail was denied. Which of the following would be admissible against *Bob*?

    (1) Bob's statement to his cellmate, "Gosh, we never should have listened to Ted and Alice. This bank robbery scheme was a terrible idea."

    (2) Carol's statement to her cellmate, "I'm never going to forgive Bob for planning this scheme."

    (3) Ted's casual statement over a game of cards to an undercover FBI agent, the day before the planned robbery, "I am playing only a small part in this—driving the get-away car. In fact, I tried to discourage him from knocking off this bank, but Bob insisted. Bob has masterminded the whole thing."

    (4) None of the above.

A: The correct answer is: (1). Bob's statement, even though it is after the conspiracy, is a personal admission by Bob admissible under Fed. R. Evid. 801(d)(2)(A). Carol's statement is being made after the conspiracy, so it does not meet the duration requirement even if a conspiracy is proved. Ted's statement is made during the conspiracy, but not in furtherance of it.

POINTS TO REMEMBER

Statements by Opposing Parties [Fed. R. Evid. 801(d)(2)]

- The statement must be offered by the party-opponent, not the party herself. (Remember: victims are not parties.)

- Statements by opposing parties are admissible even if the statement was made with no personal knowledge and was not against the party's interest at the time the statement was made.

- The statement can be:

    o   Personal;

    o   Adopted;

    o   Made by an authorized agent;

- o Made by an employee concerning the scope of her employment during her employment; or

- o Made by a co-conspirator.

- There must be some independent proof (other than the statement itself) of the existence of the agency, employment relationship, or conspiracy. Some "bootstrapping" (where the statement itself is used to establish a preliminary fact necessary to admit the statement) is permitted, but the judge cannot rely on the statement alone to establish agency, employment, or conspiracy.

Prior Statements by Witnesses [Fed. R. Evid. 801(d)(1)]

- For a prior out-of-court statement to be admissible under Rule 801(d)(1), the declarant must be a live witness subject to cross-examination. No live witness, no Rule 801(d)(1) exemption.

- All prior out-of-court statements that are *inconsistent* with the live testimony by a witness are admissible for common-law impeachment (that is to say, to demonstrate inconsistency).

- Some prior *inconsistent* statements are also admissible for their truth. To fall under Rule 801(d)(1)(A) and serve as substantive evidence (that is to say, to be admitted for their truth), these inconsistent statements must be:

- o Made under oath, subject to the penalty of perjury; and

- o Made at a trial, hearing, or other proceeding, or in a deposition.

Note: The statements did not have to be subject to cross-examination when they were made; this includes grand jury testimony.

- Fed. R. Evid. 801(d)(1)(B)(i) provides that *consistent* prior statements by the witness may be offered as substantive evidence to rebut "an express or implied charge that the declarant recently fabricated" the current in-court testimony or "acted from a recent improper influence or motive," but only if the statement was made before the motive to fabricate arose.

- A recent amendment to Fed. R. Evid. 801(d)(1)(B)(ii) expands the use of prior consistent statements to allow a party "to rehabilitate the declarant's credibility as a witness when attacked on another ground." This amendment extends the grounds for rehabilitation and the use of prior consistent statements for their truth but does not undo the timing requirement if the rebuttal relates to a charge of recent fabrication or improper motive.

- For statements of identification under Fed. R. Evid. 801(d)(1)(C), the prior statement had to concern an identification of someone by the witness. There are no formal requirements (such as an oath) for the prior identification. The prior statement of identification can be proved by someone other than the witness, such as a police officer who witnessed the identification.

CHAPTER 7

Hearsay Exceptions

§ 7.1 What Is the Effect of a Hearsay Statement that Fits within an Exception?

When an out-of-court statement is used for the truth of the matter asserted, that statement is hearsay. However, not all hearsay statements are inadmissible. If the hearsay statement fits a "not hearsay" exemption under Fed. R. Evid. 801(d)[1] or an exception under Fed. R. Evid. 803, 804, or 807, then it may be admissible even though it is used for its truth.

§ 7.2 Distinction Between Fed. R. Evid. 803 and Fed. R. Evid. 804

Fed. R. Evid. 804 exceptions require that the proponent of the evidence must first prove that the declarant is unavailable (such as being dead, too ill, subject to privilege, etc.). Fed. R. Evid. 803 exceptions have no such requirement and apply whether or not the declarant is available.

§ 7.3 Policy of Hearsay Exceptions

Evidence law admits certain hearsay statements based on the generalized assessment that some types of out-of-court statements are particularly reliable or necessary. Sometimes, however, the best explanation for a hearsay exception is that it has become enshrined in history—not that it makes a lot of practical or psychological sense.

The exceptions are applied categorically. Generally, courts do not conduct a specific inquiry into whether the policy of the exception is met in an individual case.

Fed. R. Evid. 803(6) (business records), Fed. R. Evid. 803(8) (public records), Fed. R. 804(b)(3) (declarations against interest in

---

[1]   *See* Chapter 6.

criminal cases), and Fed. R. Evid. 807 (catch-all provision) include specific trustworthiness or reliability checks. Aside from these rules, however, once the requirements of a Rule 803 or 804 exception has been met, there is no requirement of trustworthiness or test for reliability in applying the exceptions.

§ 7.4   *Requirement of Personal Knowledge*

For almost all Fed. R. Evid. 803 and Fed. R. Evid. 804 exceptions, the declarants must speak from personal knowledge.[2] This contrasts with statements by party-opponents under Fed. R. Evid. 801(d)(2), which do not require personal knowledge.

EXCEPTIONS THAT APPLY WHETHER OR NOT
THE DECLARANT IS AVAILABLE
[Fed. R. Evid. 803]

§ 7.5   *The Present Sense Impression*

[Fed. R. Evid. 803(1)]

Fed. R. Evid. 803(1) provides a hearsay exception for a "statement describing or explaining an event or condition, made while or immediately after the declarant perceived it."

Some Tweets or other simultaneous accounts of events might qualify as present sense impressions.

EXAMPLE

"Gee, the sun is in my eyes," offered to show that the Declarant was temporarily blinded by the sun.

The present sense impression exception is justified because the extremely short time span between perception and utterance allows little chance that the declarant forgot or had time to fabricate her statement. Additionally, in many cases, the person to whom the statement was addressed could check its accuracy.

When determining whether to admit a statement as a present sense impression, the trial judge must determine, as a preliminary matter under Fed. R. Evid. 104(a), if the statement was made at the time of the event or immediately afterward. Courts vary widely in the amount of time they allow to elapse before concluding that the timing limit has been reached. In the view of the author, any lapse in time more than a minute or two undermines the guarantee of

---

[2]   For Fed. R. Evid. 803(6) (business records), not everyone in the business chain of information needs to possess personal knowledge. Fed. R. Evid. 803(8)(A)(iii), which deals with public records and reports, allows findings of fact by public officials concerning events that the declarant-official did not observe personally.

trustworthiness of the statement and prohibits its admission as a present sense impression. The contents of the statement being offered may be used to establish the timing. In other words, it is permissible to bootstrap by using the utterance itself to lay its own foundation.

§ 7.6 *The Excited Utterance*

[Fed. R. Evid. 803(2)]

Fed. R. Evid. 803(2) provides an exception for a "statement relating to a startling event or condition, made while the declarant was under the stress of excitement that it caused." Often, statements are both excited utterances and present sense impressions, but the elements required for the two exceptions are distinct.

EXAMPLES

#1 "My God! The baby is in the street!" exclaimed while watching a toddler enter a busy road, offered to show that the child wandered into the street.

#2 "My God! The baby was in terrible danger there in the street," said while crying and hugging a child who had been rescued from a busy street twenty minutes earlier, offered to show that the child wandered into the street.

The first statement is both a present sense impression and an excited utterance. The second statement is an excited utterance, if it can be established that the Declarant was still under the stress of the excitement caused by seeing a toddler in the road, but is too delayed from the time of the event to be a present sense impression.

The questionable rationale of the excited utterance exception is that the stress of the excitement suspends the declarant's capacity to fabricate. A criticism of the exception arises from the fact that while sincerity may increase, perception and memory suffer during a highly stressful event.

The judge determines under Fed. R. Evid. 104(a) whether the declarant was under the stress of excitement caused by the event or condition at the time the utterance was made. In deciding this preliminary question, bootstrapping[3] is allowed: all of the circumstances can be considered, including the content of the utterance itself.

---

[3] *See* § 6.10 (discussing bootstrapping).

The excited utterance exception has no specific time limit; it is available as long as the declarant remains under the stress of the exciting event. Some courts allow a questionably long period for the declarant to remain under the stress of excitement.

§ 7.7   *Direct Evidence of Declarant's Present State of Mind or Physical Condition*

[Fed. R. Evid. 803(3)]

Fed. R. Evid. 803(3) excepts from the hearsay rule statements of the declarant's *then-existing*:

- State of mind;
- Emotion;
- Sensation;
- Physical condition; or
- Intent, plan, or motive.

EXAMPLES

"My tooth hurts." This demonstrates a physical condition.

* * *

"I don't understand hearsay." This demonstrates state of mind.

* * *

"I'm afraid of him." This demonstrates the emotion of fear.

* * *

"I'll kill him if I ever lay eyes on him again." This demonstrates intent.

* * *

"I'm going to sleep for 24 hours straight right after the bar exam." This demonstrates plan.

This exception rests on the premise that the declarant's statement was made close to the time the condition or state of mind was experienced, so the chances of memory defects or risks of fabrication are diminished. Of course, some people are unreliable in talking about their condition, feelings, or plans. Their statements are nevertheless necessary; there is really no way to know how someone is feeling either physically or emotionally other than to take her word for it.

The exception for present state of mind includes statements of present intent to do a future act, offered to show circumstantial evidence that the declarant did what she planned. In *Mutual Life Insurance Co. v. Hillmon*, 145 U.S. 285 (1892), the Declarant's statement that he was going to Colorado with Hillmon was held admissible to show that the Declarant and (more controversially) Hillmon had actually gone to Colorado.

EXAMPLES

"I'm going to my boyfriend's house." This demonstrates plan and can be used circumstantially to show the Declarant actually went to her boyfriend's house.

* * *

"I'm going out with Harry," offered against Harry to prove that the Declarant, a murder victim, did go out with Harry, who is charged with her murder. Although courts are split on this use, they tend to admit it as circumstantial evidence of Harry's whereabouts.

Fed. R. Evid. 803(3) excludes statements of memory or belief offered to show the fact remembered or believed unless it relates to the execution, revocation, identification, or terms of the declarant's will. The reason for this is that admitting backward-looking memories or beliefs would swallow up the hearsay rule entirely. The out-of-court statement, "The car went through the stop sign" should not be treated differently from the out-of-court statement "I remember that the car went through the stop sign."

EXAMPLES

The out-of-court statement, "I remember that it was Brandon who attacked me yesterday," used to prove Brandon's attack, is not covered by the Rule 803(3) exception.

* * *

The out-of-court statement, "I believe that I saw Roger hanging out at the moot-court office," used to place Roger at the moot-court office, is not covered by the exception.

* * *

The out-of-court statement, "Just yesterday I disinherited my good-for-nothing son," is admissible under Fed. R. Evid. 803(3) even though it is evidence of a memory or belief because it relates to the terms of the Declarant's will.

§ 7.8   *Statements for Medical Diagnosis or Treatment*

[Fed. R. Evid. 803(4)]

Fed. R. Evid. 803(4) creates an exception for statements made for and reasonably pertinent to medical diagnosis or treatment. The statements that fall under this exception describe medical history and past or present symptoms.

- The statement can be made by the patient, by someone representing the patient, or by the medical professional.

- Rule 803(4) does not require that the statement be made to a physician. As long as it is made for purposes of obtaining diagnosis or treatment, it could be made to anyone—an EMT, a nurse, or sometimes even a family member.

- The rule is not limited to statements of present symptoms. If made for purposes of medical diagnosis or treatment, statements of past symptoms (for example, "My right side has been hurting for a week" or "I felt numbness in my left hand") are admissible.

- The statement must be pertinent to the diagnosis. The identity of the perpetrator or tortfeasor is generally not pertinent to the medical diagnosis.

EXAMPLE

A statement "Carl stabbed me with a Civil War reenactment bayonet" would not be admissible in full because the identification of Carl is not pertinent to diagnosis or treatment. The cause of injury—bayonet— would be admissible because it is pertinent to how the wound would be treated.

The policy of the rule is that statements made for medical diagnosis tend to be particularly reliable. However, Fed. R. Evid. 803(4) does not require that the statement be made to someone who will provide medical treatment; it also admits statements made to physicians who will merely testify, not treat.

§ 7.9 *Past Recollection Recorded*

[Fed. R. Evid. 803(5)]

Fed. R. Evid. 803(5) provides a hearsay exception when:

- A witness once had knowledge of a matter in a record, but now cannot remember it well enough "to testify fully and accurately;"

- The record was made or adopted by the witness when the matter was "fresh in the witness's memory;" and

- The record accurately reflects the witness's knowledge at the time.

If the witness has a complete memory of the event, Fed. R. Evid. 803(5) does not apply. If, conversely, the witness has absolutely no memory of making the statement, the Rule is also inapplicable.

If the record is admitted under Rule 803(5), it can be read into evidence; it will not be admitted as an exhibit unless offered by the opposing party.

Fed. R. Evid. 803(5) is justified because recorded recollections are necessary when the witness has insufficient memory. Such statements are deemed trustworthy because the writing was made close to the event, and the witness who made or adopted the memorandum will be available for testimony to establish the preliminary facts that trigger the exception, such as the witness's incomplete memory. Furthermore, because the rule governs writings or memoranda, there will be no dispute about the content of the out-of-court statement.

Despite the fact that this exception falls within Rule 803, for which declarant availability is immaterial, as a practical matter the declarant must actually be available to testify to the preliminary requirements of Rule 803(5).

§ 7.10 *Refreshing Memory*

The common law traditionally permitted a party to refresh a witness's recollection. This is a non-hearsay use because the evidence is not being offered for its truth. The evidence is shown to the witness (and opposing counsel) but not to the jury. Refreshing memory survived the codification of the Federal Rules of Evidence. The technique of refreshing a witness's memory is sometimes confused with the Fed. R. Evid. 803(5) hearsay exception for recorded recollection. However, note these differences:

RECOLLECTION RECORDED [FED. R. EVID. 803(5)]	REFRESHED MEMORY
The witness does not have a sufficient memory of the events represented in the document	After being refreshed with the document, the witness's memory is sufficiently jogged so that the witness can testify from current memory
The opposing party must be shown the document	The opposing party must be shown the document
The out-of-court hearsay statement is admitted for the truth of the matter asserted, but is read into the record rather than given to the jury as an exhibit unless the opponent requests its admission as an exhibit	The out-of-court statement is not admitted at all, and used merely to refresh the witness's recollection; the jury never sees the document or hears it read into evidence
The rule applies only to writings and recordings	Memory can be refreshed with other items besides writings and recordings, such as photographs or even sounds or smells

§ 7.11 *Business Records*

[Fed. R. Evid. 803(6)]

To qualify under the business record exception to the hearsay rule, the document must be:

- "A record of an act, event, condition, opinion, or diagnosis;"

- Made "at or near the time" of the act, event, condition, opinion, or diagnosis;

- Made by a person with knowledge, or made from information transmitted by a person with knowledge;

- Made by and transmitted to someone acting in the regular course of business (this is known as the business-duty rule);

- Made "in the course of a regularly conducted" activity of a business or organization; and

- Created in the "regular practice" of that business activity.

A custodian or other qualified witness may lay the foundation for a business record, or the business record may be self-authenticating without producing a foundational witness. The exception does not apply, however, if the opponent of the evidence shows that the "source of information or the method or circumstances of preparation indicate a lack of trustworthiness." The most common example of lack of trustworthiness is a record prepared in anticipation of litigation.

The business records exception to the hearsay rule is used frequently. It is justified on the grounds that businesses possess an independent motive to be accurate for the sake of profit and viability, and that the very regularity of the business's activities ensures trustworthiness. Also, it would be expensive and impractical to have each employee who participated in the creation of a business record testify in court.

§ 7.12 *Public Records*

[Fed. R. Evid. 803(8)]

The public records exception covers records and reports concerning the activities of a governmental office or agency. It provides special protections when public records are used against the accused in criminal cases.

Fed. R. Evid. 803(8)(A)(ii) admits matters observed by a public servant pursuant to a duty imposed by law when the public servant has a duty to report. It excludes, however, matters observed by law-enforcement personnel in criminal cases.

EXAMPLES

A police officer's report that a driver was weaving and smelled of alcohol qualifies as a matter observed pursuant to a duty proposed by law. The report would nevertheless be excluded if offered in a criminal case against the accused because it was a matter observed by law enforcement personnel.

* * *

A restaurant inspector visits an establishment and spots health-code violations and illegal gambling in the back room. The written report of the health code violation leading to a civil citation or tort claim for food poisoning would be admissible under 803(8)(A)(ii). The parts of the report dealing with illegal gambling would not be admissible because supervising illegal gambling was not within the inspector's duties.

Fed. R. Evid. 803(8)(A)(iii) covers factual findings resulting from an investigation made pursuant to legal authority. Public servants may rely upon inadmissible evidence in reaching their conclusions. The exception applies both in civil and criminal cases. In criminal cases, however, only the accused may use the exception.

There is no analog to the business-duty rule in the public record exception, so the provider of the information under Fed. R. Evid. 803(8)(A)(iii) is not required to demonstrate a business duty to speak. As with the business records exception embodied in Fed. R. Evid. 803(6), the public records exception does not apply if the opponent of the evidence proves that "the source of information or other circumstances indicate a lack of trustworthiness."

The public records exception is justified because such out-of-court statements are deemed particularly reliable. Government officials are considered trustworthy, and they operate under a legal duty to be accurate. The exception is also necessary because public officials handle many matters and may not recall facts important to the determination of the suit.

Many public records are also business records, since the government is a business within the meaning of the business records exception. A comparison between the business record exception and public record exception follows:

BUSINESS RECORD	PUBLIC RECORD
Applies to any business	Applies to public agencies only
Record may be made by anyone in the business loop	Record made by public servants only
Involves regular business activity	Covers matters that are not recorded with regularity
Made at or near the time of observation	No timing requirement
Information must be both transmitted and received as part of regular business duty	Business-duty rule does not apply. Public servant can make factual findings based on inadmissible evidence, including when the source of that information had no business duty to speak

Foundation required via custodial witness or affidavit. Not all business records are self-authenticating	Self-authenticating
Trustworthiness requirement	Trustworthiness requirement

§ 7.13 *Police Records as Business Records*

As a regularly conducted activity, at least some police work would seem to qualify as business records within the meaning of the business records rule. However, there is a strong policy, expressed in the public records exception against using police records to convict an accused, which has the effect of requiring the police officer to actually take the stand in order to convict. This exception applies to business records as well, even though the business records rule contains no express prohibition of use of police records against an accused. Use of police records in the absence of an officer on the stand would raise Confrontation Clause problems in criminal cases. Use of police records in civil cases (such as routine accident reports) would not run afoul of the strong policy of requiring a cop to take the stand rather than merely using a record to convict. Such records could also be used for non-hearsay purposes, such as to refresh the cop's recollection or to impeach her.

§ 7.14 *Learned Treatise*

[Fed. R. Evid. 803(18)]

Fed. R. Evid. 803(18) allows the introduction of text from professional or scholarly published works via an expert when that expert relies on a statement in the learned treatise during direct examination or when such a statement is called to the expert's attention on cross-examination. The treatise must be shown to the expert.

A party offering the statement from the treatise must establish that the work is a reliable authority. This can be done via an expert or through judicial notice. When a controversy arises about whether the treatise is a reliable authority, the judge will determine this preliminary factual question under Fed. R. Evid. 104(a). Learned treatises can also be used to impeach experts. If admitted, the treatise excerpts may be read into evidence but may not be received as exhibits.

§ 7.15 *Ancient Documents*

[Fed. R. Evid. 803(16)]

The exception for statements in ancient documents allows the admission of documents that have been in existence for at least twenty years.

The age of the document assures that it was not prepared for admission in the present controversy. Also, this type of hearsay has traditionally been deemed especially necessary because memories fade and, given the passage of time, it might be difficult to find other evidence.

As of this writing, the Advisory Committee of Evidence Rules has unanimously proposed eliminating this exception on the grounds that the rule is unnecessary; will encompass too many electronically stored documents; and, to date, has only been tolerated because traditionally it was used so infrequently. In recommending the abrogation of Rule 803(16) the Committee noted that other exceptions, such as business records (Fed. R. Evid. 803(6)) and residual exceptions (Fed. R. Evid. 807), could serve to admit some documents formerly admitted under Rule 803(16).

EXCEPTIONS THAT ONLY APPLY IF THE DECLARANT IS UNAVAILABLE
[Fed. R. Evid. 804]

§ 7.16 *Defining Unavailability*

For a Rule 804 exception to apply, the declarant must be unavailable. Unavailability is defined as any cause that, through no fault of the proponent, prevents the witness from attending or testifying, Fed. R. Evid. 804(a).

Examples of causes for unavailability include:

- Death;

- Mental or physical disability;

- The witness is beyond the court's subpoena power and there is no other reasonable way to obtain her testimony;

- The witness invokes a privilege;

- The witness appears, asserts no privilege, but refuses to testify after being ordered to do so; and

- The witness appears and testifies that she cannot recall the subject matter.

If a proponent can foresee that the declarant will not be present at trial, she should make reasonable efforts to depose the declarant so that the opponent will have a chance to cross-examine the witness during the deposition.

§ 7.17 *Former Testimony*

[Fed. R. Evid. 804(b)(1)]

To qualify for the former-testimony exception:

- The declarant must be unavailable;

- The former testimony must have been made under oath, subject to penalty for perjury;

- In criminal cases, the party against whom the former testimony is offered must have had a similar motive and opportunity to cross-examine the witness when the former testimony was first offered. Merely having new legal theories or new strategies for cross-examination does not prevent admission of the prior testimony if the incentive for cross-examination was essentially the same; and

- In civil cases, the former testimony may be introduced if a party against whom the testimony is offered or the party's "predecessor in interest" had a similar motive and opportunity to cross-examine. The term "predecessor in interest" describes someone who had a prior interest in property that is now subject to litigation or who was otherwise in privity with a party.

EXAMPLES

Anna is convicted of wire fraud. Walter testified for the prosecution under oath at Anna's trial. Anna had ample opportunity to cross-examine Walter, which she did for two days. Anna's conviction is reversed on appeal because of a faulty jury instruction. If Walter is too sick to testify on retrial and is thus unavailable, his testimony is admissible under the former-testimony exception because it was subject to cross-examination when it was made and Anna's motive for cross-examination was the same.

* * *

Peter, a police officer, testifies at a suppression hearing regarding whether Anthony voluntarily waived the right to counsel when Anthony confessed at the police station. Anthony cross-examines Peter at the suppression hearing.

Peter dies before the criminal trial. Peter's former testimony will not be admissible at the criminal trial if the court finds that Anthony had a different motive to question Peter at the suppression hearing. At the suppression hearing, the focus would arguably have been on the circumstances of making the confession, while the trial would focus on the content of the confession.

The policy of the former testimony exception rests on the supposition that cross-examination under oath at a prior proceeding guarantees the fairness and trustworthiness of the hearsay. Also, the hearsay is particularly necessary because the declarant is unavailable. (If the declarant is available, Rule 804 does not apply.) Such former testimony may be used to impeach a declarant-witness with a prior inconsistent statement (Rule 801(d)(1)(A)) or to rehabilitate her with a prior consistent statement (Rule 801(d)(1)(B)).

Additionally, the court can admit deposition testimony of an unavailable witness under Rule 32 of the Rules of Civil Procedure if:

- The statements made in the deposition would be admissible under the Federal Rules of Evidence had they been made by a live witness at the present trial; and

- The deposition is being used against a party who was present or represented at the deposition, or at least had adequate notice of the deposition to have been present or represented.

Finally, if the prior testimony is a statement of a party-opponent, there is no requirement of witness unavailability and the prior testimony will be admitted under Fed. R. Evid. 801(d)(2).

§ 7.18 *Dying Declarations*

[Fed. R. Evid. 804(b)(2)]

To qualify for the dying declarations exception:

- The declarant must be unavailable (but not necessarily dead);

- The declarant must believe her death is imminent. Proof of that belief includes:

  o   The declarant's own statement of belief in imminent death;

  o   Evidence that the victim was told of impending death;

- o   Evidence that the victim called for a priest or other clergy; or

- o   Evidence that the injury was so grievous that the imminence of death was obvious.

- The statement must concern the cause or circumstances of death; and

- The statement is offered in a civil case or homicide prosecution. Note: Rule 804(b)(2) does not apply to crimes other than homicide.

As with most other hearsay exceptions, personal knowledge is required. Thus, a Declarant who was shot while passed out drunk and later, believing she is dying, states her suspicion of her shooter's identity, has not made an admissible dying declaration.

EXAMPLE

Victor is shot, and as he lies dying he says, "I know I'm not going to make it. Give my love to my partner and my kids. Alfred shot me. Also, Zack embezzled from our garment business." Assuming that Victor dies and is hence unavailable, the statement about the shooter qualifies as an admissible dying declaration in the homicide prosecution or the civil wrongful-death action against Alfred. The statement against Zack, offered in a prosecution for embezzlement, is inadmissible for two reasons: (1) it is a non-homicide criminal case, and (2) it does not concern the circumstance of death. The statement offered against Zack in a civil suit to recover the money will similarly fail as a dying declaration because it does not concern the cause of death.

The traditional theory behind the dying declarations exception, which dates back to seventeenth-century English law, is that no one would dare meet her maker with a lie upon her lips. Scholars question the validity of this exception, which rests on fear of hell and divine retribution, in modern secular society. Also, problems with memory, perception, and narrative may be amplified when a person is dying. Nonetheless, this time-honored hearsay exception seems alive and well.

§ 7.19 *Statements Against Interest*

[Fed. R. Evid. 804(b)(3)]

The elements of a statement against interest are as follows:

- The declarant is unavailable;

- The declarant makes a statement that she knows is contrary to her own interests regarding her:

  o Financial and property interests (statements that admit a debt or concede another's property interest);

  o Tort or contract interests (statements that potentially expose the declarant to civil liability) or

  o Penal interests (statements that expose the declarant to criminal liability).

- In criminal cases, corroborating circumstances are required.

The statements against interest exception is based on the theory that reasonable people usually do not make statements against their interests unless those statements are true. Although the common law and some states also applied the rule to personal interests in avoiding humiliation ridicule or scorn, the Federal Rules do not.

Questions sometimes arise about the status of statements that are partly disserving and partly self-serving or neutral. In *Williamson v. United States*, 512 U.S. 594 (1994), the Court endorsed a narrow view of what constitutes a statement against interest under Rule 804(b)(3). Instead of looking at the Declarant's narrative as a whole, the Court dissected the Declarant's remarks statement by statement, admitting only the inculpatory ones and not the neutral or exculpatory statements. An unavailable declarant who admits to the police her participation in the crime but minimizes her role as she inculpates another ("I was just the driver but Roxanne was the mastermind") probably does not make a statement against interest.

In criminal cases, when declarations against interest are testimonial statements made while in police custody, it is questionable whether any such declarations survive the Court's Confrontation Clause analysis.[4]

---

[4]   *See* Chapter 8 (discussing confrontation).

§ 7.20 *Forfeiture by Wrongdoing*

[Fed. R. Evid. 804(b)(6)]

The forfeiture by wrongdoing exception admits hearsay statements by an absent declarant offered against a party who intentionally caused the declarant to be unavailable.

The mere fact that the party rendered a declarant unavailable is insufficient; the party must have specifically intended to deprive the fact-finder of the witness's testimony. Such wrongdoing includes murder, intimidation, and bribery, all intended to make the witness unavailable, but it need not be criminal activity. Simple threats, bribes, or diversions are sufficient to trigger forfeiture.

The exception does not arise from the belief that such statements are necessarily reliable. Instead, forfeiture by wrongdoing emanates from the equitable principle that parties should not benefit from their own bad acts. Courts tend to apply the rule cautiously because it deprives a party of an important procedural (and, in criminal cases, constitutional) right.

OTHER HEARSAY EXCEPTIONS

§ 7.21 *The Residual Exception to the Hearsay Rule*

[Fed. R. Evid. 807]

Fed. R. Evid. 807 creates a "residual" or "catch-all" exception. The exception is designed to address new and unexpected situations where an out-of-court statement seems particularly trustworthy and necessary but does not fit into any established hearsay exception. It also allows exceptions to hearsay law to develop.

To qualify under Rule 807, the hearsay evidence must:

- Constitute a "material" fact (a requirement that merely restates the rule of relevance);

- Provide "guarantees of trustworthiness" that are "equivalent" to those of the established exceptions (it is unclear what this means);

- Be "more probative" on the point for which it is offered than any other evidence that can reasonably be obtained;

- Be in the "interests of justice" and in accordance with the purposes of the Federal Rules of Evidence; and

- Be presented only if the opponent of the evidence receives notice or if failure to notify was excusable, thereby guarding against unfair surprise.

As to the second requirement above, does the hearsay statement admitted under Rule 807 have to be as reliable as an excited utterance (not very reliable) or as former testimony (highly reliable because taken under oath and subject to cross-examination)? The rule is unclear on this point.

As to the third requirement above, generally, the Evidence Rules do not require the proponent to provide the most probative evidence; the evidence has to simply be relevant and pass Rule 403. The added restriction limits the residual exception to cases of particular need.

Rulings based on Fed. R. Evid. 807 have no precedential value. Each case must be decided on its own unique facts, applying the Rule 807 criteria and assessing the reliability of the evidence and the need for the hearsay.

In the past, Rule 807 was frequently (and inappropriately) used in child sex-abuse prosecutions, where prosecutors attempt to admit child hearsay, and for introducing grand jury testimony where the declarant is no longer available. Since the Supreme Court expanded the reach of the Sixth Amendment in *Crawford v. Washington*, 541 U.S. 36 (2004),[5] the utility of Rule 807 has declined in criminal cases where the declarant is unavailable.

Despite a generally permissive trend in admitting evidence under the residual exception, there may be limits to how far courts will go. When evidence almost fits under one of the established exceptions, but not quite, this is sometimes called "near-miss" hearsay. Some courts have excluded near-miss hearsay, concluding that Congress did not intend for the evidence to be admitted. An example would be a declaration made in belief of imminent death offered to name the perpetrator in an assault case. Because the current dying declaration rule only applies to homicides and civil cases, this would be a "near miss."

§ 7.22　*Hearsay Within Hearsay*

[Fed. R. Evid. 805]

Sometimes the declarant's out-of-court statement will incorporate another out-of-court statement. For example, a hospital record might contain the patient's account of the cause of the accident. The patient's oral statement to the nurse constitutes the first level of hearsay; the nurse's written statement in the hospital record describing what the patient said constitutes the second level. Or, a waiter might report to his husband what he heard a diner say at the restaurant. There, the first level of hearsay is the diner's out-

---

5　*See* § 8.3 (discussing *Crawford*).

of-court statement; the second level of hearsay is the waiter's report to his husband. In both cases, if the out-of-court statement is offered to prove the truth of the matter asserted, the record has hearsay within hearsay.

Fed. R. Evid. 805 provides that hearsay within hearsay is admissible if each level of hearsay falls under an exception or exemption to the hearsay rule, or if it is not hearsay at all.

EXAMPLES

A Plaintiff seeks to prove that the governor was behind her ejection from the state fair. She offers into evidence a statement by a state fair employee that the governor had ordered the Plaintiff to be ejected. The state fair employee's statement is admissible because it is a party-opponent's statement, which is exempted as "not hearsay" under Fed. R. Evid. 801(d)(2)(D). The statement-within-a-statement of the governor is admissible because it is not hearsay; it was not offered for the truth of the matter asserted, but instead offered for the effect on the listener. Alternatively, the governor was also making a statement by a party opponent. Therefore, the witness can repeat what the state fair employee says.

* * *

Sam tells his partner Donna that he just ran over a child and was so upset that he left the scene of the accident. Donna immediately calls her mother, and in an agitated state cries into the phone, "Oh no! Sam just ran over a child!" Donna's mother tells the story to a police officer. May the police officer testify at Sam's criminal trial for negligent homicide? The answer is no. Although some of the hearsay within hearsay is admissible, one link in the chain is not.

Sam ———> Donna ———> Donna's –> Police Officer
                                Mother

Opposing	Excited	???
Party's	Utterance	
Statement		

Donna's mother could testify about what Donna said even though she would be testifying as to hearsay within hearsay, because every link of the chain can be admitted. Sam's original declaration is a statement by an opposing party, Fed. R. Evid. 801(d)(2)(A). Donna's repetition of that statement is an excited utterance, Fed. R. Evid. 803(2). Therefore, Donna's mother could testify about what Donna told her that Sam said. However, the statement from Donna's mother to the police officer, if offered for its truth, is hearsay and is subject to no exemption or exception. Hence, the police officer may not testify as to what Donna's mother told him.

 HEARSAY EXCEPTIONS CHECKLIST

Hearsay Definition

1.   Is the statement hearsay at all? (Check Chapter 5 Hearsay Definition Checklist.)

   If yes: See whether it fits under a Rule 801(d) exemption. (Check Chapter 6, Prior Statements by Witnesses and Statements by Party-Opponents.) Even if it does fit under a Rule 801(d) exemption, it is worth assembling a list of all the ways the statement would be admissible as an exception to the hearsay rule, just in case the judge disagrees with one of your approaches. Go to Step 2.

   If no: No need to fit it under a hearsay exception. However, if the question is close regarding whether the statement is hearsay, you might choose to develop alternative arguments. For example, "This is not hearsay at all, your Honor, because I'm not offering the out-of-court statement for its truth. However, even if it were hearsay, it would fall under the following exemptions and exceptions . . . "

RULE 804 EXCEPTIONS (DECLARANT MUST BE UNAVAILABLE)

Definition of Unavailability [Fed. R. Evid. 804(a)]

2.   Is the declarant unavailable? Rule 804(a) defines unavailability as including death, illness, privilege, refusal under penalty of contempt to testify, total memory loss of the declarant, or the declarant's being outside the court's subpoena power.

   If yes: Go to Step 3.

   If no: Go to Step 11.

Former Testimony [Fed. R. Evid. 804(b)(1)]

3. Did the unavailable declarant make a formal statement under oath, subject to cross-examination, in a deposition or prior proceeding?

    If yes: Go to Step 4.

    If no: The statement cannot fit the former-testimony exception, Fed. R. Evid. 804(b)(1). Go to Step 5.

4. Did the party against whom the testimony was offered (or, in a civil case, a predecessor in interest of the party) have a similar motive and opportunity to cross-examine the declarant?

    If yes: The statement is admissible for its truth under the former-testimony exception, Fed. R. Evid. 804(b)(1). There will be no Confrontation Clause problem if this is offered against the accused in a criminal case, because although the statement was testimonial, the accused had the motive and opportunity to cross-examine. *See* Chapter 8 on Confrontation. Go to Step 5.

    If no: The statement cannot fit the former-testimony exception, Fed. R. Evid. 804(b)(1). Go to Step 5.

Dying Declaration [Fed. R. Evid. 804(b)(2)]

5. Did the unavailable declarant believe her death was imminent?

    If yes: Go to Step 6.

    If no: The statement cannot fit the dying declaration exception, Fed. R. Evid. 804(b)(2). Go to Step 8.

6. Does the statement concern the events that led to the declarant's belief that she was dying?

    If yes: Go to Step 7.

    If no: The statement cannot fit the dying declaration exception, Fed. R. Evid. 804(b)(2). Go to Step 8.

7. Is the case a homicide or a civil case?

    If yes: The statement is admissible for its truth under the dying declaration exception, Fed. R. Evid. 804(b)(2). There will probably be no Confrontation Clause problem if this is offered against the accused in a criminal case. *See* § 8.6. Go to Step 8.

    If no: The statement cannot fit the dying declaration exception, Fed. R. Evid. 804(b)(2), which does not apply to any crimes but homicide. Go to Step 8.

Statements Against Interest [Fed. R. Evid. 804(b)(3)]

8. Did the unavailable declarant knowingly make a statement so contrary to her financial, property, tort, contract, or penal interests that no one would say such a thing unless it was true?

    If yes: Go to Step 9.

    If no: The statement cannot fit the statement against interest exception, Fed. R. Evid. 804(b)(3). Go to Step 10.

9. Is this a criminal case?

    If yes: The statement fits the statement against interest exception, Fed. R. Evid. 804(b)(3), only if there is corroboration of the statement's trustworthiness. If the statement was testimonial, there may be a constitutional objection. *See* Chapter 8 on Confrontation. Go to Step 10.

    If no: The statement is admissible for its truth as a statement against interest, Fed. R. Evid. 804(b)(3). Go to Step 10.

Forfeiture by Wrongdoing [Fed. R. Evid. 804(b)(6)]

10. Did the party against whom the unavailable declarant's statement is offered intentionally render the declarant unavailable or acquiesce in the conduct of another to make the declarant unavailable?

    If yes: The party has forfeited the right to object to the hearsay under Fed. R. Evid. 804(b)(6). The confrontation right is also forfeited. *See* § 8.5. Go to Step 11.

    If no: The forfeiture by wrongdoing exception does not apply, Fed. R. Evid. 804(b)(6). Go to Step 11.

RULE 803 HEARSAY EXCEPTIONS (DECLARANT AVAILABILITY IMMATERIAL)

Present Sense Impression [Fed. R. Evid. 803(1)]

11. Did the declarant make the statement as she perceived the event or immediately thereafter?

    If yes: The statement is admissible as a present sense impression under Rule 803(1) and may fit other exceptions. Go to Step 12.

    If no: Go to Step 12.

Excited Utterance [Fed. R. Evid. 803(2)]

12. Did the declarant make a statement relating to a startling event or condition? (Examples include crimes, traffic accidents, fights, etc.)

If yes: Go to Step 13.

If no: Go to Step 14.

13. When she made the statement, was the declarant still under the stress of excitement caused by the startling event or conditions?

If yes: The statement is admissible as an excited utterance under Rule 803(2) and may fit other exceptions. Go to Step 14.

If no: Go to Step 14.

Then-Existing State of Mind [Fed. R. Evid. 803(3)]

14. Did the declarant make a statement about her current mental or physical condition, sensation, emotion, thought, or plan?

If yes: Go to Step 15.

If no: Go to Step 17.

15. Was the statement a statement of then-existing memory or then-existing belief to prove the fact remembered or believed? (Examples of such statements of memory or belief: "I believe he went swimming," to prove the person went swimming, or, "I remember that the drink tasted funny," to prove the drink tasted funny.)

If yes: The statement is not admissible under Rule 803(3), the then-existing mental, emotional, or physical condition exception, unless it fits the exception for wills. Go to Step 16.

If no: The statement is admissible under Rule 803(3). Go to Step 17.

16. Did the statement of memory or belief relate to the existence, validity, or terms of the declarant's will?

If yes: The statement is admissible under the then-existing mental, emotional, or physical condition exception. Go to Step 17.

If no: The statement is not admissible under the then-existing mental, emotional, or physical condition exception, but it might fit under another exception. Go to Step 17.

Statement Made for Medical Diagnosis or Treatment [Fed. R. Evid. 803(4)]

17. Was the statement one describing medical symptoms or treatment made for the purpose of medical diagnosis?

If yes: Go to Step 18.

If no: It is not admissible under the statements for medical diagnosis or treatment exception, Fed. R. Evid. 803(4). Go to Step 19.

18. Was the statement pertinent to the medical diagnosis?

If yes: It is admissible under the statements for medical diagnosis or treatment exception, Fed. R. Evid. 803(4), even if the doctor was not a treating physician. Comments that are not pertinent to diagnosis will be redacted. Go to Step 19.

If no: It is not admissible under the statements for medical diagnosis or treatment exception, Fed. R. Evid. 803(4), but it might fit under another exception. Go to Step 19.

Recorded Recollection [Fed. R. Evid. 803(5)]

19. Has the declarant made or adopted a record of a matter about which she once had knowledge but now can only partly remember?

If yes: Go to Step 20.

If no: The exception for past recollection recorded, Fed. R. Evid. 803(5), does not apply. Note: if the declarant's memory can be jogged by a record, it could be used for the non-hearsay purpose of refreshing recollection, and if so, much been shown to the opposing party. Go to Step 21.

20. Was the record made or adopted when the matter was still fresh in the declarant's mind?

If yes: The record is admissible as a past recollection recorded, Fed. R. Evid. 803(5). It will normally be read into the record as testimony, rather than entered as a physical exhibit (unless it is offered by the opposing party). Go to Step 21.

If no: The exception for past recollection recorded, Fed. R. Evid. 803(5), does not apply. Note: if the declarant's memory can be jogged by the record, the offering attorney could use the record for the non-hearsay purpose of refreshing recollection. Go to Step 21.

Business Records [Fed. R. Evid. 803(6)]

21. Is the out-of-court statement a record of regularly conducted business activity where it was the regular practice of the business to make such a record?

If yes: Go to Step 22.

If no: The exception for business records, Fed. R. Evid. 803(6), does not apply. Go to Step 25.

22. Was the record made by a person with knowledge, or made from information transmitted by a person with knowledge?

    If yes: Go to Step 23.

    If no: The exception for business records, Fed. R. Evid. 803(6), does not apply. Go to Step 25.

23. Was the source of the information part of the regular business loop? In other words, did the source of the information possess a business duty to speak or otherwise participate in creating the record?

    If yes: Go to Step 24.

    If no: The statement fails the business-duty rule. The exception for business records, Fed. R. Evid. 803(6), does not apply. Go to Step 25.

24. Can the opponent of the evidence prove that the source of information or the method or circumstances of preparation indicates a lack of trustworthiness? (The most common example of lack of trustworthiness is a record prepared in anticipation of litigation.)

    If yes: The exception for business records, Fed. R. Evid. 803(6), does not apply. Go to Step 25.

    If no: The exception for business records, Fed. R. Evid. 803(6), applies, unless the record is a police report offered by the government in a criminal case. Go to Step 25.

Public Records and Reports [Fed. R. Evid. 803(8)]

25. Is the hearsay statement a record or report concerning the activities of a government agency?

    If yes: Go to Step 26.

    If no: The exception for public records and reports, Fed. R. Evid. 803(8), does not apply. Go to Step 28.

26. Does the governmental record or report involve any of the following?

    - Activities of the government agency;

    - Matters observed pursuant to a duty imposed by law when the public servant has a duty to report, excluding matters observed by law enforcement personnel; or

    - Factual findings resulting from an investigation made pursuant to legal authority. (The underlying evidence used by public servants in reaching their conclusion need not be admissible.)

If yes: Go to Step 27.

If no: The exception for public records and reports, Fed. R. Evid. 803(8), does not apply. Go to Step 28.

27. Can the opponent of the evidence prove that the source of information or the method or circumstances of preparation indicate a lack of trustworthiness? (Examples of lack of trustworthiness include records prepared in anticipation of litigation or records that rely heavily on inadmissible hearsay.)

    If yes: The exception for public records and reports, Fed. R. Evid. 803(8), does not apply. Go to Step 28.

    If no: The exception for public records and reports, Fed. R. Evid. 803(8), applies. Go to Step 28.

Learned Treatises [Fed. R. Evid. 803(18)]

28. Does the out-of-court statement come from a learned treatise?

    If yes: It is admissible under Fed. R. Evid. 803(18) once a foundation has been established that the work is a reliable authority and can be used to impeach experts. If admitted, the treatise excerpts may be read into evidence but may not be received as an exhibit.

    If no: Fed. R. Evid. 803(18) does not apply. Go to Step 29.

Ancient Documents [Fed. R. Evid. 803(16)]

29. Does the out-of-court statement arise from a document that is 20 or more years old?

    If yes: It is admissible under the ancient documents exception, Fed. R. Evid. 803(16). In 2016, the Evidence Advisory Committee proposed to abrogate this rule, so double check that it is still operative.

    If no: Go to Step 30.

Residual Exception [Fed. R. Evid. 807]

30. Have you tried every step in this checklist and still cannot figure out a way to get the hearsay statement in?

    If yes: Go to Step 31.

    If no: The checklist has generated at least one way that the out-of-court statement can be used for its truth. Stop here unless you wish to argue in the alternative that Fed. R. Evid. 807 also applies to admit the evidence.

31. Does the otherwise inadmissible, relevant hearsay evidence:

- Provide "guarantees of trustworthiness" that are "equivalent" to those of established exceptions;

- Offer evidence that is more probative on the point for which it is offered than any other evidence that can reasonably be obtained; and

- Serve the "interests of justice" by its admission?

If yes: Go to Step 32.

If no: The out-of-court statement is not admissible under the residual exception, Fed. R. Evid. 807, and the hearsay evidence will not come in.

32. Did the proponent of the evidence provide the opposing party with notice or demonstrate to the court that its failure to do so was excusable?

If yes: The hearsay statement is admissible for its truth under the residual exception, Fed. R. Evid. 807, but the ruling will have no precedential value.

If no: The out-of-court statement is inadmissible hearsay.

ILLUSTRATIVE PROBLEMS

■ PROBLEM 7.1 ■

Q: Alvin is accused of money laundering. The chief evidence offered by the Prosecution is the testimony of Wanda, who made a sworn statement at the police station, subject to penalties of perjury. Ignoring issues of confrontation, under what circumstances would Wanda's sworn statement be admissible under the hearsay rules if Wanda does not appear at trial?

A: Wanda's statement is hearsay.

Wanda's out-of-court statement is hearsay, even though sworn and subject to penalties of perjury, if used to prove the truth of the matter asserted. One justification for excluding such hearsay as a general matter is that the trier-of-fact does not have the benefit of hearing Wanda's statement challenged by cross-examination. However, its status as hearsay does not necessarily mean it is not admissible. The next step is to examine hearsay exemptions and exceptions.

None of the Rule 801(d) "not hearsay" exemptions apply.

Wanda is unavailable as a witness, so the Fed. R. Evid. 801(d)(1) exemptions do not apply. Wanda is not a party, so Fed. R. Evid. 801(d)(2) does not apply to her out-of-court statement. Even if Wanda were a co-conspirator of Alvin, her statement to the police was certainly not made in furtherance of the conspiracy, so it cannot fall under Fed. R. Evid. 801(d)(2)(E).

None of the Rule 803 exceptions apply, either.

Looking at the Rule 803 exceptions where the declarant's availability is immaterial, the out-of-court statement is unlikely to be an excited utterance under Fed. R. Evid. 803(2) because of the formality surrounding the police question. Whatever stress Wanda was under had long passed, and she was calm enough to sit and make a formal statement. Her statement cannot be admitted as a statement of then-existing state of mind under Fed. R. Evid. 803(3) because it consists of facts remembered or believed. It is not a business record under Fed. R. Evid. 803(6) because Wanda was not involved in police business and had no business duty to speak. It fails as a public record or report because Fed. R. Evid. 803(8) specifically excludes matters observed by police in criminal cases.

Wanda may be unavailable under Rule 804.

The fact that Wanda did not appear at trial does not necessarily mean she is unavailable under Rule 804(a). Assuming, however, that the Prosecutor made appropriate efforts to subpoena Wanda and have Wanda testify, or that Wanda is too sick to testify, or, worse yet, that she is dead, she would qualify as unavailable, thereby triggering the Rule 804 exceptions.

The only Rule 804 exception that might apply is forfeiture by wrongdoing, Fed. R. Evid. 804(b)(6), and more facts would be needed to fit within that exception.

Wanda's statement, though under oath, fails to qualify as former testimony under Fed. R. Evid. 804(b)(1) because it was not cross-examined when it was made and, less significantly, because it was not made at a hearing, proceeding, or deposition, but rather at the police station. Wanda's statement is not a dying declaration under Fed. R. Evid. 804(b)(2) because it was not made while she thought her death was imminent. It is also not a declaration against interest, Fed. R. Evid. 804(b)(3), because there is no indication that she made the statement against her penal or pecuniary interests. Even if she did incriminate herself somewhat, it is likely that she portrayed herself in the best light when she spoke with the police.

If Wanda is unavailable because Alvin intentionally made her so with threats or bribes, or by creating some physical impediment to her testimony (hopefully not cement overshoes), then the statement might be admissible through the forfeiture by wrongdoing exception, Fed. R. Evid. 804(b)(6). However, the question presents insufficient information to make the determination. The policy of this rule is the equitable principle that a party should not benefit from her wrongful action. The judge, using Fed. R. Evid. 104(a), would determine the preliminary question of whether Alvin made Wanda intentionally unavailable.

Nothing in the facts indicates that Wanda's statement is so reliable and unusual that resort to the Rule 807 residual hearsay exception would be warranted.

Finally, Fed. R. Evid. 807, the residual evidence rule—the last refuge of a party desperate to admit hearsay when no other exception has availed—will not work to admit this hearsay. Un-cross-examined statements to police are quintessential examples of untrustworthy hearsay. The current evidence rules insist that the declarant be present to be examined about the prior statement under Fed. R. Evid. 801(d)(1), or that the statement made at a proceeding or deposition was cross-examined when made as required by Fed. R. Evid. 804(b)(1). Neither safeguard is present, and this is not the type of oddball case for which Rule 807 was designed.

Conclusion.

Wanda's statement is inadmissible hearsay unless Alvin intentionally rendered her unavailable to prevent Wanda from testifying.

■ PROBLEM 7.2 ■

Q: Pamela was badly injured when a truck, driven by Devin, rear-ended her car at a stoplight. She makes the following statement to an emergency medical technician on the scene: "Oh my God! Help me! I may not make it. My head is killing me. That truck driver did not even slow down. I wasn't wearing my seatbelt because it was just a short trip to the grocery store." Two days after the accident, Pamela's head injury leads to a debilitating stroke that affects her memory and speech. She is unable to communicate or testify. How might her statement be used in the civil lawsuit of Pamela versus Devin concerning the accident?

A: Pamela's statement is hearsay.

Pamela's statement is hearsay because it is an out-of-court statement offered to prove the truth of the matters asserted in the statement. Pamela's representative would wish to use the statement to prove Pamela's head pain and the fact that the truck did not slow down when it rear-ended her. Devin would wish to use her statement to show that Pamela was not wearing a seatbelt, which in some jurisdictions is an affirmative defense that reduces the defendant's liability. One justification for excluding such hearsay as a general matter is that the trier-of-fact does not have the benefit of directly hearing Pamela's statement, observing her demeanor, or benefiting from information elicited on cross-examination. However, the status of the statement as hearsay does not necessarily mean it is not admissible. The next step is to examine hearsay exemptions and exceptions.

Pamela's statement could be used against her because she is a party.

Because Pamela is a party, Fed. R. Evid. 801(d)(2)(A) would allow Devin to introduce Pamela's statement about not wearing a seatbelt as a statement by a party-opponent if it was relevant to his defense. Devin need not show that Pamela was aware that the statement was against interest at the time it was made. Although Pamela is clearly unavailable under Rule 804(a) because she is too disabled to testify, it is not clear that she would meet the strictures of the declarations-against-interest exception because she might not have been aware that what she was saying might have been against her penal or litigation interests.

None of the Fed. R. Evid. 801(d)(1) exemptions apply.

None of the Fed. R. Evid. 801(d)(1) exemptions apply because Pamela is not available as a witness.

Pamela's entire statement is admissible as an excited utterance.

Looking at the Rule 803 exceptions where the declarant's availability is immaterial, we find that Pamela's entire statement is probably admissible as an excited utterance under Fed. R. Evid. 803(2). The accident was a startling event, and Pamela was probably still under the stress of the event when she made statements concerning the event. The "Oh My God!" part of her statement can be used to "bootstrap" the hearsay by supporting the preliminary finding by the court under Rule 104(a) that she was indeed excited.

Pamela's statements about head pain will also fall under Fed. R. Evid. 803(1), 803(3), and 803(4).

Pamela's statement about head pain will satisfy the present sense impression exception of Fed. R. Evid. 803(1) because it was made as she perceived the pain. Similarly, her statement about head pain is admissible as a then-existing physical condition under Fed. R. Evid. 803(3). Her statement about pain will also qualify as statement made for medical diagnosis or treatment under Fed. R. Evid. 804. It does not matter whether the EMT was a doctor; it is sufficient that he was a logical person from whom to request medical assistance.

Pamela's statements about fault will not fall under Fed. R. Evid. 803(1), 803(3), or (probably) 803(4).

Pamela's statements about the truck driver's failure to stop, although admissible as an excited utterance, will not qualify under the present sense impression, the then-existing state of mind, or the statements made for medical diagnosis exceptions. It fails Fed. R. Evid. 803(1) (present sense impression) because she is reporting an event too distant in the past. Pamela did not make her statement about the truck's failure to stop "immediately" after she perceived it.

Similarly, because of the timing, Pamela is not reporting a then-existing perception, but a fact remembered, which is excluded by Fed. R. Evid. 803(3). The passage of time makes such post-accident statements of fault generally seem unreliable, and they do not fit within the hearsay exceptions for Fed. R. Evid. 803(1). However, if Pamela was still under the stress of excitement when she made the statement, it may qualify as an excited utterance under Fed. R. Evid. 803(2).

Finally, unless one could credibly argue that the truck's driving error (as opposed to the fact of the impact) was pertinent to Pamela's diagnosis, that part of the statement is also not admissible under Fed. R. Evid. 803(4). If, however, the nature of the impact and its speed are pertinent to diagnosis, such as to determine whether an injured driver might have an acute subdural hematoma, and if medical professionals routinely request this information, it might be admissible under Fed. R. Evid. 803(4).

Pamela's statement is possibly admissible as a dying declaration.

As noted, because of her disability, Pamela is clearly unavailable under Rule 804(a), so it is worthwhile to explore whether her statement was a dying declaration under Fed. R. Evid. 804(b)(2). The judge would have to determine under Fed. R. Evid. 104(a) whether Pamela believed her death to be imminent. The judge could rely on inadmissible evidence. Factors include:

(1)　Her own statement about whether she would make it;

(2)　Her request for help, indicating that she had not determined that all attempts to cheat death were futile;

(3)　The surrounding circumstances, such as whether Pamela appeared to be severely injured; and

(4)　What was said to Pamela.

Reassuring statements by the EMT would undermine the likelihood that Pamela believed she was dying. If it is possible to establish Pamela's belief in her impending death, the dying declaration will apply even though she did not die. To qualify under this exception, the Declarant has to be unavailable, but not necessarily dead. Since this is a civil case, and Pamela made the declaration about the cause of what she believed was going to kill her, the evidence would be admissible under Fed. R. Evid. 804(b)(2) if the foundational requirement of the Declarant's belief in imminent death is met.

Pamela's statement will not be admissible under forfeiture by wrongdoing.

Even though Devin made Pamela unavailable by hitting her with his truck and affecting her brain function, the exception for forfeiture by wrongdoing, Fed. R. Evid. 804(b)(6), does not apply because Devin did not intentionally cause Pamela's absence in order to prevent her testimony.

Conclusion.

Devin will be able to admit Pamela's statement about not wearing a seatbelt as a statement by a party-opponent if it is material to the lawsuit. Pamela's statements as to her injury and the truck's failure to stop will be admissible as excited utterances, indicating the far reach of this exception. Pamela's statements might also be admissible as dying declarations if the judge determines that Pamela believed in her own impending death. Pamela's statements about her headache and pain would also be admissible as present sense impressions, statements of a then-existing physical condition, and statements made for medical diagnosis.

POINTS TO REMEMBER

- When a hearsay statement fits within an exception, the statement can be offered for its truth.

- For exceptions under Fed. R. Evid. 804, the declarant must be unavailable. For exceptions under Fed. R. Evid. 803, it does not matter whether the declarant is available.

- Generally, declarants must possess personal knowledge concerning the subject of their statements. (For business records, not everyone in the business loop needs personal knowledge.)

Exceptions that Apply Only if the Declarant Is Unavailable [Fed. R. Evid. 804]

- For a Rule 804 exception to apply, the declarant must be unavailable.

- Unavailability is defined as any cause that, through no fault of the proponent, prevents the witness from attending or testifying. Examples of causes for unavailability include the following:

  o Death;

  o Mental or physical disability;

  o The witness is beyond the court's subpoena power and there is no other reasonable way to obtain her testimony;

  o The witness invokes a privilege;

  o The witness appears, asserts no privilege, but refuses to testify after being ordered to do so; or

  o The witness appears and testifies that she cannot recall the subject matter.

- The former-testimony exception, Fed. R. Evid. 804(b)(1), admits former testimony given under oath and subject to cross-examination from an unavailable declarant. To qualify for the former-testimony exception:

  o *In criminal cases*: The party against whom the former testimony is offered must have had a similar motive and opportunity to cross-examine the witness when the former testimony was first offered.

  o *In civil cases*: The former testimony can be introduced if a party against whom the testimony is offered or the party's "predecessor in interest" had a similar motive and opportunity to cross-examine. The term "predecessor in interest" describes someone who had a prior interest in property that is now subject to litigation or who was otherwise in privity with a party.

- The dying declarations exception, Fed. R. Evid. 804(b)(2), admits statements by declarants who believe death is imminent, and whose statements concern the cause or circumstance of the impending death.

  o The declarant does not actually have to die to qualify for this exception; she just has to believe at the time of making the statement that she was about to die and to be currently unavailable.

  o Fed. R. Evid. 804(b)(2) applies to homicide criminal cases and civil cases. It does not apply to crimes other than homicide.

- The declarations against interest exception, Fed. R. Evid. 804(b)(3), admits statements by an absent declarant that are so contrary to the declarant's own interest that the declarant would not have made the statement unless it were true.

  o Fed. R. Evid. 804(b)(3) applies to financial and property interests, tort or contract interests, and penal interests. The rule does not apply to social interests such as statements that subject the declarant to hatred or humiliation.

  o In criminal cases, corroborating circumstances supporting the trustworthiness of the statement are required.

  o When an absent declarant's narrative is mixed, containing neutral, inculpatory, and exculpatory statements, the court will analyze the remarks statement by statement, admitting only the inculpatory ones.

  o Although some statements by party-opponents are also possible declarations against interest, it is easier to admit them under Fed. R. Evid. 801(d)(2) because the rule for admitting statements by party-opponents does not require personal knowledge or knowledge at the time it was made that the statement was against interest.

- The forfeiture by wrongdoing exception, Fed. R. Evid. 804(b)(6), admits hearsay statements by an absent declarant offered against a party who has intentionally procured (or acquiesced in wrongfully causing) the unavailability of the declarant as a witness. The focus is on the intent of the party, who must have intended to deprive the fact-finder of the witness's testimony.

Exceptions—Declarant Availability Immaterial [Fed. R. Evid. 803]

- The present sense impression exception, Fed. R. Evid. 803(1), admits hearsay statements describing or explaining an event or condition made while or immediately after it was perceived. Timing is crucial. The statement must be made during the event or immediately afterwards.

- The excited utterance exception, Fed. R. Evid. 803(2), admits hearsay statements relating to a startling event or condition made when the declarant was still experiencing the stress of excitement. There is no formal timing requirement, but the declarant must still feel the effects of the stress caused by the startling event or condition.

- The then-existing state of mind exception, Fed. R. Evid. 803(3), admits direct evidence of the declarant's mental state or physical condition at the time of the incident in question.

  o It includes any direct statement of a current thought, sensation, emotion, or plan of the declarant. Note: Some statements that indirectly indicate the declarant's state of mind are not hearsay at all.

  o Except in statements related to testamentary wills, Rule 803(3) excludes statements of the declarant's memory or belief.

  o Courts are divided about the admissibility of a current statement of the declarant's plan to circumstantially prove the actions of another. This is known as the *Hillmon* question.

- The exception for statements for medical diagnosis or treatment, Fed. R. Evid. 803(4), admits statements describing medical history and past or present symptoms, made for and reasonably pertinent to medical diagnosis or treatment.

  o The statement can be made either by the patient (or someone representing the patient) or by the medical professional.

  o Rule 803(4) is not limited to statements of present symptoms.

  o The statement must be pertinent to the diagnosis.

  o Rule 803(4) applies to treating as well as testifying physicians.

- The past recollection recorded exception, Fed. R. Evid. 803(5), admits a document or record where the witness once had knowledge of the matter, but at trial cannot remember it well enough "to testify fully and accurately."

  o The record must have been made or adopted by the witness when the matter was "fresh" in the witness's memory.

  o The record must accurately reflect the witness's knowledge at the time it was made.

  o The witness must have an incomplete memory of the event; Rule 803(5) does not apply if the witness has absolutely no memory of making the statement.

  o If the record is admitted under Rule 803(5), it can be read into evidence; it will not be admitted as an exhibit unless offered by the opposing party.

      o   Rule 803(5) is different from refreshing memory, which is a non-hearsay use of the record. A present recollection refreshed is not offered into evidence, but shown to the witness to jog her memory.

- The business records exception, Fed. R. Evid. 803(6), admits records of regularly conducted business activity.

      o   These include records of acts, events, conditions, opinions, or diagnoses.

      o   Record must be made "at or near the time" of the act, event, condition, opinion, or diagnosis.

      o   Record must be made by a person with knowledge, or made from information transmitted by a person with knowledge.

      o   Record must be made and based on information provided by someone acting in the regular course of business; this is known as the business-duty rule.

      o   Creating the record must have been the "regular practice" of that business activity.

      o   A custodian or other qualified witness may lay the foundation for a business record, or the business record may be self-authenticating without producing a foundational witness.

      o   Fed. R. Evid. 803(6) does not apply if the evidence's opponent can show that the "source of information or the method or circumstances of preparation indicate a lack of trustworthiness." The most common example of lack of trustworthiness is a record prepared in anticipation of litigation.

      o   Even though some police reports might seem to fall under Fed. R. Evid. 803(6), the provision in Fed. R. Evid. 803(8)(A)(ii) excluding matters observed by law enforcement personnel applies to business records as well.

- The public records exception, Fed. R. Evid. 803(8), admits records and reports concerning the activities of an office or agency.

      o   Fed. R. Evid. 803(8)(A)(ii) admits matters observed pursuant to a duty imposed by law when the public servant has a duty to report. It excludes matters observed by law-enforcement personnel for use in a criminal case.

      o   Fed. R. Evid. 803(8)(A)(iii) covers factual findings resulting from an investigation made pursuant to legal authority.

The underlying evidence used by public servants in reaching their conclusions need not be admissible. It applies to civil cases and findings offered against the government in criminal cases.

o   The public records exception has no business-duty rule.

o   The public records exception allows the court to exclude evidence that otherwise satisfies the rule if the opponent can show that "the sources of information or other circumstances indicate lack of trustworthiness."

- The learned treatise exception, Fed. R. Evid. 803(18), admits text from professional or scholarly published works, once a foundation has been established that the work is a reliable authority.

o   Learned treatises can also be used to impeach experts, but the treatise must be shown to the expert witness.

o   The treatise is not an exhibit. If admitted, the treatise excerpts may be read into evidence, but they may not be received as exhibits.

- The ancient documents exception, Fed. R. Evid. 803(16), admits statements in documents that are 20 years old or older. The Evidence Rules Advisory Committee has recommend abrogating this exception.

The Residual Exception [Fed. R. Evid. 807]

- The residual exception to the hearsay rule is the last place to look when a party is trying to admit hearsay and nothing else works.

- To qualify under Rule 807, the hearsay evidence must:

o   Provide "guarantees of trustworthiness" that are "equivalent" to those of the established exceptions;

o   Be "more probative" on the point for which it is offered than any other evidence that can reasonably be obtained; and

o   Be in the "interests of justice" and in accordance with the purposes of the Rules.

- To admit a statement under Rule 807, the proponent of the evidence must send the opposing party notice or demonstrate to the court that its failure to do so was excusable.

- Rulings based on Fed. R. Evid. 807 have no precedential value.

Hearsay Within Hearsay [Fed. R. Evid. 805]

The hearsay within hearsay rule allows the admission of multiple hearsay statements, or hearsay within hearsay, if each part of the combined statements is either not hearsay at all or conforms to an exemption under Fed. R. Evid. 801(d) or to an exception under Fed. R. Evid. 803, 804, or 807.

CHAPTER 8

Confrontation

§ 8.1   *Introduction to the Confrontation Clause*

The Confrontation Clause of the Sixth Amendment applies to federal and state criminal trials. It provides: "In all criminal prosecutions, the accused shall enjoy the right . . . to be confronted with the witnesses against him." Until *Crawford v. Washington*, 541 U.S. 36 (2004), the court construed the Confrontation Clause to provide little more than the protections otherwise assured by the hearsay rule.[1] *Crawford* gave the Confrontation Clause independent meaning, but it also confused confrontation doctrine and raised questions about the constitutionality of some traditional hearsay exceptions involving absent declarants.

§ 8.2   *Comparing Hearsay and Confrontation*

HEARSAY	CONFRONTATION
Applies to civil and criminal	Applies to criminal only
Can be raised by any party	Is the right of the accused, not of the prosecutor
Focuses on accuracy and reliability	Rejects using accuracy or reliability as a surrogate for actual confrontation, and insists, with limited exceptions, upon the accused's right to cross-examine witnesses under oath in court. Is grounded in the belief that a specific, essential process—confrontation—has unique social and procedural value.

---

[1]   Under the rule set forth in *Ohio v. Roberts*, 448 U.S. 56 (1980), the Confrontation Clause was satisfied if the out-of-court statement bore "adequate 'indicia of reliability.'" Such reliability derived from a "firmly rooted hearsay exception" or "particularized guarantees of trustworthiness." *Roberts* essentially collapsed the confrontation standard onto the hearsay rules; by satisfying traditional hearsay rules, the prosecutor almost always satisfied the Confrontation Clause.

§ 8.3   Crawford v. Washington

In *Crawford*, authored by the late Antonin Scalia, the Supreme Court of the United States held that an out-of-court "testimonial" statement may be used against the accused only if the declarant is either:

- Available for cross-examination; OR

- Proved to be unavailable and the testimonial statement was previously subject to cross-examination by the accused.

Crawford focused its holding on whether the out-of-court statement used against the accused constituted a "testimonial statement." Unfortunately, *Crawford* did not actually define what it meant by "testimonial." One definition cited (but not fully endorsed) by *Crawford* is that testimonial statements are those "made under circumstances which would lead an objective witness reasonably to believe that the statement would be available for use at a later trial." Some statements are indisputably testimonial, including:

- Testimony at a preliminary hearing;

- Grand jury testimony;

- Testimony at a former trial;

- Police interrogations;

- Affidavits prepared for trial.

*Non*testimonial statements receive no constitutional protection whatsoever, and their use in criminal cases is checked only by the hearsay rule.

§ 8.4   *Exploring What Is a Testimonial Statement: Ongoing Emergencies and Primary Purposes*

Post-*Crawford*, courts around the country have struggled with questions concerning which out-of-court statements are "testimonial." In particular, they wrestled with whether statements made by domestic violence victims to police at the scene of the incident are "testimonial." If such statements are testimonial, courts cannot admit them against the accused unless the witness is available to testify or the accused had an opportunity to cross-examine. As a practical matter, victims of domestic violence often recant or refuse to testify. In addition, there are often no other witnesses to the actual battery besides the victim and the accused.

Therefore, without the victim's in-court testimony, the prosecutor often has no case.

In *Davis v. Washington*, 547 U.S. 813 (2006), the court held that the statement to police by a victim of domestic violence was nontestimonial because it was not intended to provide testimony. Instead, the situation and the statement itself "objectively indicated its primary purpose was to enable police assistance to meet an ongoing emergency." The court contrasted the facts of *Davis* with the facts of its companion case, *Hammon v. Indiana*, in which it deemed the statements of the domestic violence victim to be testimonial.

TESTIMONIAL STATEMENT IN *HAMMON*	NONTESTIMONIAL STATEMENT IN *DAVIS*
Circumstances objectively indicate that there was no "ongoing emergency."	Declarant's statements were "[m]ade in the course of police interrogation under circumstances objectively indicating that the primary purpose of the interrogation is to enable police assistance to meet an ongoing emergency."
Declarant's statements "were neither a cry for help nor the provision of information enabling officers immediately to end a threatening situation."	Declarant's statements were "necessary to be able to *resolve* the present emergency, rather than simply to learn . . . what had happened in the past."
The primary purpose of the interrogation was to "establish or prove past events potentially relevant to later criminal prosecution."	Declarant's statements were "speaking about events *as they were actually happening,* rather than 'describ[ing] past events.'"

Another factor for assessing the testimonial nature of a statement is its formality; the more formal, the more likely the statement is testimonial. The court emphasized, however, that intention, not formality, was the key inquiry.

Justice Thomas has advocated a narrow, bright-line definition of testimonial statements that exclusively looks to history, formality, and solemnity. His consistent approach, which no other Justice has adopted, would deem only "formalized testimonial materials, such as affidavits, depositions, prior testimony, or confessions" testimonial statements under the *Crawford* standard.

In 2011, the court again addressed the question of continuing emergency in *Michigan v. Bryant*, 562 U.S. 344 (2011). In *Bryant*, as the police awaited medical help, they surrounded a bleeding gunshot victim, questioning him repeatedly about the event and learning the name of the shooter. The Victim died shortly thereafter. Quoting *Davis*, the court held that, with the possibility of a shooter on the loose, the primary purpose of the interrogation was to enable police assistance to meet an ongoing emergency. The court cited the Victim's medical condition and the type of weapon used as factors in determining whether an ongoing emergency existed. Therefore, the Victim's identification and description of the shooter and the location of the shooting were not testimonial statements and their admission at Bryant's trial did not violate the Confrontation Clause. The majority's references to reliability deeply troubled Justice Scalia, who for the first time wrote a dissent in a major post-*Crawford* confrontation case.

The *Bryant* majority explained that to determine the primary purpose of a statement made by a victim at the scene of a criminal investigation, the court should examine the police's perspective and the surrounding circumstances, in addition to the victim's perspective. The court also considered the level of formality (which was low, since the Victim bled to death on the ground of a gas station); but, as in *Davis*, the mere fact that the encounter was informal did not render it nontestimonial.

In *Ohio v. Clark*, ___ U.S. ___, 135 S. Ct. 2173 (2015), Justice Alito, writing for the court, held that a three-year-old victim's statements to his teacher identifying the Accused as his batterer were not testimonial. The primary purpose of the child's statements was to get help, not to get the Accused in trouble. Even though teachers are mandatory reporters, that obligation alone does not convert a conversation between teacher and student into a testimonial report to law enforcement.

§ 8.5   *Forfeiture by Wrongdoing:* Giles

In *Giles v. California*, 554 U.S. 353 (2008), the court addressed the conditions whereby an accused forfeits the confrontation right. In *Giles*, the Accused was charged with murdering his girlfriend, who had previously made tearful statements to police about Giles's past violence and threats of future violence. Three weeks after the statements were made, Giles killed her, claiming that he acted in self-defense. At his murder trial, Giles supported his self-defense claim by describing the Victim as "jealous, vindictive, aggressive, and violent." To rebut Giles's self-defense claim and impeach his testimony, the state introduced into evidence the Victim's uncross-examined statements to police.

The Justices examined whether by killing the Victim, something the Accused acknowledged that he did (allegedly in self-defense), the Accused forfeited his right to confront her prior statements. The court ruled that, to fall within the forfeiture doctrine, the Accused must *intend* to prevent the witness from testifying. *Giles* held that not every homicide case automatically opens the door to admitting the victim's former testimonial statements. To do so would ignore the traditional common-law intent requirement of forfeiture and deprive the Accused of his confrontation rights.[2]

In his concurrence in part, Justice Souter also expressed concern about the unseemliness of allowing a trial judge to determine a preliminary fact (that the Accused made the Victim unavailable by murdering her) that also encompasses an ultimate fact for the jury. Although trial courts often find preliminary facts by a preponderance of the evidence, Justice Souter was troubled that a judicial finding on this issue could vitiate a constitutional right. Additionally, Justice Souter argued that a long-term dynamic of abuse might count as forfeiture.

The dissent noted the anomalous results of the majority's approach. In domestic violence cases where the victim has made previous statements incriminating the accused, the majority's rule creates a disturbing incentive for the accused batterer. A batterer who strikes in anger (not necessarily to silence his victim in future proceedings) is better off killing his victim. If he merely intimidates her into refusing to testify, the hearsay will come in; if he kills her in anger, his hearsay will not be admissible.

§ 8.6   *Dying Declarations*

Dicta in *Crawford*, *Giles*, and *Bryant* indicate that dying declarations[3] may present an exception to the rule set out in *Crawford*.

Not all dying declarations will be testimonial, but some clearly are. Normally under the *Crawford* scheme, when an out-of-court

---

[2]   The dissent questioned *Giles*'s focus on the Accused's subjective intent to make the Declarant unavailable and instead advocated an objective test: whether a reasonable Accused would recognize that his actions would render the witness unavailable. The dissent argued that such an objective test would be consonant with the equitable notion of forfeiture—that the Accused should not benefit from his own wrongdoing.

[3]   *See* § 7.18 (discussing dying declarations).

statement by an absent declarant is testimonial, it cannot be used against the accused unless there is cross-examination at the time it was made. When a victim who has since died makes a dying declaration that is intended to incriminate the accused, it would seem to be prohibited by *Crawford's* approach. However, *Crawford* was based in large part on an attempt to discern the founders' original intent. Dying declarations were clearly admissible at the time the Sixth Amendment was written, so it is hard to argue that the Confrontation Clause was intended to prohibit them. The issue of a testimonial dying declaration is open, but the court's dicta imply that such dying declarations would be admissible.

§ 8.7 *Lab Reports and Confrontation:* Melendez-Diaz, Bullcoming, *and* Williams

In addition to statements made at the scene of domestic violence, laboratory reports present some difficult and recurring confrontational questions.

In *Melendez-Diaz v. Massachusetts*, 557 U.S. 305 (2009), the court held 5–4 that a lab analyst's notarized certificate attesting that a substance was cocaine was "testimonial." Because the lab analyst was never called as a witness by the government, and in fact no live witness testified, the admission of the lab report violated the Accused's right to confrontation. Scalia, writing for the majority, explained that the lab reports, even though they resembled business records, fell within the "core class of testimonial statements," because it was prepared for use at trial against the Accused.

The court found unpersuasive the attempts to distinguish the type of testimonial evidence in *Crawford* from scientific lab reports that arise out of a post-crime forensic inquiry by a nonaccusatory, neutral party who was reporting near-contemporaneous observations.

The dissent criticized the majority for leaving important questions unanswered: most notably, the majority failed to clarify who, among the many scientists, technicians, and engineers who generated a positive-for-cocaine result, must be available for confrontation.[4] The dissent further portrayed the entire *Crawford* jurisprudence as devolving into a "body of formalistic and wooden rules, divorced from precedent, common sense, and the underlying purpose of the Clause."

---

[4] Clifford Fishman has amusingly and accurately referred to this as the "Ghostbusters question" ("Who you gonna call?"). CLIFFORD S. FISHMAN, A STUDENT'S GUIDE TO HEARSAY (Fall 2012 update).

In *Bullcoming v. New Mexico*, 564 U.S 647 (2011), the Accused was arrested for drunk driving. The Accused's gas chromatography indicated a .21 blood alcohol level, sufficient for a charge of aggravated DWI. Unlike in *Melendez-Diaz*, the Prosecutor called a live witness, a lab technician who was familiar with the procedure and technology but who had not observed or supervised the actual test in this case. The technician who performed the procedure was not proved unavailable (he was on unpaid leave for unexplained reasons). The court found that the certification of the blood alcohol level through the testimony of an analyst who did not sign the certification or observe the test reported in the certification violated the Confrontation Clause.[5] The dissent viewed the requirement of calling the technician who filled out the form "a hollow formality."

A year later in *Williams v. Illinois*, ___ U.S. ___, 132 S. Ct. 2221 (2012), the court heard the third in the triad of forensic lab-report cases. An independent commercial DNA research group (not a government crime lab) analyzed and reported on DNA from a rapist's semen. An expert witness testified that the DNA profile of semen matched the DNA profile of the Accused gathered in another case. No one from the commercial DNA group that created the DNA profile testified. The Supreme Court delivered a near-incomprehensible opinion holding that the expert's testimony did not violate the Confrontation Clause. Justice Alito explained this result: (1) the expert did not offer the crime lab's finding for its truth, and experts are allowed under Fed. R. Evid. 703 to rely on inadmissible evidence to reach their conclusions; and (2) the lab result did not inculpate anyone specific, it just generated a DNA profile with no targeted accused in mind. The court divided 4–1–4, with Justice Thomas agreeing that the Confrontation Clause was not violated, but only because of his singular, very narrow view of the confrontation right, which he applies only to highly formal statements. Justice Thomas did not agree with any of Justice Alito's reasons for finding that the independent lab report did not violate the Confrontation Clause. Justice Breyer, who also joined in the result, conceded that he was deviating from the court's prior precedents and essentially following the dissents in *Melendez-Diaz* and *Bullcoming*. *Williams* is extremely long, confusing, and essentially unhelpful in determining future precedent.

§ 8.8   *Methods of Confrontation*

In addition to whether the Confrontation Clause applies, an important related question arises concerning *how* the actual confrontation must occur. For instance, where a child witness is a

---

[5]   *See* § 11.5 (discussing Fed. R. Evid. 703 and the basis of expert opinions).

victim of a crime and cannot face the stress of looking the accused in the eye, is face-to-face interaction nevertheless mandated by the Confrontation Clause?

In 1988, in *Coy v. Iowa*, 487 U.S. 1012 (1988), the court struck down an Accused's conviction where a screen had been erected to shield the Victim-witness from the Accused. The court relied on "the irreducible literal meaning of the Clause," which guarantees the "right to meet face-to-face all those who appear and give evidence at trial." Reasoning that it is harder to lie to someone's face, the court held that the face-to-face component of confrontation, like the right to cross-examine, ensures "the integrity of the fact-finding process."

Just two years later, however, in *Maryland v. Craig*, 497 U.S. 836 (1990), the court permitted the use of one-way, closed-circuit television allowing the Accused to hear the testimony and suggest questions, preventing eye contact between the traumatized child witness and the Accused. In explaining the apparent retreat from *Coy*, Justice O'Connor held that the purposes of the Confrontation Clause were satisfied by the witness's physical presence, oath, subjection to cross-examination, and the availability of demeanor evidence. She explained that the Sixth Amendment's preference for face-to-face confrontation "must occasionally give way to considerations of public policy and the necessities of the case."

Justice Scalia dissented, stating, "Seldom has this Court failed so conspicuously to sustain a categorical guarantee of the Constitution against the tide of prevailing current opinion." Although the issue has not yet reached the Supreme Court, it is questionable whether *Craig*, with its focus on the excoriated policy of reliability, remains viable post-*Crawford*.

 CONFRONTATION CHECKLIST

1. Is this a criminal case?

    If yes: Go to Step 2.

    If no: The Confrontation Clause does not apply. In civil cases, the rules of evidence alone will control whether the statement is admissible.

2. Is the evidence being offered against the accused?

    If yes: Go to Step 3.

    If no: The Confrontation Clause does not apply.

3. Does the issue involve a statement made out-of-court?

   If yes: Go to Step 4.

   If no: If a live witness is testifying about what she did or saw, and her testimony is subject to cross-examination, then the Confrontation Clause is not implicated.

4. Is the out-of-court statement being used for its truth?

   If yes: Go to Step 5.

   If no: The Confrontation Clause does not apply.

5. Is there a way to admit the statement under the hearsay rules?

   If yes: Go to Step 6.

   If no: You do not need to worry about confrontation because the hearsay bar will prevent the admission of the out-of-court-statement. (In an exam you should analyze the Confrontation Clause issue anyway, particularly if the hearsay question is close.)

6. Is the declarant currently available for cross-examination under oath at the current trial?

   If yes: Then there is no confrontation problem.

   If no: Go to the Step 7.

7. Was there an opportunity for the accused to cross-examine the statement at some previous time?

   If yes: There is no confrontation problem. The obvious example here is former testimony that was cross-examined at the prior trial, hearing, or deposition.

   If no: Go to Step 8.

8. Is the statement a formal, solemn one (i.e., a sworn affidavit, answer to police interrogation at the stationhouse, former testimony, or part of a deposition)?

   If yes: Its admission violates the Confrontation Clause.

   If no: The statement may still be testimonial. For all Justices other than Justice Thomas, formality and solemnity are factors that contribute to rendering a statement testimonial, but they are not necessary to find that a statement falls within the Confrontation Clause. Go to Step 9.

9. Is the statement "testimonial," e.g., would a reasonable person expect that the prosecutor would use it against the accused in a criminal trial? Alternatively, is the statement's primary purpose to report a crime or collect evidence?

If yes: Go to Step 10.

If no: Because it is *non*testimonial, the Confrontation clause does not apply.

Note: There is significant disagreement about when an ongoing emergency exists, whose perspective matters (just the declarant's, or the declarant's and the listener's), and how much context should be considered. In cases involving lab reports, the Supreme Court Justices disagree about the status of statements that experts use to form their opinions but do not introduce into evidence.

10. Did the accused intentionally make the declarant unavailable in order to prevent the declarant from testifying?

If yes: Even though the out-of-court statement is testimonial and would normally fall under the Confrontation Clause, the forfeiture exception applies and the declarant's statements are admissible. There is growing discussion about how forfeiture works in the context of a long-time violent relationship.

If no: Go to Step 11.

11. Is the statement a dying declaration (i.e., a statement made by a victim of homicide concerning the cause of her believed impending death with the subjective expectation that she will soon die)?

If yes: The Supreme Court in dicta has stated this may be an exception to the Confrontation Clause.

If no: The statement is testimonial and is barred by the Confrontation Clause.

ILLUSTRATIVE PROBLEMS

■ PROBLEM 8.1 ■

Q: Vicky calls Emergency 9-1-1 because her ex-boyfriend, Alan, has entered her house without permission and is breaking items and threatening to injure her. Alan spots Vicky on the phone, pushes her to the ground, kicks Vicky, kicks her dog, and stomps on Vicky's cell phone. After Alan leaves, Vicky calls the police again on a neighbor's phone. She informs the officer that she is bruised, but OK, and that she plans to go in the following day to make a report. Vicky does indeed go to the police station the next day and makes a full report outlining Alan's misconduct. The following week, Alan calls Vicky to apologize. He sends two dozen roses and some organic dog biscuits for Vicky's dog. He sends her a check for a new smart phone and offers to pay Vicky's cell phone bills for a year. Alan begs Vicky not to testify against him because any conviction would constitute a "third strike" that would lead to a long jail sentence (and would prevent him from paying for her phone). After talking to Alan, Vicky informs the police and the district attorney that she is no longer interested in pressing charges and will not participate in Alan's prosecution. The Prosecutor wishes to go forward with the case anyway. He subpoenas Vicky, but on the day of the trial she refuses to testify. As part of Alan's prosecution, the Prosecutor wishes to introduce: (1) Vicky's statement to the 9-1-1 officer: "Help! My ex-boyfriend, Alan Jones, broke into my home and he is destroying things. I'm afraid he is going to hurt me!"; and (2) Vicky's sworn, signed, and written statement, given in the police station the day after the incident, that Alan destroyed her property, intimidated her, and committed battery. Will Vicky's out-of-court statements be admissible?

A: <u>Vicky's statement during her 9-1-1 call is probably admissible hearsay under the excited utterance and present sense impression exceptions.</u>

Any analysis regarding admissibility of an out-of-court statement must always begin with hearsay. If the statement cannot overcome the hearsay bar, then, as a practical matter, there will be no issue of confrontation. Vicky's 9-1-1 qualifies as an excited utterance under Fed. R. Evid. 803(2). Her statement concerns a startling event and was made under the stress of that event. Under hearsay law, Vicky's availability is immaterial and she need not be present to have her statement admitted. Hence, her statement on the phone at the crime scene would be admitted as an exception to the hearsay rule. Given the fact that she was narrating events as they occurred, her statement also meets the requirements of the present sense impression exception, Fed. R. Evid. 803(1).

<u>Admitting Vicky's 9-1-1 statement probably would not violate the Confrontation Clause because it was not testimonial in that it was made for the purpose of requesting help during an ongoing emergency.</u>

Post-*Crawford*, the mere fact that the Prosecutor can admit the 9-1-1 statement as an excited utterance does not satisfy the constitutional question of confrontation, which must be analyzed separately. The confrontation standard announced in *Crawford* requires that in order to admit a testimonial statement, the declarant must either be available for cross-examination concerning the statement, or, if the declarant is unavailable, the declarant must have been previously subject to cross-examination by the accused concerning the statement. For Vicky's 9-1-1 statement, our analysis would consider whether the statement at the scene was testimonial.

If it was a testimonial statement, it could not be introduced under *Crawford* because Vicky is not subject to confrontation and Alan never had an opportunity to cross-examine her about this statement. It appears, however, that the statement is not testimonial because Vicky's primary purpose was to secure assistance, not to create testimony. In this respect, the scenario resembles the facts in *Davis*, where the court admitted the statement from the domestic violence victim's 9-1-1 call. Therefore, Vicky's 9-1-1 statement would probably be admitted even if she refuses to testify.

<u>Vicky's statement at the police station is inadmissible hearsay unless it falls under forfeiture by wrongdoing.</u>

Vicky's statement to police the next day probably cannot be considered an excited utterance—too much time has passed for Vicky to still be operating under the stress of the startling event. It certainly cannot fall within the narrow timing requirements of the present sense impression exception. It does not qualify as an 803(3) statement of current mental condition because it is a fact remembered. The only hearsay exception that might fit her statement after the emergency had subsided would be forfeiture by wrongdoing, Fed. R. Evid. 804(b)(6). If Vicky is truly unavailable (something that would require more factual inquiry), then her statement might be admitted if Alan intentionally rendered her unavailable by bribing her with a free cell phone and free use of it for a year in an attempt to dissuade her from testifying. Per Rule 804(b)(6), the Prosecutor would have to prove that Alan intended to render Vicky unavailable.

<u>If Vicky did not testify because Alan intentionally made her unavailable as a witness, Alan may have forfeited his confrontation right.</u>

Vicky's statement at the police station was unquestionably testimonial, even under Justice Thomas's narrow definition of the term. It is a formal statement generated with the assistance of the government that the Declarant fully expects will be used in court against the Accused. The only possible way for admitting this statement is forfeiture of the confrontation right, as discussed in *Giles*. The constitutional forfeiture analysis resembles the hearsay analysis for forfeiture by wrongdoing. *Giles* indicates that the constitutional question turns on whether Alan intended to make Vicky unavailable. Here, the question of forfeiture centers on bribery of a potential witness. Equally difficult is the question of when a domestic violence perpetrator renders a declarant-victim unavailable because of threats. Given a history of violence between the Accused and the Declarant, even subtle threats might be very effective.

■ **PROBLEM 8.2** ■

Q: Police answer a silent alarm in a liquor store and come upon Derek, a salesman at the liquor store, who is bleeding profusely, and Arthur, who has been knocked out cold on the floor of the liquor store. Derek explains that Arthur attempted to rob the store. Derek managed to hit Arthur with a bottle, but not before Arthur had fired a shot at him. At the scene, Derek states the following to police:

> I was in Afghanistan, and I've seen men shot before. I know that I'm going to die of this wound. I have no hope of making it. I just want you to take my statement and convict Arthur, who came in to rob the store. The man lying here on the ground is Arthur Anderson, whom I know from the pool hall. Arthur pulled out a gun and announced it was a robbery. When I moved to hit him with the bottle, he shot me. I am positive of my identification and I swear that he initiated the violence by pulling out a gun. Please tell my Mom that I love her and that my last thoughts were of her.

Derek does indeed die. Arthur is charged with robbery and murder, but claims that he was only defending himself, not robbing the store. Arthur claims that Derek, who suffered from PTSD as a veteran of the war in Afghanistan, started to behave menacingly by waving a bottle at him, and that Arthur pulled out his gun and shot Derek in self-defense as Derek hurled the bottle. Based on his prior crimes (two recent robberies of liquor stores), the government believes that Arthur did indeed rob and kill Derek without provocation. May the government introduce Derek's statement?

A: <u>Although hearsay, Derek's statement will be admissible as an excited utterance or a dying declaration.</u>

Derek's statement is hearsay if offered for its truth. Because Derek is dead, Arthur will have no opportunity to cross-examine Derek. Arthur, although he was physically present when Derek made his declaration, was unconscious and hence was unable to conduct any meaningful cross-examination. Nevertheless, Derek's statement will be admissible hearsay because his statement qualifies as a dying declaration under Fed. R. Evid. 804(b)(2). He is currently unavailable, he was aware of his impending death when he made his out-of-court declaration, and his statement concerns the cause of his death in a homicide case. The statement might also be an excited utterance under Fed. R. Evid. 803(2). The robbery was a startling event and Derek was still under the stress of the event when he made his statement about what happened.

Derek's statement is testimonial but will probably be admitted notwithstanding a Confrontation Clause challenge.

Applying the *Crawford* standard, Derek's statement is testimonial because his primary purpose is to testify against Arthur, not seek help. There was no opportunity to cross-examine Derek's testimonial statement, so it appears to fail the *Crawford* test. However, dying declarations were recognized at the time of the founders as an exception to the confrontation right. Dicta in *Crawford*, *Giles*, and *Bryant* indicate that the Supreme Court might recognize this exception if it pursues the policy of seeking the original intent of the founding fathers in interpreting the Sixth Amendment Confrontation Clause. The fact that the investigation rested on potentially inadmissible prior-act evidence does not affect the hearsay or Confrontation Clause analysis.

POINTS TO REMEMBER

- The general rule of *Crawford*: If a statement is testimonial, then either the witness must be available for cross-examination or the accused must be unavailable and have had an opportunity to cross-examine the witness at another time.

- The following are clearly testimonial:

  o Affidavits;

  o *Ex parte* in-court testimony;

  o Uncrossed depositions and other prior sworn testimony that the accused was unable to cross-examine;

  o Formal stationhouse statements or other custodial examinations;

  o Lab reports indicating by affidavit or certification the illegal nature of a substance; and

  o Statements made at the scene of a crime after the emergency has passed.

- Some statements are clearly nontestimonial and hence outside constitutional protection:

  o Statements made during an emergency to secure assistance;

  o Casual remarks made to friends;

  o Statements of co-conspirators in furtherance of a conspiracy;

  o Medical reports prepared for treatment purposes;

- o   Regularly kept business records (but not those of forensic laboratories or others prepared in anticipation of litigation);

- o   A clerk's certification that a copy is a true and complete copy of an original on file in the clerk's office; and

- o   Documents prepared in the regular course of maintaining and calibrating laboratory equipment.

- Forfeiture is the only exception to this new definition that the Supreme Court has considered fully. To forfeit the confrontation right, the accused must have made the witness unavailable with the intent of preventing the witness's testimony.

- Justice Thomas has remained steadfast in his very narrow view of testimonial statements, which he limits to formal extrajudicial statements such as affidavits, depositions, prior testimony, or confessions.

Remaining Open Questions

- Three cases dealing with forensic reports still have not clarified whom the prosecution must call regarding lab reports.

- Another unsolved question (especially with child witnesses) concerns what constitutes an adequate opportunity for cross-examination. Post-*Crawford*, some courts have found that entirely unresponsive children are unavailable for Confrontation Clause purposes.

- Admission of testimonial dying declarations has been approved in dicta. The Supreme Court has indicated that because dying declarations constituted an exception at the time of the founders, they will be admissible even when they are testimonial, but the Court has provided no actual decision on this question.

- Although the court has clarified that forfeiture requires an intent to make the witness unavailable, the nature of the showing necessary to prove forfeiture is still open. It is unclear what behavior qualifies as purposely making a witness unavailable, particularly in cases involving an extended violent relationship between the witness and the accused.

CHAPTER 9

Competence

§ 9.1   *Who Is a Competent Witness?*

[Fed. R. Evid. 601]

A competent witness is someone who is allowed to take the witness stand because she can understand the solemnity of the oath and communicate meaningfully. An incompetent witness may not testify.

§ 9.2   *The Federal Rules of Evidence Presume Competence*

Fed. R. Evid. 601 states that every person is competent to be a witness except as otherwise provided by the rules. The competence bar is very low.

Under Fed. R. Evid. 601, the following people would be deemed incompetent:

- Profoundly mentally handicapped people who do not possess language or understanding;

- Preverbal children; and

- Witnesses who refuse to take an oath or affirmation, Fed. R. Evid. 603.

§ 9.3   *How Are Witness Deficits Handled?*

Deficits in witnesses are generally handled by impeachment, not by prohibiting the testimony entirely. The common law rendered some people, such as the mentally ill, children, and the parties to the lawsuit, incompetent to testify. The modern approach, adopted by the Federal Rules of Evidence, allows such folks to testify as witnesses, but uses impeachment to display the potential problems with their testimony.

Witnesses who have impaired perception, mental illness, or memory failure are allowed to testify and can be impeached. The liabilities of such witnesses will affect the weight and credibility of their testimony but will not prohibit their taking the witness stand altogether.

§ 9.4   What Happens in Diversity Cases?

[Fed. R. Evid. 601]

Fed. R. Evid. 601 provides that in diversity cases,[1] the state competence rule will apply in federal court. This deference to state competence rules reflects policies of comity and discourages litigants from forum shopping.

§ 9.5   Lay or Expert Testimony by an Attorney or Judge in the Case

[Fed. R. Evid. 605]

According to Fed. R. Evid. 605, a judge cannot testify in a case over which she presides. Ethical rules prevent an attorney from being a witness in a case she tries.[2]

§ 9.6   Juror Testimony

[Fed. R. Evid. 606]

Sensibly, jurors may not testify as lay or expert witnesses in cases in which they are impaneled, Fed. R. Evid. 606(a).

Jurors are also not competent to testify about their deliberations. However, jurors may testify about the following under Fed. R. Evid. 606(b)(2):

- Whether extraneous prejudicial information was improperly brought to the jury's attention;

- Whether improper outside influences were introduced to the jury (such as the fact that a juror googled a party, or a juror received a bribe or a threat from a party). Note: alcohol or drug use in deliberation is not considered an "outside influence," *Tanner v. United States*, 483 U.S. 107 (1987); and

---

[1]   Diversity cases may be brought in federal court because the opposing parties are citizens of different states and the amount-in-controversy requirement has been met. In diversity actions, state law provides the substantive law that will guide the outcome of the case in federal court. Federal law usually governs procedure, but in the case of Rules 501 (privilege) and 601 (competence), the rule makers decided to follow state law on these issues in cases arising out of state law.

[2]   *See* Model R. Prof. Conduct 3.7 (addressing the question of lawyer as witness).

- Whether there was a mistake in entering the verdict on the verdict form.

COMPETENCE CHECKLIST

1. Does federal law apply to the substance of the case?

   If yes: Go to Step 2.

   If no: According to Fed. R. Evid. 601, determinations of competence will be governed by state law.

2. Is the witness willing to take an oath or make an affirmation?

   If yes: Go to Step 3.

   If no: The witness may not testify.

3. Does the witness understand the solemnity of the oath and the difference between truth and a lie?

   If yes: Go to Step 4.

   If no: The witness is incompetent to testify.

4. Is the witness able to comprehend and communicate?

   If yes: Go to Step 5.

   If no: The witness is incompetent to testify.

5. Is the witness testifying as a lay or expert witness the judge, a juror, or a lawyer in the case?

   If yes: The witness is incompetent to testify.

   If no: Go to Step 6.

6. Is the witness a juror testifying about the jury deliberations in the case?

   If yes: Go to Step 7.

   If no: The witness is competent. She may, however, be impeached for lack of truthful character, bias, or deficits in her thinking, memory, or perception.

7. Does the witness's testimony about deliberations concern an alleged mistake in entering the verdict on the verdict form?

   If yes: The witness is competent to testify.

   If no: Go to Step 8.

8.   Does the witness's testimony about deliberations concern the introduction of extraneous prejudicial information?

If yes: The witness is competent to testify.

If no: Go to Step 9.

9.   Does the witness's testimony about deliberations concern any improper outside influence? This does not include the jurors' use of illegal drugs or alcohol while deliberating.

If yes: The witness is competent to testify.

If no: The witness is incompetent to testify.

ILLUSTRATIVE PROBLEM

■ PROBLEM 9.1 ■

Q: Audrey is convicted for interstate transfer of stolen goods. After a guilty verdict is handed down, Fred, the jury foreperson, expresses his deep regret to Audrey's attorney. He tells her the following:

> Audrey seems like an awfully nice person and I sincerely hope that she gets rehabilitated. I believe the verdict is just, but I wouldn't blame you for feeling bad about it. After all, Stella, juror number 1, came dead drunk every day of the deliberations. Paul, juror number 2, read newspaper accounts even though he was specifically instructed not to by the judge. Jane, Juror number 3, seemed to have cut a deal with the Prosecutor over an unrelated check forgery.

Audrey immediately moves for a hearing to investigate juror misconduct. Will Fred be competent to testify as to what occurred in the jury room? How should the judge rule?

A: As a general rule, jurors are not competent to testify about their deliberations [Fed. R. Evid. 606(b)(1)].

This rule stems from a desire to protect full and frank deliberations, avoid juror harassment, encourage jury service, and promote finality. Also, like the parents of errant teenagers who prefer not to know what their kids are up to, we may be scared to discover what really transpires in jury deliberations.

The rule against inquiring into jury deliberations allows for certain exceptions.

The first exception is administrative, relating to a mistake in transmitting the jury's verdict, Fed. R. Evid. 606(b)(2)(C) and does not apply here. The exceptions concerning introduction of extraneous prejudicial information and improper outside influence apply to testimony about two of the jurors in Audrey's case, Fed. R. Evid. 606(b)(2)(A) and Fed. R. Evid. 606(b)(2)(B).

The behavior of Stella, the drunken juror, does not fall within any exception.

Although Stella's drunken behavior is reprehensible, neither she nor Fred, the foreperson, may offer competent testimony about her behavior, demeanor, or capacity during deliberation. Rule 606(b)(2)(B), which allows inquiry into the any improper outside influence that was brought to bear on any juror, does not apply to these facts. According to the Supreme Court in *Tanner,* the alcohol Stella ingested was an internal influence, not an external one, and thus does not fit into the exceptions of Rule 606(b)(2). One justification for this result is that there are many substances, (including food and prescription drugs) that can affect cognition and ability to focus. It might be hard to distinguish an angry juror from a hungry one, and the policy of noninterference with jury deliberations would be compromised if the juror's state of mind, as affected by outside substances, presented sufficient reason to intrude on jury deliberations.

Testimony can be taken about Paul's access to forbidden newspaper accounts of the trial.

By accessing forbidden media, Paul was subject to extraneous improper information. To fall within the exception of Rule 606(b)(2)(A), however, the judge would first have to determine that the newspaper article was potentially prejudicial. If the piece is innocuous, the judge will not allow Paul to be questioned. If, however, the newspaper contained prejudicial information unknown to the jury (such as Audrey's prior crimes), then inquiry into the matter, including Paul's testimony, would be appropriate.

Jane may be questioned about her undisclosed deal with the Prosecutor and whether it affected her deliberation.

The deal with the Prosecutor constitutes an outside influence that was potentially brought to bear on Jane. Jane will be deemed competent to testify about the deal because it falls within the Fed. R. Evid. 606(b)(2)(B) exception.

POINTS TO REMEMBER

- The Federal Rules of Evidence presume a witness's competence. Anyone who can communicate and understand the solemnity of the oath is competent to testify, unless proven otherwise.

- Generally, deficits in witnesses are handled by impeachment— not by prohibiting the testimony entirely.

- In diversity cases, state competence rules will apply in federal court, Fed. R. Evid. 601.

- A judge cannot testify in a case over which she presides, Fed. R. Evid. 605.

- An attorney for a party cannot be a witness in a case she litigates.

- A juror cannot be a fact or expert witness in a case in which she is impaneled, Fed. R. Evid. 606(a).

- Jurors are incompetent to testify about their deliberations, Fed. R. Evid. 606(b)(1). However, jurors may:

  o Testify about the introduction of extraneous prejudicial information;

  o Testify about an improper outside influence; or

  o Testify that there was a mistake in reporting the actual verdict, Fed. R. Evid. 606(b)(2).

CHAPTER 10

Privileges

§ 10.1 *What Is a Privilege?*

An evidentiary privilege can limit a party's ability to: (1) demand information about specific communications made within certain relationships or (2) interrogate some witnesses entirely.

Common evidentiary privileges include:

- Lawyer-client privilege;

- Work-product/trial-preparation privilege;

- Therapist-patient privilege;

- Spousal privileges;

- Privilege against self-incrimination; and

- Clergy-penitent privilege.

The holder of the privilege controls decisions about its use. Only the holder of the privilege may decide whether to claim or to waive it, although the privilege can be inadvertently waived. Privileges are distinct from ethical duties such as the professional obligations of lawyers and doctors. Professional ethical codes may impose additional limits on the dissemination of confidential client or patient information.

§ 10.2 *Policy of Privileges*

Privilege excludes otherwise admissible evidence because the value of the evidence is deemed less important than the preservation of certain rights and social relationships. Many privileges are based on the utilitarian notion that they promote socially valuable communication, especially open communication between a professional and the privilege holder. Privileges can also be understood as respecting the dignity of individuals and preserving personal and professional relationships.

§ 10.3　*Which Privilege Law Applies in Federal Court?*

[Fed. R. Evid. 501]

Fed. R. Evid. 501 provides that in diversity cases, state privilege rules apply in federal court. When federal substantive law (federal crimes, constitutional questions, and federal statutes or regulations) applies, courts will rely on the federal common law to determine the scope of the privilege. Fed. R. Evid. 501 states that federal privilege law is governed by common law and interpreted "in the light of reason and experience."

§ 10.4　*The Lawyer-Client Privilege*

The lawyer-client privilege protects confidential conversations related to legal advice (as opposed to business, political, or personal advice) between a lawyer and her client. A third-party presence may serve to destroy the confidentiality of the communication. However, attorney support staff, translators, and other necessary third parties do not waive the privilege.

The lawyer-client privilege protects only confidential *communications*, not acts or observations. Information about the fact of employment or the identity of the client is generally not covered by the privilege. Additionally, it covers only the confidential communications, not the underlying information upon which those communications are based.

EXAMPLE

A business owner engages in a loud conversation with her attorney in a crowded line at Starbucks. Even if the business owner was seeking legal advice and intended her statement to be confidential, her communication is not privileged because no reasonable person would expect confidentiality under the circumstances.

The privilege is held by and may be waived by the client; however, certain Evidence Rules and Civil Procedure Rules limit the consequences of accidental disclosure. The privilege may also be waived when the holder of the privilege puts privileged material in issue. Testimony by the privilege holder concerning privileged material constitutes waiver.

The lawyer-client privilege does not include communications made in furtherance of an ongoing crime or fraud, nor does it apply to any relevant communications when a lawyer and client litigate against each other (for example, in a malpractice action by the client, or a suit for fees by the attorney).

The privilege survives the death of the client. It applies to corporate clients as well as individuals. In *Upjohn Co. v. United States*, 449 U.S. 383 (1981), the Supreme Court rejected a narrow control-group test that would have applied the lawyer-client privilege only to top corporate management, but it did not fully elucidate the proper standard for corporations.

§ 10.5 *The Limited Protection for a Lawyer's Work Product and Other Matters Prepared in Anticipation of Litigation*

Attorney work product is protected by a federal common-law privilege, *Hickman v. Taylor*, 329 U.S. 495 (1947). Under Fed. R. Civ. P. 26(b)(3), which codified most of the common-law privilege, a party may not obtain discovery of documents and tangible things prepared "in anticipation of litigation" by a lawyer or other agent of the opposing party. Fed. R. Civ. P. 26(b)(3) expands the privilege to include preparation materials made by people other than lawyers. If the document or tangible thing was routinely collected, and not specifically created in anticipation of litigation, the work-product privilege does not apply, and the material is discoverable.

The privilege is a qualified one and can be overcome by a showing of "substantial need" and a showing that the party is unable, without undue hardship, to obtain the substantial equivalent of the necessary work product from other sources. The court will conduct a balancing test to determine whether the qualified privilege applies.

Mental impressions, opinions, or legal theories of a party's attorney or other representative concerning the litigation are similarly inadmissible even when the tangible work product is, Fed. R. Civ. P. 26(b)(3)(B).

ATTORNEY-CLIENT PRIVILEGE	WORK-PRODUCT PRIVILEGE
Material that is covered by the lawyer-client privilege cannot be discovered even upon a showing of special need	Material that is covered by work-product protection can be discovered upon a showing of special need, except for material that would reveal mental impressions
Only confidential communications are covered.	A much larger category of material is covered by the work-

The attorney-client privilege covers confidential communications to the lawyer seeking legal advice or services.	product protection, which includes more than just confidential communications.
The privilege applies whether or not litigation is expected.	The work-product privilege applies only to information gathered in "anticipation of litigation."
The lawyer-client privilege covers communication to lawyers only.	Fed. R. Civ. P. 26 expands upon the common-law privilege and includes others besides lawyers who generate work-product in anticipation of litigation, including the party or the party's agent (such as a claim adjuster).

§ 10.6 *Disclosure by Mistake*

[Fed. R. Evid. 502]

Inadvertent revelation of privileged material—such as mistakenly turning over a privileged document during discovery—traditionally resulted in waiver of the privilege.

In 2008, Congress enacted Fed. R. Evid. 502 to address the problem of inadvertent disclosure. It applies to disclosures of attorney-client privilege or work product in all federal court proceedings. Under Fed. R. Evid. 502, a disclosure does not result in a waiver of the attorney-client privilege if the disclosing party acted in accordance with three requirements outlined in Fed. R. Evid. 502(b):

- The disclosure was inadvertent;

- The privilege holder took reasonable steps to prevent a disclosure; and

- The privilege holder promptly took reasonable steps to rectify the inadvertent disclosure.

§ 10.7 *Physician-Patient Privilege*

Most states recognize a general physician-patient privilege. However, there is no such federal privilege.

§ 10.8   *Psychotherapist-Patient Privilege*

In *Jaffee v. Redmond*, 518 U.S. 1 (1996), the Supreme Court, as directed by Fed. R. Evid. 501, interpreted the principles of the common law "in the light of reason and experience" to establish the federal therapist-patient privilege. The privilege promotes the policy of encouraging candor, which, in turn, leads to more effective therapy and a safer and happier society. The court noted the experience of the states, all of which provide some form of a therapist-patient privilege.

§ 10.9   *Marital Privileges*

There are two distinct spousal privileges: (1) the testimonial privilege, an absolute privilege against adverse spousal testimony; and (2) the confidential-communication privilege (also known as the "pillow-talk privilege").

A key requirement of both spousal privileges is a legal marriage. Couples who merely cohabitate without the benefit of marriage are not covered by the privilege.

Adverse Spousal Testimonial Privilege

The adverse spousal testimonial privilege prevents an individual from being compelled to take the witness stand against her spouse for *any* reason, regardless of whether the testimony concerns communication with or just facts about the spouse (for example, a spouse who came home at 3:00 am with blood on her shirt). The testimonial privilege only applies if the couple is married at the time the testimony is sought. It is designed to protect the peace and harmony of an existing marriage. In federal court, it is a common-law privilege restricted to criminal cases. Almost all states also restrict the privilege to criminal matters where a spouse is the accused. Historically, the adverse spousal testimonial privilege derived from the privilege against *self*-incrimination, where the wife's identity was legally merged into the husband's. Today, the privilege is gender-neutral.

Under federal common law as most recently elucidated by *Trammel v. United States*, 445 U.S. 40 (1980), the witness-spouse, not the accused-spouse, holds the privilege. If the witness-spouse wishes to testify against the accused-spouse, the accused-spouse cannot prevent it. Not all states follow the *Trammel* doctrine. Some states make the accused-spouse the holder of the privilege, while others make both spouses joint holders, so both have to agree to waive the privilege for the witness-spouse to testify.

The testimonial privilege does not apply in divorce actions or in cases involving an alleged crime by one spouse against the other or against their children. The testimonial privilege can be waived.

EXAMPLE

Sylvia was in the car when Jehiel was stopped for making an illegal U-turn through a red light while speeding. Jehiel is charged with the crime of reckless driving. Under the federal approach, if they are married at the time of the trial, Sylvia could invoke the adverse testimonial privilege so that she could avoid testifying against her husband. Here, the privilege applies even if Jehiel's driving was done in public and the spouses did not speak while driving. If Sylvia wished to take the stand, however, she could, because under *Trammel* she owns the privilege.

The Privilege for Marital Confidences ("Pillow-Talk Privilege")

The privilege for marital confidences only applies to communication that was shared confidentially during the marriage. Unlike the adverse spousal testimonial privilege, the pillow-talk privilege survives and continues even after the termination of the marriage by divorce or death.

The privilege is held by the spouse who transmitted the confidence. Even if the witness-spouse wishes to testify, she cannot do so regarding confidences shared during the marriage.

If the holder of the privilege calls her spouse to testify about a marital confidence, the privilege for that confidential communication is waived and the content of the testimony no longer can be controlled. Accidental disclosure to persons outside the marriage can result in a waiver of the privilege. The presence of a third party during the communication, including children, can also waive the privilege.

The privilege for marital confidences encourages spouses to confide in one another, and it is rooted in respect for marital privacy.

EXAMPLE

While they are married, Sylvia confides in her husband, Jehiel, that she has committed a crime. At her trial, she is able to invoke the privilege successfully and prevent Jehiel from testifying about the conversation, even if he is willing to testify against her. She may invoke the privilege even if they divorced after the confidential communication and were not married at the time of Sylvia's trial.

§ 10.10 *The Privilege Against Self-Incrimination*

A person can claim the Fifth Amendment privilege against self-incrimination only when facing a potential criminal charge. One cannot invoke the privilege merely to avoid humiliation. It is a personal privilege that cannot be claimed on behalf of another person.

The witness may lose the right to invoke the privilege because the danger of incrimination has been removed through acquittal, conviction, application of double jeopardy to the underlying charge, or a grant of immunity.

The privilege applies only to "testimonial" incrimination, and does not prohibit other compelled conduct. For example, a person may be compelled to sign a release of bank records, appear in a lineup, or give a blood sample, even though doing so may incriminate her.

A corporation or other organization cannot claim the privilege.

The accused in a criminal case has the right not only to refuse to answer self-incriminating questions, but also to refuse to take the witness stand at all.

Witnesses in civil cases may exercise the privilege to refuse to answer on grounds that their testimony could subject them to criminal charges. They must, however, take the stand to claim the privilege.

§ 10.11 *Other Privileges*

Other relationships for which evidentiary privileges may apply include:

- Clergy-penitent. Courts widely recognize a privilege for confidential communications between parishioners and clergy. It is part of the federal common law of privilege, and it is codified in state law.

- Journalist-source. Several jurisdictions have recognized a privilege for journalists and other news gatherers. In *Branzburg v. Hayes*, 408 U.S. 665 (1972), the Supreme Court rejected a general privilege for journalists, holding that the First Amendment does not protect journalists from testifying before a grand jury. Some federal courts recognize a qualified First Amendment journalists' privilege in criminal cases, resting on Justice Powell's concurrence in *Branzburg*.

- Accountant-client. A few states recognize an accountant-client privilege, but there is no such privilege under federal law.

    PRIVILEGES CHECKLIST

1. Does federal law apply to the substance of the case?

    If yes: Go to Step 2.

    If no: According to Fed. R. Evid. 501, any privilege will emerge from state privilege law when state law supplies the rule of decision, such as in diversity cases. State privilege law is often statutory and can vary significantly from federal law.

Spousal Testimony

2. Is the privilege being asserted in response to an attempt to obtain a spouse's testimony via deposition, police inquiry, in-court witness statement, or other formal mechanism to extract information about the other spouse?

    If yes: Go to Step 3.

    If no: Spousal privilege is not involved. Go to Step 8 to see if any other privileges might apply.

3. Is the couple currently married?

    If yes: Go to Step 4.

    If no: No adverse testimonial spousal privilege applies. Go to Step 6 to see if the confidential spousal communication privilege applies.

4. Is this a criminal case?

    If yes: Go to Step 5.

    If no: Adverse spousal testimonial privilege does not apply. Go to Step 6 to see if the confidential spousal communication privilege applies.

5. Does the spouse from whom the adverse testimony is sought wish to testify?

    If yes: Under the Supreme Court's opinion in *Trammel*, no adverse spousal privilege applies because the testifying spouse holds the privilege and may choose to waive it and testify. Go to Step 6 to see if the confidential spousal communication privilege applies.

If no: The adverse spousal testimonial privilege will apply in federal court unless the case involves a crime by one spouse against the other or against their children. Go to Step 6, because the confidential communication spousal privilege may also apply.

6. Does the potential testimony relate to a confidential communication made between spouses while they were married?

If yes: Go to Step 7.

If no: No spousal confidential communication privilege applies. If you found an adverse spousal privilege, go to Step 7. If neither type of spousal privilege exists, go to Step 8 to scan for other potential privileges.

7. Has the spousal confidential communication privilege been waived or abrogated by:

- Inadvertent waiver;

- Waiver by testimony or disclosure;

- Joint participation in a crime or fraud; or

- Domestic violence?

If yes: The privilege does not apply.

If no: Depending on your analysis above, one or both spousal privileges apply.

Work-Product Privilege

8. Is the privilege being asserted regarding a matter prepared in anticipation of litigation?

If yes: Go to Step 9.

Note: Under the Federal Rules of Civil Procedure, work product has been expanded beyond attorneys to include consultants, insurers, agents, etc.

If no: The work-product privilege does not apply. Scan for other potential privileges. Go to Step 12.

9. Does the privilege being asserted seek to protect the mental impressions of an attorney?

If yes: The privilege is absolute and is protected by federal common law under *Hickman* and Fed. R. Civ. P. 26(b)(3)(B). For tangible aspects of the work product, go to Step 10.

If no: Go to Step 10.

10. Has the party seeking the work product articulated substantial need for the information and demonstrated that it cannot obtain the information otherwise without undue hardship?

   If yes: In its discretion, the trial court can order disclosure of the work product.

   If no: Go to Step 11.

11. Has the work product been disclosed to a third party, including expert witnesses?

   If yes: The privilege may have been waived. Go to Step 12 to examine whether an attorney-client privilege exists.

   If no: The work-product privilege will apply. Go to Step 12 to examine whether an attorney-client privilege exists.

Attorney-Client Privilege

12. Does the privilege concern a communication between lawyer and client?

   If yes: Go to Step 13.

   If no: The attorney-client privilege does not apply. Scan for other privileges. Go to Step 17.

13. Did the communication concern legal (as opposed to business, personal, or political) advice?

   If yes: Go to Step 14.

   If no: The attorney-client privilege does not apply. Go to Step 17.

14. Was the communication intended to be confidential and to include only the lawyer, client (including a corporate client), and necessary support staff such as secretaries and translators?

   If yes: Go to Step 15.

   If no: The attorney-client privilege has been waived and does not apply. Go to Step 17.

15. Was the confidentiality of the communication accidentally breached through error or compromised by eavesdropping despite the lawyer and client's reasonable precautions?

   If yes: The inadvertent disclosure will probably not waive the privilege. Go to Step 16.

   If no: Go to Step 16.

16. Has the attorney-client privilege been waived or abrogated by:

   • Intentional disclosure to the third-party;

- Waiver because of testimony;

- Joint participation in a crime or fraud; or

- A lawsuit between lawyer and client?

If yes: Then the privilege does not apply. Go to Step 17.

If no: The attorney-client privilege applies. Go to Step 17.

Privilege Against Self-Incrimination

17. Does the person asserting the Fifth Amendment privilege against self-incrimination face a potential criminal charge?

    If yes: Go to Step 18.

    If no: No privilege against self-incrimination exists. Check for other privileges. Go to Step 20.

18. Is the person asserting the privilege on her own behalf?

    If yes: Go to Step 19.

    If no: Only the individual herself can assert a privilege against self-incrimination. It cannot be asserted on another's behalf. Go to Step 20.

19. Is the person asserting the privilege against self-incrimination the accused in a criminal case?

    If yes: The accused may assert the privilege against self-incrimination and refuse to take the stand entirely. Go to Step 20.

    If no: The witness may assert the privilege against self-incrimination but will have to do so under oath at the hearing, deposition, or proceeding. Go to Step 20.

Other Privileges

20. Does the privilege involve other professionals such as:

    - Clergyperson;

    - Therapist.

    If yes: Go to Step 21.

    If no: If you have not identified any other privilege, you are probably all out of privileges to assert.[1] Answer the question. If you have identified another privilege above, go to Step 21.

---

[1] This work does not address national security privilege or executive privilege. And, of course, the federal courts could create new common-law privileges.

21. Has the privilege been waived or abrogated by:

- Disclosure to the third party;

- Waiver by testimony; or

- Joint participation in a crime or fraud?

If yes: Then the privilege does not apply.

If no: The federal common law recognizes a privilege of confidential communications with these professionals who are ethically bound to respect confidences.

ILLUSTRATIVE PROBLEMS

■ PROBLEM 10.1 ■

Q: Sarah is accused of robbing Chase Bank. (1) Jerry, her husband of three years, watched her unload bags of money and destroy the top and bottom bills in each pile. (2) In the kitchen, in front of Sarah's nephew, Fred, Sarah told Jerry, "I'm glad I pulled this job; now we can afford to send Junior to Indiana University Maurer School of Law." (3) Sarah whispered to Jerry that night in bed, "With all the cash I got today, we'll be able to take that trip to French Lick, Indiana, that we've always dreamed of." Which of the above (1, 2, and 3) would Jerry be allowed to testify to in a criminal case?

A: In a federal criminal case, Jerry would be allowed to testify to his observations (1) if he wished to do so, but Jerry could assert the adverse spousal testimonial privilege and refuse to testify.

Jerry's observations of Sarah's activity (1) is protected by the adverse spousal testimonial privilege, which prevents a witness from involuntarily taking the stand against her spouse in a criminal matter. Under federal common law, the witness spouse holds this privilege. Only the holder of the privilege may decide whether to claim or to waive it. Therefore, if Jerry wishes to testify against Sarah in her federal criminal case, Sarah cannot prevent him from testifying to statement 1. It does not matter that no verbal statements were exchanged between Sarah and Jerry.

Some states make the witness-spouse the holder of the privilege, others make the accused-spouse the holder of the privilege, and still other states make both spouses joint holders. If Sarah held the privilege, or it were a jointly-held privilege, Sarah could prevent Jerry from testifying. Therefore, whether or not Jerry may testify about Sarah's activity (1) in a state criminal case would depend upon the jurisdiction.

Because watching Sarah unpack bags of money involved no confidential communication, the "pillow-talk" privilege for confidential spousal communication between married people does not apply.

Sarah's statement 2 in the kitchen would be privileged if Jerry asserted the adverse spousal testimonial privilege, but it is not protected by the spousal confidential communications privilege because confidentiality has been waived.

Jerry, as Sarah's husband, could assert the adverse spousal testimonial privilege and refuse to testify against his wife. However, Jerry may also waive the privilege and testify about the statement. Fred enjoys no such privilege and could be called.

Although statement 2 looks as if it would be protected by the privilege for marital confidences made during a couple's marriage, the presence of a third party during the communication renders the statement non-confidential, and waives the privilege. Although Sarah holds the privilege and would normally be able to prevent Jerry from testifying to statement 2, Fred's presence in the kitchen during the transmission waives the privilege and allows Jerry to testify.

Statement 3 is protected by both privileges.

Sarah's statement to Jerry in bed is covered by both the adverse spousal testimonial privilege (held by Jerry) and the privilege for marital confidences (held by Sarah). The confidential communication privilege is applicable to confidences made between a couple during their marriage. The privilege is held by the spouse who makes the confidence, in this case, Sarah. Because the privilege is held by the spouse transmitting the confidence, Jerry cannot testify against her about this confidential communication.

■ **PROBLEM 10.2** ■

Q:　Given the same facts from Problem 10.1, would Jerry be allowed to testify to would Sarah's actions (1) and statements 2 and 3 in a civil action for return of the money, assuming that Sarah embezzled it over a long time?

A:　Jerry would be allowed to testify to what he observed and to statement 2 in a civil trial. Generally, the adverse marital testimonial privilege is restricted to criminal cases, so it would likely not apply at all in a civil trial. Therefore, Jerry would only be prevented from testifying to statement 3, which is protected by the privilege for marital confidences. Fred's presence still serves to waive the privilege for marital confidences as to statement 2.

■ PROBLEM 10.3 ■

Q: Given the same facts from the previous two problems, how would your answers change if it turns out that Jerry and Sarah had never been legally married because Jerry had never divorced his first wife Jennifer, a fact known to Sarah?

A: If it turned out that Jerry and Sarah had never been married, Jerry would be allowed to testify to his observation and both statements. A key requirement of both spousal privileges is a legal marriage. If their marriage was not legal, Jerry and Sarah would have neither the protection of the marital testimonial privilege nor the protection of the privilege for marital confidences.

■ PROBLEM 10.4 ■

Q: How would your answers to the question above change if the filthy lucre ruined a great relationship and at the time Jerry is asked to testify, he and Sarah, who had been legally married at the time of these events, are now divorced?

A: Even if Jerry and Sarah were divorced by the time they get to trial, Jerry would still be prevented from testifying to statement 3, which is protected by the privilege of marital confidences. The privilege is applicable to confidences made during the marriage and continues even after the marriage terminates. Therefore, it makes no difference whether Jerry and Sarah divorced before Jerry testifies, so long as the confidence was made while they were legally married.

Any testimonial privileges that Jerry would attempt to raise as to his observation of Sarah and Sarah's statement in the kitchen (2) will not succeed. The spousal testimonial privilege only applies if the marriage is intact when one of the spouses is testifying. It does not outlive the marriage. Statement 3 is a confidential spousal communication and Sarah could prevent Jerry from testifying about it.

POINTS TO REMEMBER

- Under Fed. R. Evid. 501, state privilege rules apply in diversity cases, and federal common law applies in cases applying federal substantive law.

- Federal privilege law is governed by common law and interpreted in the "light of reason and experience."

- In the event of a disclosure made by mistake, certain Evidence and Civil Procedure Rules may limit the consequences of accidental disclosure.

- The holder of the privilege decides whether to claim or waive a privilege.

Lawyer-Client Privilege

- Protects confidential communications between lawyer and client regarding legal advice.

- May be waived by the client or by putting privileged material in issue.

- Although a third party's presence may serve to destroy the confidentiality of the communication, the presence of attorney support staff, translators, and other necessary third parties does not.

- Survives the death of the client.

- Applies to corporate clients as well as individuals.

- The lawyer-client privilege does not protect:

  o The underlying information upon which the privileged communications are based;

  o Acts or observations;

  o Communications made in furtherance of a future or ongoing crime or fraud; or

  o Any relevant communications when a lawyer and client litigate against each other.

Work-Product Protection

- Protected by a federal common-law privilege and by Rule 26 of the Federal Rules of Civil Procedure.

- Applies only to information gathered in anticipation of litigation.

- Material that is covered by work-product protection can be discovered with a showing of special need (except for mental impressions, conclusions, or opinions concerning the litigation).

Physician/Psychotherapist-Patient Privileges

- While most states recognize a general physician-patient privilege, federal law does not.

- There is, however, a federal therapist-patient privilege.

Marital Privileges

- There are two distinct spousal privileges: testimonial privilege and the privilege for marital confidences (pillow-talk privilege). Each requires a legal marriage.

- The testimonial privilege is an absolute privilege preventing a spouse from being forced to the witness stand in any capacity against the other spouse while they are still married. It is restricted to criminal cases.

- Under federal common law, the witness-spouse holds the testimonial privilege and may testify against the other spouse if the witness-spouse so desires. Which spouse holds the testimonial privilege under state law varies by jurisdiction.

- The privilege for marital confidences applies only to confidences that were made during the marriage. It continues to remain in force even after the marriage ends. The privilege is held by the spouse who transmitted the confidence.

- The privilege for marital confidences is waived if:

  o The holder of the privilege calls the other spouse to testify about marital confidences;

  o Accidental disclosure was made to persons outside the marriage; or

  o A third party is present during the confidential communication.

Privilege Against Self-Incrimination

- A person can claim the Fifth Amendment privilege against self-incrimination during police interrogations, depositions, and at trial if answering the question might subject her to a potential criminal charge. Immunity, acquittal, and double jeopardy remove the potential of a criminal charge.

- It is a personal privilege that cannot be claimed on behalf of another.

- The accused in a criminal case has a right not only to refuse to answer self-incriminating questions, but also to refuse to take the witness stand at all. Witnesses in civil cases may exercise the privilege but must take the stand in order to do so.

CHAPTER 11

Opinion Evidence and Expert Testimony

§ 11.1 *Lay Opinion*

[Fed. R. Evid. 701]

Historically, American evidence law permitted witnesses to testify about facts only. Drawing conclusions and forming opinions was the exclusive purview of juries and judges. However, the line between "facts" and "opinions" is a fine and probably pointless one to draw, and the Federal Rules of Evidence now allow limited opinion testimony from lay witnesses.

Fed. R. Evid. 701 provides that a lay (non-expert) witness may offer an opinion or inference if the lay witness's opinion is:

- Rationally based on the witness's perceptions;

- Helpful to the finder-of-fact because it:

  o Clarifies the witness's testimony; or

  o Aids in the determination of a disputed fact; and

- Not based on expert, scientific, technical, or other specialized knowledge.

If the witness is essentially giving expert testimony, then Fed. R. Evid. 702, which deals with experts, will govern, rather than Rule 701.

EXAMPLE

Samantha, a lay witness, can testify that the Plaintiff looked tired, even though it may seem more of an opinion than a fact. More persuasive testimony would include the underlying facts upon which Samantha's opinion was based (for instance, that the Plaintiff had bags under her eyes, yawned frequently, and had trouble focusing). But, even without such detail, the trial judge should admit

Samantha's lay opinion if it is rationally based on her perceptions and helpful to the fact-finder.

§ 11.2 *The* Frye *"General Acceptance" Standard for Scientific Testimony and the* Daubert *Test*

The *Frye* test, a common-law test that some federal circuits continued to apply even after the adoption of the Federal Rules, and some states apply to this day, requires that expert scientific testimony enjoy "general acceptance in the particular field in which it belongs," *Frye v. United States*, 293 F. 1013, 1014 (D.C. Cir. 1923). Proponents of the *Frye* test praise the standard because it limits the admission of "junk science" by restricting expert testimony to what the expert community generally accepts. Opponents of the *Frye* test argue that the inherently conservative standard excludes new reliable science that has yet to be accepted by the cautious and conservative scientific community. Additionally, the *Frye* test admits expertise such as handwriting analysis, which historically experts had generally accepted but is now considered dubious.

Daubert v. Merrell Dow Pharmaceuticals, 509 U.S. 579, 589 (1993), held that the *Frye* test was "incompatible with the Federal Rules of Evidence," holding that the liberal standard of assisting the trier-of-fact, encompassed in Fed. R. Evid. 702, rejected the more restrictive *Frye* standard. However, *Frye* still governs scientific testimony in some state courts.

§ 11.3 *Overview of Expert Testimony*

[Fed. R. Evid. 702]

Fed. R. Evid. 702 governs experts and defines expertise broadly. Experts can be qualified through:

- Knowledge;
- Skill;
- Expertise;
- Training; or
- Education.

An expert need not possess fancy degrees or certifications. A car mechanic can be an expert; so can a nursery school teacher. One federal court deemed a habitual marijuana user an expert regarding the quality and origin of the marijuana in question, *United States v.*

Johnson, 575 F.2d 1347, 1362 (5th Cir. 1978). His mother must have been so proud.

Expert testimony must help the jury to understand the evidence or to determine a fact. Although expert testimony is not limited to information entirely beyond the knowledge of jurors, the expert testimony must add value and not just relate information that reasonable fact-finders would already know.

Courts must evaluate the methodology and scientific conclusions of an expert. In addition to helping the fact-finder understand the evidence or determine a disputed fact, Fed. R. Evid. 702 requires that the trial judge must determine that:

- The testimony is based upon sufficient facts or data;

- The testimony is the product of reliable principles and methods; and

- The expert has applied the principles and methods reliably to the facts of the case.

This last element arguably augments the *Daubert* standard, which addressed the expert's principles and methodology but not the expert's actual application of those principles.

§ 11.4 *The Trial Judge as Gatekeeper*

Under *Daubert*, trial judges serve as gatekeepers, responsible for independent screening of the reliability of the so-called science and of the expert witnesses. *Daubert* listed five non-exclusive factors that trial courts could use in determining the value of expert testimony. Trial judges should examine whether:

- The theory or technique underlying the expert testimony can be and has been tested;

- Controls and standards were maintained;

- The theory has been subject to peer review and publication;

- There is a known error rate; and

- The theory is accepted in the scientific community. (This last factor is essentially the *Frye* test, which has become one, rather than the sole, factor.)

The Advisory Committee Note to the 2000 Amendment of Rule 702 acknowledged and approved of some additional factors, including whether:

- Experts are able to testify about matters from their independent research, or opinions they developed expressly for purposes of testifying at trial;

- The expert has adequately accounted for obvious alternative explanations; and

- The field of expertise claimed by the expert is known to reach reliable results for the type of opinion the expert would give.

Daubert applies to more than just scientific expertise. Experts who base their testimony on specialized experience rather than formal scientific training must also use a demonstrably valid methodology, *Kumho Tire Co. v. Carmichael*, 526 U.S. 137 (1999).

Appellate courts review trial courts' determinations concerning admission of expert testimony under an abuse-of-discretion standard.

§ 11.5   *The Basis of Opinion Testimony by Experts*

[Fed. R. Evid. 703, 705]

Fed. R. Evid. 703 provides that an expert's opinion testimony may derive from:

- Personal knowledge;

- Any information the expert has learned in preparation for testimony; or

- Training and study.

Fed. R. Evid. 703 clarifies that the information used to form the testifying expert's opinion need not be otherwise admissible at trial as long as "experts in the particular field would reasonably rely on those kinds of facts or data in forming an opinion on the subject." Functionally, Rule 703 grants experts the discretion to reach conclusions in the manner that they normally would outside the courtroom. Experts may rely on hearsay, character evidence, and unauthenticated documents if doing so is the accepted method of gathering information in their field.

Just because experts may rely on inadmissible evidence to reach their expert conclusions, however, does not mean that such experts may directly convey those inadmissible facts to the jury. They cannot become conduits for hearsay and other inadmissible evidence.[1]

Therefore, as a general rule, experts may not testify on direct examination about the inadmissible evidence on which they relied.

---

[1]   These same principles also apply to the Rules' treatment of factual findings by public officials under Fed. R. Evid. 803(8)(A)(iii). *See* § 7.12.

Fed. R. Evid. 703 allows the proponent of the expert to present otherwise inadmissible facts or data underlying her opinion only if, in the discretion of the court, the probative value of those facts or data in helping the jury evaluate the expert's opinion substantially outweighs the risk of prejudice to the opposing party in making that inadmissible evidence known to the jury. This is a high standard and will not often be met.

The limitation on admitting the basis for the expert's testimony applies only to the proponent of the expert. Fed. R. Evid. 705 provides that on cross-examination, the opposing party may inquire into the facts or data forming the basis of the expert witness's opinion, regardless of whether such facts or data would be otherwise admissible.

§ 11.6 *Opinions on the Ultimate Issue at Trial*

[Fed. R. Evid. 704]

Fed. R. Evid. 704 provides that, in general, both lay witnesses and experts may offer opinions about the ultimate issue in the case.

EXAMPLE

A citizen sues Alice, a police officer, and the Missouri town she works for, claiming that Alice used excessive force in making an arrest. An expert witness in police brutality could testify that Alice used only the force reasonably necessary and that Alice's behavior reflected proper training and supervision—even if those are ultimate issues in the case. The police expert could not, however, testify that Alice acted lawfully, complied with Missouri state law, or had a legal duty to arrest the Plaintiff. Rule 704 does not allow an expert to rest her opinion on unexplored legal criteria.[2]

Fed. R. Evid. 704(b) creates an exception to this general rule, prohibiting expert testimony on the mental state of an accused relating to a criminal element or defense. For instance, a police officer cannot testify as an expert about the accused's intent to distribute drugs in the accused's possession. This exception, known as the Hinckley Amendment, was passed in response to the conflicting expert psychiatric testimony concerning the sanity of John Hinckley, who shot President Reagan. When Hinckley was found not guilty by

---

[2]   The facts of this example are drawn from *Richman v. Sheahan,* 415 F. Supp. 2d 929 (N.D. Ill. 2015).

reason of insanity, Congress amended the evidence rule to include Rule 704(b).

§ 11.7 *Legal Conclusions*

Courts tend to reject expert opinions that are essentially legal conclusions unless the witness is a legal expert. For example, a medical expert may be allowed to state that a physician did not meet the standard of care expected of a reasonable physician, but she may not testify that the physician acted "negligently."

OPINIONS AND EXPERTS
CHECKLIST

Lay Opinion

1. Is the opinion rationally based on the witness's perceptions?

    If yes: Go to Step 2.

    If no: The lay opinion is not admissible.

2. Is the lay opinion helpful to the finder-of-fact because it clarifies the witness's testimony or helps to determine a disputed fact?

    If yes: Go to Step 3.

    If no: The lay opinion is not admissible.

3. Is the witness testifying as an expert?

    If yes: The portion that is lay testimony may be admitted as such but the expert testimony must be qualified separately and is not lay testimony. Go to Step 4.

    If no: The lay opinion is admissible.

Expert Opinion

4. Is the witness qualified by her education, experience, knowledge, or skill to render an expert opinion?

    If yes: Go to Step 5.

    If no: The witness may not offer expert testimony.

5. Does the expert's opinion derive from any of the following:

    •   Personal knowledge;

    •   Any information the expert learned in preparation for testimony; or

    •   Training and study?

If yes: The witness is qualified as an expert. Go to Step 6.

If no: The witness may not offer expert testimony.

6.   Does the expert's opinion rely on inadmissible evidence?

If yes: Go to Step 7.

If no: Go to Step 8.

7.   Do experts in the field reasonably rely on those kinds of facts or data?

If yes: The expert's opinion may be admissible even if the expert relied on inadmissible evidence. The fact that the expert may rely on inadmissible evidence does not mean that the expert may repeat such evidence in court, thereby serving as a conduit for inadmissible evidence. The expert may provide the otherwise inadmissible evidence upon which she relied only if the probative value in helping the jury evaluate the opinion substantially outweighs its prejudicial effect. Such information may also be inquired into on cross-examination, Fed. R. Evid. 705. Go to Step 8.

If no: The judge as gatekeeper should reject the expert's testimony.

8.   Is the expert's opinion based on sufficient facts or data?

If yes: Go to Step 9.

If no: The witness may not offer expert testimony.

9.   Is the expert's opinion the product of reliable principles and methods? Factors include whether:

- The theory or technique underlying the expert testimony can be and has been tested;

- Controls and standards were maintained;

- The theory has been subject to peer review and publication;

- There is a known error rate;

- The field of expertise claimed by the expert is known to reach reliable results for the type of opinion the expert would give;

- The theory is accepted in the scientific community.

If yes: Go to Step 10.

If no: The witness may not offer expert testimony.

10. Did the expert apply the scientific or technical principles correctly?

If yes: Go to Step 11.

If no: The witness may not offer expert testimony.

11. Is this expert testifying in a criminal case about the mental state of the accused relating to a criminal element or defense?

If yes: That part of the expert's testimony is prohibited by the Hinckley Amendment, Rule 704(b).

If no: The expert testimony is admissible. If the expert is also a fact witness, go to Step 2 to work through that aspect of the testimony.

ILLUSTRATIVE PROBLEM

■ PROBLEM 11.1 ■

Q: The Prosecutor wishes to call Caroline, who has a master's degree in social work, as an expert witness in a child sex-abuse trial. Caroline has not interviewed the child-victim, nor has she served as the child-victim's therapist. Caroline regularly teaches a university course, leads continuing education for social workers on child sexual abuse, is familiar with the psychological literature, and has an extensive clinical practice dealing with young victims of sexual abuse. Caroline will testify as to some unique aspects of children's memory and communication, particularly the trouble child witnesses have remembering dates and the sequence of events. The Accused objects to Caroline's testimony, arguing that she is not a psychiatrist, her testimony is based on inadmissible hearsay, and her testimony addresses the ultimate issue of whether the child was abused.

A: The judge should overrule all three objections and permit Caroline to testify regarding child victims' cognitive and communication challenges as witnesses.

Caroline can be deemed an expert even though she is not a psychiatrist and does not have a Ph.D. in psychology.

Fed. R. Evid. 702 makes it clear that an expert can be qualified by experience and specialized knowledge, not just by academic degrees. Caroline's experience as a teacher and lecturer, her clinical experience, and her knowledge of the psychological literature qualify her as an expert. Because of problems of cost and expert availability, the evidence rules are flexible and do not require the best expert, but simply someone with the requisite expertise.

Caroline's testimony may rest on inadmissible evidence.

Fed. R. Evid. 703 permits experts to rely on inadmissible evidence if experts in the field reasonably and regularly do so. Caroline's opinion is formed in part through her clinical work with victims and in part from her academic studies. The texts she has read to gain her knowledge are hearsay (although some of them might qualify under the exception for learned treatises, Fed. R. Evid. 803(18)). To the extent that Caroline learned about the newest research by attending an academic conference, everything she learned at the conference was also hearsay, but it was the type of information reasonably relied on by experts in the field of child psychology.

Caroline's testimony does not address the ultimate issue in the case (which in any case is often permitted), but instead educates the jury about important background material of which they might not otherwise be aware.

It is rarely a good objection to protest that the witness's testimony goes to the ultimate issue in the case. Testimony as to the ultimate issue is prohibited only where the witness testifies about the mental state of the accused as it affects an element or defense in the criminal case. Fed. R. Evid. 704(b).

A better objection is where the expert testifies beyond her actual knowledge and expertise. Had Caroline testified that in her professional opinion the child was being truthful, or that based on her behavior, the child suffered sexual abuse, Caroline would have been inappropriately vouching for the witness and testifying beyond her expertise.

However, Caroline did no such thing. Instead she offered expert testimony to help the jury understand the child's testimony and behavior. A child who cannot remember times, dates, and frequencies of abuse might seem to the finder-of-fact like a poorly coached liar. Caroline's testimony will elucidate children's cognitive development and their general inability at young ages to ground events in the calendar (unless it happened on the child's birthday or Christmas). Caroline's testimony will assist the jury in interpreting the child's inability to name dates and times, undermining the Accused's attempt to portray the child as an inconsistent liar.

POINTS TO REMEMBER

Lay Opinion

Under Fed. R. Evid. 701, lay witnesses may provide opinion testimony if such testimony is:

- Rationally based on the witness's own perceptions;

- Helpful to the finder-of-fact by clarifying the lay witness's testimony or aiding in the determination of a disputed fact; and

- Not based on expert, scientific, technical, or specialized knowledge.

Experts

- Experts are qualified by their education, experience, knowledge, or skill. Under Fed. R. Evid. 702, the label "expert" has broad application and is not limited to those with advanced degrees.

- An expert's testimony must help the jury understand evidence or determine a fact.

- An expert's opinion may derive from:

  o Personal knowledge;

  o Any information the expert learned in preparation for testimony; or

  o Training and study.

- Expert opinion may be based on inadmissible evidence, as long as it is the type of information reasonably used by experts in the field. But generally, the expert may not testify on direct examination about the inadmissible evidence upon which they relied. An opposing party may inquire into such underlying facts and data.

- Trial judges evaluate the methodology and scientific conclusions of the expert by determining whether:

  o The testimony is based upon sufficient facts or data;

  o The testimony is the product of reliable principles and methods; and

  o The expert has applied the principles and methods reliably.

- Trial judges conduct an independent screening of expert witnesses. Factors include whether:

  o The theory or technique underlying the expert testimony can be and has been tested;

  o Controls and standards were maintained;

  o The theory has been subject to peer review and publication;

  o There is a known error rate;

  o The theory is accepted in the scientific community;

o   The expert is able to testify about matters growing naturally and directly out of her independent research or whether her opinions were developed expressly for purposes of trial testimony;

o   The expert has adequately accounted for obvious alternative explanations; and

o   The field of expertise claimed by the expert is known to reach reliable results for the type of opinion the expert would give.

Ultimate Issues

Except in criminal cases regarding expert testimony about the accused's state of mind, both lay and expert witnesses may present opinions about an ultimate issue in the case.

CHAPTER 12

Judicial Notice

§ 12.1 *Role of Judicial Notice*

[Fed. R. Evid. 201]

Judicial notice is a shortcut in proof that reduces the time and expense of having to prove obvious facts at trial. By taking judicial notice, the court relieves the party offering the evidence of the burden of proving the adjudicative fact. Lawyers use judicial notice to prove facts that are "not subject to reasonable dispute" but are nevertheless difficult or expensive to prove under the evidence rules, Fed. R. Evid. 201(b). For instance, the judge could take judicial notice that January 27, 2016 was a Wednesday. Without this shortcut of judicial notice, the hearsay and authentication issues surrounding admission of a calendar would prove time-consuming and complicated.

§ 12.2 *Adjudicative Versus Legislative Facts*

Under Fed. R. Evid. 201(a), judicial notice is available only for "adjudicative facts," a fairly unhelpful term that the rules do not define. "Adjudicative facts" are best understood as facts that arise out of the litigation and that concern the immediate parties. As the Advisory Committee explains, "Adjudicative facts are simply the facts of the particular case." Adjudicative facts are contrasted with "legislative facts," which are facts and arguments that arise out of general lawmaking and policy assessment. Legislative facts are those that "have relevance to legal reasoning and the lawmaking process," such as the interpretation of a statute or the contours of a common-law rule. Assessment of such legislative facts often relies on general social, economic, or other facts.

To illustrate the difference: whether there was a full moon on the night of the alleged rape is an adjudicative fact that the trial judge could decide with reference to an almanac. Whether rape shield law excludes prior rape allegations by the victim is a legislative fact and is not covered by Rule 201.

§ 12.3 When Should a Court Take Judicial Notice of an Adjudicative Fact?

[Fed. R. Evid. 201(b)]

The court may judicially notice a fact that is not subject to reasonable dispute. As stated by Fed. R. Evid. 201(b), the fact must also be either:

- Generally known within the trial judge's jurisdiction, Fed. R. Evid. 201(b)(1); or

- "[A]ccurately and readily determined from sources whose accuracy cannot reasonably be questioned," Fed. R. Evid. 201(b)(2).

Just because a judge happens to know an adjudicative fact does not make it appropriate for judicial notice unless it fits into one of the two categories above.

For example, everyone knows that the Empire State Building is in New York City, or that smoking causes health problems, so a judge could take judicial notice of those facts if they are relevant to the case, Fed. R. Evid. 201(b)(1). However, many might not know that as of the publication of this text, the Indiana Hoosiers last won the NCAA Men's College Basketball championship in 1987. Although this fact may not be generally known throughout the United States, one can easily determine its accuracy via reliable sources; it is therefore still subject to judicial notice under Fed. R. Evid. 201(b)(2).

§ 12.4 How Should Judicial Notice Be Raised?

[Fed. R. Evid. 201(c)]

If a lawyer requests judicial notice and supplies the trial court with the "necessary information," the judge must take judicial notice of the fact, Fed. R. Evid. 204(c)(2). The court may also take judicial notice on its own, even if no lawyer so requests, Fed. R. Evid. 204(c)(1).

§ 12.5 Timing of Judicial Notice; Opportunity to Be Heard

[Fed. R. Evid. 201(d)]

A court may take judicial notice of an adjudicative fact "at any stage of a proceeding" under Fed. R. Evid. 201(d), but the party opposing judicial notice has a right to be heard as provided by Fed. R. Evid. 201(e).

§ 12.6 *Ability to Contest*

[Fed. R. Evid. 201(e)]

A party against whom a fact is judicially noticed is entitled "to be heard on the propriety of taking judicial notice and the nature of the fact to be noticed," Fed. R. Evid. 201(e).

§ 12.7 *Effect on the Jury*

[Fed. R. Evid. 201(f)]

In criminal cases, jurors may (but are not required to) accept a judicially-noticed fact, Fed. R. Evid. 201(f). In civil cases, jurors must accept the judge's instruction that judicially noticed facts are conclusively true, Fed. R. Evid. 201(f).

 JUDICIAL NOTICE CHECKLIST

1. Does the evidence concern an adjudicative fact?

   If yes: Go to Step 2.

   If no: Judicial notice is not appropriate.

2. Is the adjudicative fact subject to reasonable dispute?

   If yes: Judicial notice is not appropriate.

   If no: Go to Step 3.

3. Is the fact generally known in the jurisdiction?

   If yes: Judicial notice is appropriate. Go to Step 5.

   If no: Go to Step 4.

4. Can the fact be accurately and readily determined from reliable sources?

   If yes: Judicial notice is appropriate. Go to Step 5.

   If no: The court should not grant judicial notice.

5. Did a party make a motion?

   If yes: The judge should grant judicial notice if, after hearing objections, the judge feels the criteria have been met. Go to Step 6.

   If no: The judge may take judicial notice sua sponte if the opposing party has been given a chance to speak. Go to Step 6.

6.   What is the effect if a judge grants judicial notice?

In criminal cases: The jury may, but does not have to, accept the fact as conclusively proved.

In civil cases: The jury must accept the fact as conclusively proved.

ILLUSTRATIVE PROBLEM

■ PROBLEM 12.1 ■

Q: Pamela, the Plaintiff in a civil paternity action, alleges that David is the father of her child and demands child support. Pamela offers a properly authenticated lab report analysis of DNA evidence showing that the child and Peter are a match. May the judge take judicial notice of the science behind paternity testing?

A: Because the accuracy of DNA testing is widely known and is not subject to reasonable dispute, the judge can take judicial notice of the process of identifying paternity through DNA and no expert need testify about the underlying science.

POINTS TO REMEMBER

- Judicial notice applies only to adjudicative facts, which are, facts that arise out of the litigation and concern the immediate parties.

- The adjudicative facts to be judicially noticed cannot be subject to reasonable dispute.

- Adjudicative facts must either be:

  o   Generally known in the jurisdiction; or

  o   Accurately and readily determined from reliable sources.

- Judicial notice may be initiated by a party or by a judge.

- The party against whom the judge takes judicial notice has a right to be heard.

- Judicial notice has conclusive effect in civil cases.

- In criminal cases the jury may, but does not have to, accept the fact as conclusively proved.

CHAPTER 13

Burdens and Presumptions

§ 13.1 *Burdens*

"Burden of proof" is an inexact term that can refer to either the burden of *persuasion* or the burden of *production* in civil cases.

The Burden of Persuasion

The party with the burden of *persuasion* must convince the trier-of-fact to the appropriate level of certainty that she deserves to win. The burden of persuasion never shifts between the parties, and remains constant throughout the litigation. The plaintiff bears the burden of persuading the fact-finder that her claim is valid and meets the necessary standard of proof. In civil cases, the burden of persuasion is usually a preponderance of the evidence (that is to say, more likely than not), but it can be a higher standard, such as clear and convincing evidence. Concomitantly, the civil defendant carries the burden of persuading the fact-finder that her affirmative defense is valid and meets the necessary standard of proof. In a criminal case, the prosecutor bears the burden of proving each element of the crime beyond a reasonable doubt.

The Burden of Production

The burden of *production* concerns the trial court's role as screener of evidence. Without prejudging whether the party with the burden of persuasion will ultimately be able to meet that burden, the judge applies a lower standard to determine whether the party has offered sufficient evidence to justify letting a particular claim go forward.

The party carrying the burden of production must present sufficient evidence to demonstrate that a reasonable jury could find for her on that claim or issue. To meet its burden of production, the party must establish the prima facie elements of a claim or defense.

§ 13.2 *Presumptions in Civil Cases*

[Fed. R. Evid. 301]

A *presumption* is a substantive legal rule whereby proof of a designated fact establishes by necessary inference the existence of another fact. You are of course familiar with the presumption of innocence in criminal law. The Federal Rules of Evidence, however, apply only to civil presumptions. (Congress rejected a proposed rule for criminal presumptions.)

A party seeking to take advantage of a presumption must offer evidence sufficient to meet the burden of production as to each foundational fact.

Under Fed. R. Evid. 301, presumptions are not absolute and a party may rebut a presumption by producing facts that contradict the presumption. Rule 301 does not, however, shift the burden of persuasion, which remains on the party who possessed it originally. Examples of presumptions include the business judgment rule, which presumes that directors act in the best interests of the corporation, and the presumption of validity for patents issued by the United States Patent and Trademark Office.

When the presumption is not rebutted, the judge will inform the jury that the fact at issue has been proven.

§ 13.3 *Presumptions in Diversity Cases*

[Fed. R. Evid. 302]

In a civil case where state law supplies the rule of decision, that is to say, a case in federal court under diversity jurisdiction, state substantive law will govern the effect of a presumption.

     PRESUMPTIONS CHECKLIST

1.   Is this a civil case?

     If yes: Go to Step 2.

     If no: The Federal Rules of Evidence do not apply to presumptions in criminal cases.

2.   Does the substantive civil law provide a presumption?

     If yes: Go to Step 3.

     If no: The rules concerning presumptions do not apply to your evidence.

3. Does state law provide the rule of decision in this case? Is this claim in federal court under diversity jurisdiction?

If yes: Follow state law on presumptions, Fed. R. Evid. 302.

If no: Go to Step 4.

4. Has the party seeking to benefit from the presumption provided sufficient evidence of the presumption's foundational facts to meet the burden of production?

If yes: Go to Step 5.

If no: The party may not receive the benefit of the presumption.

5. Has the party against whom the presumption is offered rebutted the presumption?

If yes: The presumption has no effect.

If no: Go to Step 6.

6. Has the party seeking to benefit from the presumption provided sufficient evidence of the presumption's foundational facts to meet the burden of persuasion?

If yes: The jury will be instructed about the presumption and directed to follow the presumption. In a bench trial, the judge will set out the foundational facts and rely on the presumption to reach her ruling.

If no: The presumption does not apply.

ILLUSTRATIVE PROBLEM

■ PROBLEM 13.1 ■

Q: Ned is suing Harry and Wanda for visitation of five-year-old Kathy, whom Ned alleges is his biological daughter. According to Ned, Kathy was conceived when Ned had a romantic affair with Wanda, his married next-door neighbor. Ned claims that he, not Wanda's husband Harry, is Kathy's father. Wanda and Harry have been married for fifteen years. Ned is suing for visitation and claims that his constitutional right to have a relationship with his daughter has been violated. Under the relevant state law, a man who was married to a woman when she became pregnant is presumed to be the child's father. What should the court do regarding the presumption?

A: First Harry and Wanda must provide sufficient evidence to meet the burden of production regarding the foundational facts of the paternity presumption. To take advantage of the presumption, they must demonstrate the foundational fact that they were married at the time of Kathy's conception, something that will be easy to do. This establishes the presumption and shifts the burden to Ned to overcome the paternity presumption. Ned can rebut the presumption with evidence of his paternity, such as DNA tests showing that he is the biological father. Ned will be able to assert his paternity and the court will then address Ned's rights and duties as Kathy's biological father.[1]

POINTS TO REMEMBER

- The burden of *persuasion* is the quantum of evidence necessary to convince the trier-of-fact to the appropriate level of certainty that the party with the burden deserves to win.

- The burden of persuasion never shifts between the parties; it remains constant throughout the litigation.

- The burden of *production* concerns whether the party has offered sufficient evidence to justify letting a particular claim go forward. To meet its burden of production, the party must establish the prima facie elements of a claim or defense.

- A *presumption* is a substantive legal rule whereby proof of a designated fact establishes by necessary inference the existence of another fact.

- The Federal Rules of Evidence apply only to civil presumptions.

- A party seeking to take advantage of a presumption must offer evidence sufficient to meet the burden of production as to each foundational fact.

- Under Fed. R. Evid. 301, presumptions are not absolute and a party can rebut a presumption by producing facts that contradict the presumption.

- When the presumption is not rebutted, the judge will inform the jury that the fact at issue has been proven.

- In a civil case where state law supplies the rule of decision, that is to say, a case in federal court under diversity jurisdiction, Fed. R. Evid. 302 dictates that state substantive law will govern the effect of a presumption.

---

[1]   The very interesting constitutional questions that arise concerning the right to parent are addressed in *Michael H. v. Gerald D.*, 491 U.S. 110 (1989).

CHAPTER 14

Authentication

§ 14.1 *General Principle of Authentication*

[Fed. R. Evid. 901(a)]

A party must authenticate any tangible thing that she intends to offer into evidence. Whether it is a document, a recording, a gun, a baggie full of cocaine, or a work of art, it must first be authenticated. Both real evidence (items that were actually involved in the events that gave rise to the litigation) and demonstrative evidence (items such as a gun that resembles the gun used in the crime, a map of the accident location, or a chart) must be authenticated.

As Fed. R. Evid. 901(a) indicates, the authentication question is simple: Is the item what its proponent claims it is?

Authenticating an item is a two-step process in which:

(1) The judge decides whether a reasonable jury could find the item to be what the proponent claims it to be, and if so,

(2) The jury, as it deliberates, decides whether the evidence is sufficient to determine that the item is, in fact, authentic.

EXAMPLE

In a lawsuit for breach of contract, the Defendant claims that the contract the Plaintiff introduced (and is suing over) contains a forgery of the Defendant's signature and is not the contract that the Defendant actually signed. In considering the foundational question of authentication, if the judge believes that no jury could find that it is the Defendant's signature, then the document is inauthentic, and the judge will exclude the contract. Generally, however, if a legitimate question exists concerning the authenticity of the contract, the question of the signature will go to the jury, especially if it is an ultimate issue in the case.

Authentication should not present a major hurdle unless the attorney is unprepared or a genuine question exists about the item's legitimacy. In civil cases, pretrial practice usually requires identification of documents and exhibits before trial so that many hearsay and authentication issues can be hashed out in advance.

§ 14.2 Self-Authentication

[Fed. R. Evid. 902]

Some items are self-authenticating. Fed. R. Evid. 902 lists items that will be admitted into evidence without any outside evidence of authenticity. Examples include the following:

- Various official, public, or acknowledged documents, certified or with signature and seal;

- Newspapers;

- Trade inscriptions;

- Commercial paper; and

- Certified business records.

The opponent of a self-authenticating document bears the burden of raising authenticity questions. For example, under Fed. R. Evid. 902(11) and (12) business records are authenticated by a certificate, but the opponent is given "a fair opportunity" to challenge both the certificate and the underlying record.

As of this writing, the Advisory Committee on Evidence Rules has proposed two additional types of self-authenticating evidence. The first, proposed Fed. R. Evid. 902(13), would allow self-authentication of machine-generated information, upon submission of a certification prepared by a qualified person. The second, proposed Fed. R. Evid. 902(14), would provide a similar certification procedure for a copy of data taken from an electronic device, media, or file. These proposals shift the burden of production (but not the burden of persuasion) to the opponent regarding disputes over the authenticity of such electronic evidence.[1]

§ 14.3 How to Authenticate Non-Self-Authenticating Items

[Fed. R. Evid. 901(b)]

Most items are not self-authenticating and require evidence of authenticity. Fed. R. Evid. 901(b) provides ten "illustrations" designed to show the kind of evidence that meets the authentication requirement. The list is not exclusive, and, maddeningly, the

---

[1]   See § 13.1 (discussing burdens of production and persuasion).

compilation of illustrations is not a list of rules. Unlike hearsay, which is very technical and categorical, authentication is ultimately more flexible and practical, but less uniform and predictable.

Examples of authentication methods include but are not restricted to the following:

- Testimony of a witness with knowledge (including a party who wishes to introduce the evidence), Fed. R. Evid. 901(b)(1).

- Non-expert opinion about handwriting. A non-expert may offer her opinion that the handwriting is genuine if she is familiar with the handwriting and that familiarity was not acquired for the current litigation, Fed. R. Evid. 901(b)(2).

- Comparison by an expert witness or the trier-of-fact. An expert witness or the trier-of-fact compares the item with an authenticated specimen. For instance, the jury could compare the defendant's signature on her driving license with her purported signature on the contract, Fed. R. Evid. 901(b)(3).

- Distinctive characteristics and the like. This includes the appearance, contents, substance, internal patterns, or other distinctive characteristics of the item, which, taken together with all the circumstances, indicate its authenticity. For instance, a will refers to a family member by a pet name that only the genuine testator used. As another example, the contents of a reply letter can, on its own, authenticate the letter, Fed. R. Evid. 901(b)(4).

- An opinion by a person with knowledge identifying a person's voice, Fed. R. Evid. 901(b)(5).

- Evidence about a telephone conversation, or evidence that a call was made to the number assigned at the time to:

  o A particular person, if circumstances (including self-identification) show that the person answering was the one called; or

  o A particular business, if the call was made to a business and the call related to business reasonably transacted over the telephone, Fed. R. Evid. 901(b)(6).

- Evidence about public records. This includes evidence that a document was filed in a public office as authorized by law, or a purported public record is from the office where items of this kind are kept, Fed. R. Evid. 901(b)(7).

- Evidence about ancient documents or data compilations. This includes documents and data over twenty years old— as you may remember from the hearsay exception, according to evidence law, if you are over twenty, you are ancient—found where it would be expected to be, in a condition that creates no suspicion about its authenticity, Fed. R. Evid. 901(b)(8).

- Evidence describing a process or system and showing that it produces an accurate result. For instance, in admitting the contents of a security camera at an ATM where no one can testify as to the nature of the scene, it will suffice to explain the process by which the camera is activated, the scene recorded, and the film processed. Similarly, the authentication of x-rays, MRIs, and CAT scans requires proof that the process produces an accurate result, Fed. R. Evid. 901(b)(9).

- Methods allowed by a federal statute or a rule prescribed by the United States Supreme Court, Fed. R. Evid. 901(b)(10).

The above are merely illustrations and do not directly address newer authentication questions, particularly those involving email and social media (such as Twitter and Facebook). Most commonly, courts have cited Fed. R. Evid. 901(b)(4) (distinctive characteristics and the like) in authenticating the Facebook pages of people who allegedly brag on their pages about crimes they are later charged with committing. If a statement is indeed the accused's statement, there is little hearsay problem, for it is a statement by a party-opponent. The real challenge will be authenticating the email, Facebook page, or other social media. Photos of the accused and her pet, her birthday, and other distinctive characteristics may suffice. Courts have, however, expressed concern about the possibility of faking or hijacking someone else's Facebook page.

§ 14.4 *Chain of Custody*

Real evidence is authenticated by showing that the exhibit in court is the actual item in question and that it has not undergone any significant change.

When the item of real evidence is not particularly distinctive— one vial of crystal meth looks pretty much like another—or when its condition at the time of testing or trial is crucial, the most effective way to authenticate the exhibit is to provide a chain of custody tracing who has handled the evidence and where it has been.

§ 14.5 *Demonstrative Exhibits*

Demonstrative evidence illustrates and clarifies a witness's oral testimony. To create a foundation for demonstrative evidence, the witness must demonstrate familiarity with whatever is depicted and she must testify that the exhibit fairly and accurately represents the subject.

The most common objection to demonstrative evidence used for an illustrative purpose is that it is misleading. For example, diagrams that appear to be but are not actually to scale, or a photograph taken under different lighting or seasonal conditions, can mislead the jurors about the nature of the scene.

§ 14.6 *Photograph*

Authenticating a photograph is usually very easy. A person familiar with the scene can testify that it is a fair and accurate depiction. There is no need to produce the photographer or, if it was produced in the pre-digital age, the negative.

  AUTHENTICATION CHECKLIST

1. Is the evidence in question a tangible item such as a document, recording, weapon, etc.?

    If yes: Go to Step 2.

    If no: Authentication rules do not apply.

2. Is the item self-authenticating under Fed. R. Evid. 902?

    If yes: The item is authenticated.

    If no: Go to Step 3.

3. Does the proponent contend that the item is the actual item at issue in the case?

    If yes: Go to Step 4.

    If no: Go to Step 5.

4. Is there sufficient evidence for a judge to believe that the jury would find the item authentic? Examples of evidence sufficient to persuade a jury that the item is what its proponent claims include the following:

    • Testimony of a witness with knowledge;

    • Non-expert opinion about handwriting;

- Comparison by an expert witness or the trier-of-fact of a known authentic handwriting with the handwriting in question;

- Distinctive characteristics and the like;

- Opinion about a voice;

- Evidence about a telephone conversation, or evidence that a call was made to the number assigned at the time to:

  o   A particular person; or

  o   A particular business;

- Evidence about public records filed in a public office as authorized by law or a purported public record from the office where items of this kind are kept;

- Evidence about ancient documents or data compilations;

- Evidence describing a process or system and showing that it produces an accurate result; and

- Methods allowed by a federal statute or a rule prescribed by the Supreme Court.

Note: The above are illustrations, and a party seeking to authenticate evidence is free to rely on the general principle of Rule 901(a), that the evidence is what its proponent claims it to be, to argue that the item is what the proponent claims it to be.

If yes: The judge should allow the jury to consider the evidence.

If no: The judge will sustain an objection for lack of authentication and the evidence will be inadmissible.

5.   Is the tangible item offered as demonstrative evidence (such as a chart, map, or replica) and authenticated by a witness who demonstrates familiarity with whatever is depicted, and who testifies that the exhibit fairly and accurately represents the subject?

If yes: The demonstrative evidence has been authenticated and the judge should allow the jury to consider the evidence.

If no: The judge should not admit the demonstrative evidence and should sustain an objection as to authenticity.

ILLUSTRATIVE PROBLEMS

■ PROBLEM 14.1 ■

Q: Farmer Old MacDonald has died. He left a document, dated thirty years ago, deeding the farm to his son, Ronald. How might the document be authenticated?

A: The authentication question is essentially whether a jury could find that the item—in this case, the deed—is what its proponent claims it to be. There are many avenues for authenticating the document, and the authentication task should be easy.

- First, if the deed is introduced as a document from the proper public record office with the appropriate signature and seal, or is otherwise a certified copy, it may be self-authenticating under Fed. R. Evid. 902.

- Second, even without the sign and seal, evidence that it was filed in a public office or that it is from the proper county office where such items are kept would authenticate it under Fed. R. Evid. 901(b)(7).

- Third, a witness with knowledge (including Ronald himself) could authenticate the document, Fed. R. Evid. 901(b)(1).

- Fourth, the deed might contain unique nomenclature or other distinctive characteristics to indicate its authenticity, such as reference to the property's water source by the traditional family's designation, "Hamburgler's Crick," Fed. R. Evid. 901(b)(4).

- Fifth, because the document is ancient—more than twenty years old—and can be authenticated as per the illustration in Fed. R. Evid. 901(b)(8) by showing (1) that the document is in unsuspicious condition for a document of its age and (2) that it was found in a place where it was expected to be.

■ PROBLEM 14.2 ■

Q: In a civil action for damages based on a car accident, the Plaintiff wishes to introduce a picture of the scene to show that the Defendant had a stop sign, and the Plaintiff did not. How can the Plaintiff authenticate the photo?

A: Any witness with knowledge can testify that the photo is a fair and accurate representation of the accident scene. However, the photo would be objectionable if it were taken in winter (when the stop sign was visible) and not in late spring (the time of the accident) when the stop sign was obscured by the leaves of an overhanging tree.

POINTS TO REMEMBER

- All tangible items, both real and demonstrative, must be authenticated.

- The authentication question is simple: Is the item what its proponent claims it is? Fed. R. Evid. 901(a).

- Authenticating an item is a two-step process wherein: (1) the judge decides whether a reasonable jury could find the item to be what the proponent claims it to be, and if so, (2) the jury, as it deliberates, decides whether the evidence is sufficient to determine that the item is, in fact, authentic.

- Some items are self-authenticating, including:

  o Various official, public, or acknowledged documents;

  o Newspapers;

  o Trade inscriptions;

  o Commercial paper; and

  o Certified business records.

- Technically, there are no authentication "rules." Instead Fed. R. Evid. 901(b) provides ten "illustrations" designed to demonstrate what meets the authentication requirement. Examples of authentication methods include but are not restricted to the following:

  o Testimony of a witness with knowledge;

  o Non-expert opinion about handwriting;

  o Comparison by an expert witness or the trier-of-fact;

  o Distinctive characteristics and the like;

  o Opinion about a voice;

  o Evidence about a telephone conversation, or evidence that a call was made to the number assigned at the time to:

    ▪ A particular person; or

    ▪ A particular business;

  o Evidence that public records were filed in a public office as authorized by law or a purported public record is from the office where items of this kind are kept;

  o Evidence about ancient documents or data compilations;

  o Evidence describing a process or system and showing that it produces an accurate result; and o   Methods allowed by a federal statute or the Supreme Court.

- Authenticating emails, Facebook pages, or other social media pages can be tricky, and it is usually accomplished through identifying distinctive characteristics, Fed. R. Evid. 901(b)(4). Courts have expressed concern about the possibility of faking or hijacking someone else's Facebook page.

- To create a foundation for demonstrative evidence, the witness must demonstrate familiarity with whatever is depicted, and she must testify that the exhibit fairly and accurately represents the subject.

- To authenticate a photograph, someone familiar with the scene can testify that it is a fair and accurate depiction. There is no need to produce the photographer or, if it was produced in the pre-digital age, the negative.

CHAPTER 15

The Best Evidence Rule

[Fed. R. Evid. 1001–1006]

§ 15.1 *Overview of the Best Evidence Rule*

The "best evidence" rule requires that an original writing, photograph, or recording be produced if the proponent of the evidence wishes to "prove the contents" of the item. The rule applies only to writings, photographs, and recordings. Generally, producing a mechanically reproduced duplicate will satisfy the rule. Therefore, the rule represents not so much a competition between an original and a copy, but rather a competition between producing the actual document, photograph, or recording versus merely providing and relying upon testimony about such items. Essentially, the best evidence rule expresses a preference for providing the trier-of-fact with a writing, photograph, or recording rather than just allowing testimony about the contents of the item.

The best evidence rule also:

- Excuses failure to produce the document, photograph, or recording if the evidence is lost or destroyed;

- Is not the "best" rule of evidence—it is really just an OK rule that ultimately does little to prevent mistakes or fraud in the oral reporting of the contents of documents, photographs, and recordings; and

- Has little effect on the course of a trial if lawyers plan ahead and arrive to court prepared. If a lawyer properly prepares her case, the only circumstance in which the best evidence rule should actually exclude evidence is when her client has destroyed such evidence in bad faith. (Destruction of evidence may be a separate crime, but our focus is on the admissibility of statements regarding the document.)

§ 15.2 *To What Types of Items Does the Best Evidence Rule Apply?*

[Fed. R. Evid. 1001]

The best evidence rule applies to writings, recordings, and photographs. "Photographs" include film. The best evidence rule does not reach all tangible evidence. It does not include, for example, a knife, an automobile, or a work of art (all of which still need to be authenticated even though they do not fall under the best evidence rule).[1]

§ 15.3 *When Is the Proponent Trying to "Prove the Contents" of a Writing, Photograph, or Recording?*

[Fed. R. Evid. 1002]

A proponent attempts to "prove the contents" of a writing, photograph, or recording when either:

(1) The law requires that the writing, recording, or photograph be introduced; or

(2) The proponent strategically chooses to mention and rely upon the document.

The best evidence consideration of "proving the contents of a writing" is different from the hearsay issues of using a document for the "truth of the matter asserted." A party trying to offer proof of a libelous document would be attempting to prove the contents of the writing but not the truth of the matter asserted in the writing.

Examples of the law requiring the writing, recording, or photograph to be introduced include contracts that must be introduced under the parol evidence rule and libelous statements that defamation law requires the plaintiff to enter into evidence.

EXAMPLE

In a prosecution for making terroristic threats, the Prosecutor attempts to establish the nature of the statements made in the Defendant's newspaper. An FBI agent read the threats in the newspaper and is prepared to testify about what was written. The newspaper itself is not offered into evidence or shown to the jury. The judge should sustain a best evidence objection because by talking about the item in the newspaper, the FBI agent is trying to prove

---

[1]   *See* Chapter 14 (Authentication).

the contents of the article. If, however, the Defendant had destroyed all the copies, then the agent could testify about them.

The best evidence rule does not require producing the writing, recording, or photograph merely because the item happens to exist. If a witness is testifying about the underlying event based on knowledge from a source other than the writing, recording, or photograph, then the witness is not trying to prove the contents, and the best evidence rule does not apply. The principal concern of the best evidence rule is the danger of mistake or fraud in the oral reporting (or human copying) of the contents of writings, photographs, and recordings.

EXAMPLES

Beyoncé lends Jay Z $500. Jay Z writes an IOU for the money and gives the IOU to Beyoncé. After months without repayment, Beyoncé sues Jay Z for the $500. If Beyoncé says at trial, "Jay Z owes me money, and I have an IOU to prove it," but does not enter the IOU into evidence, Jay Z may successfully object on grounds of best evidence, unless the receipt has been lost or is in Jay Z's possession. The principle is that if Beyoncé wants to talk about the contents of the IOU, she must prove its contents by introducing the physical document. However, if Beyoncé merely testifies as to the loan and never mentions the IOU, then Jay Z cannot prevent her testimony by raising an objection that the IOU is the "best evidence."

* * *

A robbery is caught on videotape. If an eyewitness who was present at the robbery is asked, what the robber looked like, the response should not trigger a best evidence objection. The testimony is about what the witness saw, not what is on the videotape. A best evidence objection would be appropriate if a witness who viewed the videotape is asked, "What does the videotape indicate about the robber's appearance?" By soliciting testimony about the contents of the videotape, the party sponsoring the evidence is attempting to prove the content of the video, and the video itself must be produced.

§ 15.4 *When Do the Rules Insist on an Original (as Opposed to a Mechanically Duplicated Copy)?*

[Fed. R. Evid. 1003]

Generally, it is a mistake to think of the rule as preferring an original over a duplicate. Although historic concerns about mistakes in hand-copying prompted the rule, today few concerns are raised about mechanical duplicates. A "duplicate," which according to Fed. R. Evid. 1001 is a counterpart produced by photographic, electric, or other process that accurately reproduces the original, is usually "admissible to the same extent as the original," Fed. R. Evid. 1003. However, the original (rather than a duplicate) is required if a reasonable question is raised about the duplicate's authenticity or if there is something unfair about using the duplicate, Fed. R. Evid. 1003.

§ 15.5 *When Non-Production Is Allowed*

[Fed. R. Evid. 1004]

The prohibition against proving the contents of a writing, recording, or photograph without producing the original does not apply when the writing, recording, or photograph is:

- Collateral, that is to say tangential, to a controlling issue;

- Lost or stolen;

- Destroyed in good faith;

- In someone else's hands and not obtainable by judicial process; or

- In the possession of the party making the objection, and the opponent had notice to produce it, by the pleadings or otherwise.

If the proponent satisfies the judge that the original is missing or that there is some other valid excuse for not producing the original, the proponent can prove the contents of the original either by oral testimony or by producing a copy.

§ 15.6 *Preference for Certified Copies of Public Documents*

[Fed. R. Evid. 1005]

Fed. R. Evid. 1005 indicates a clear preference for copies that are certified[2] or that are presented through the testimony of a witness who has compared the copy with the original. Other evidence of the contents of a public record is admissible only if the certified or compared copy cannot be obtained by the exercise of due diligence.

 BEST EVIDENCE CHECKLIST

1. Is the item in question a writing, recording, or photo, and therefore something that falls within the best evidence rule, Fed. R. Evid. 1001?

   If yes: Best evidence rule applies. Go to Step 2.

   If no: Best evidence rule does not apply.

2. Is the proponent trying to prove the contents of the document? Fed. R. Evid. 1002.

   • Is the introduction of the document, photo, or recording legally required (for example, by the parole evidence rule or the law of defamation)?

   • Alternatively, as a matter of trial strategy, has the litigant chosen to rely on a writing, recording, or photo?

   If yes to either: Best evidence rule applies. Go to Step 3.

   If no to both: Best evidence rule does not apply.

3. Is the writing, recording, or photo "closely related to a controlling issue"? Fed. R. Evid. 1004.

   If yes: Best evidence rule applies. Go to Step 4.

   If no: It is collateral and the best evidence rule does not apply.

4. Is there any reason that a duplicate would be unfair, or is there any question about authenticity? Fed. R. Evid. 1003.

   If yes to either: The proponent must provide the original. Go to Step 5.

   If no to both: A mechanical duplicate will suffice. Go to Step 5.

---

[2] Certification is made pursuant to Fed. R. Evid. 902(4).

5.   Is the referenced document a public record? Fed. R. Evid. 1005.

If yes: Best evidence rule prefers a certified copy but will accept other evidence if the proponent, acting with reasonable diligence, cannot provide one. Go to Step 6.

If no: Best evidence rule applies. Go to Step 6.

6.   Is there a legitimate excuse for not applying the best evidence rule (for example, if the writing, photo, or recording is either lost or in the hands of the opponent)? Fed. R. Evid. 1004.

If yes: Other evidence is permissible.

If no: Evidence may be excluded by the best evidence rule.

ILLUSTRATIVE PROBLEMS

■ PROBLEM 15.1 ■

Q: In a prosecution for display of an obscene film, the Prosecutor attempts to establish the nature of the film seized from the Defendant by calling Officer Silver, who viewed the tapes. Officer Silver, who was "shocked and sickened," describes in detail the action of the film in question, "Betty Does Bloomington." The film itself is neither offered into evidence nor shown to the jury. The Defendant makes a best evidence objection. How should the judge rule?

A: The judge should sustain the best evidence objection. The film counts as a photograph under the rule and hence must be shown to the jury rather than merely described by the witness if the proponent of the evidence is trying to prove the contents of the film. By calling the witness to discuss the action in the film, the Prosecutor is attempting to prove its contents. Therefore, the jury must be allowed to view the film—and any unaltered version will do, because all unaltered copies of the film would count as originals. The film is certainly closely related to a controlling issue in the case. Only if the originals were all lost or destroyed through no fault of the Prosecutor would the best evidence rule not apply.

■ PROBLEM 15.2 ■

Q: Thelma is picked up by the police and charged with criminal restraint. After being read her rights, she states that she is ready to confess. The interviewing officer calls in a stenographer to take down her statement. In front of the officer and the police stenographer, Thelma confesses to locking patrolman Joe Friday in a trunk to avoid arrest on unrelated charges. At Thelma's criminal trial, the prosecution calls the interviewing officer to testify as to what Thelma said. Thelma raises a best evidence objection that the transcript is the best evidence of her confession. How should the court rule?

A: Although there is a transcript of Thelma's confession that colloquially might be "better" evidence than the memory of the interviewing officer, there is no legitimate best evidence objection here. The officer is not trying to prove the contents of the transcript. Rather, the transcript is an alternate source of information. Since the officer is relying on his own memory, and not the transcript, he is not trying to prove the contents of the transcript. The best evidence rule does not apply.

■ PROBLEM 15.3 ■

Q: Imagine the same facts as Problem 15.2, but instead of the interviewing officer, the Prosecutor wishes to call Officer Frank Gannon, who was not present during the confession but reviewed the recorded confession and is prepared to testify as to what Thelma said. Thelma raises a best evidence objection. How should the court rule?

A: Officer Gannon has no personal knowledge of what Thelma said, so his testimony could only be about what the transcript provides. Therefore, Officer Gannon is trying to prove the contents of the transcript and the best evidence objection should be sustained. The Prosecutor should move to admit the transcript as evidence so the finders-of-fact can judge what the transcript says for themselves.

POINTS TO REMEMBER

- The best evidence rule applies when a proponent wishes to prove the contents of a writing, photograph, or recording.

- Essentially, the best evidence rule expresses a preference for providing the fact-finder with the actual writing, photograph, or recording rather than witness testimony about its contents.

- A proponent wishes to prove the contents of a writing, photograph, or recording when:

  o Law requires that the writing, photograph, or recording be introduced; or

  o The proponent strategically chooses to rely upon the document.

- Generally, a mechanically reproduced document will satisfy the requirement for the original. However, Fed. R. Evid. 1003 requires the original itself if a reasonable question is raised concerning authenticity or if there is something unfair about using the duplicate.

- The rule excuses failure to produce the original when evidence is lost or destroyed in good faith.

CHAPTER 16

Evidence on Appeal

§ 16.1 *Appealing the Trial Court's Mistakes in Admitting or Excluding Evidence*

Parties deserve a fair trial, not a perfect one. Because fallible human beings try and judge cases, almost every trial may contain evidentiary mistakes. Some mistakes, particularly those appropriately objected to, can be serious enough to require a new trial or a revision of the verdict. But not every error qualifies as reversible.

§ 16.2 *"Harmless Error"*

[Fed. R. Evid. 103(a)]

If an error does not affect a substantial right of a party, then the error, even if objected to, is harmless. Harmless error is not prejudicial and does not require reversal. In other words, if the other evidence in the case is strong enough that it is likely that the result would have been the same even without the improperly admitted evidence (or with the improperly excluded evidence), then the error was harmless. If there is a substantial chance that the jury could not have reached the same verdict without the evidentiary error, then the error is not harmless. The precise standard for harmless error varies with the type of case, the type of evidence, and the jurisdiction.

§ 16.3 *The Importance of Timely Objection*

[Fed. R. Evid. 103(a)(1)]

In addition to showing that the mistake mattered, which is to say that it was not harmless, a party must also object promptly if the trial court makes a mistake concerning evidence. Such an objection puts the court on notice and permits it to correct the error, or at least mitigate the damage with a limiting instruction.

§ 16.4 *Offer of Proof*

[Fed. R. Evid. 103(a)(2)]

If a party wishes to introduce evidence and the trial court refuses to admit it, the party should inform the court of what it wants to prove by making an offer of proof and creating a record (outside the hearing of the jury) of what the evidence would show. The party should address any evidentiary objections and explain why the evidence is admissible.

§ 16.5 *Providing the Correct Reason*

The objection or offer of proof must provide the court with the correct reason for the admissibility of the evidence. If an attorney argues at trial that a piece of evidence is inadmissible, she must state the specific ground for exclusion. Failure to do so will limit the ability to appeal on that evidentiary point. The goal is to allow the trial court to correct errors on the spot; that is less likely to happen if the advocate offers the wrong reasons for admission or exclusion.

EXAMPLE

Petunia objects to evidence, arguing that it is hearsay, which it is not. The evidence is, however, excludable as improper character evidence. If the trial court overrules the hearsay objection, Petunia would generally not be able to argue for reversal, because she failed to object with the proper reason. This is generally true even if the disputed evidence would have affected the outcome. Only if the evidentiary ruling was plain error (see below) would the appellate court reverse.

§ 16.6 *Plain Error*

[Fed. R. Evid. 103(e)]

A substantial error that affects a party, even if unobjected to, can be reversed in egregious cases where the mistake is obvious and plain. Even if a party fails to object or objects but fails to state the correct grounds, the appellate court may "take notice of a plain error affecting a substantial right," Fed. R. Evid. 103(e). Courts rarely recognize plain error, and parties should not count on this standard to save them from failure to take adequate procedural steps in the trial court.

§ 16.7 *Standards of Review on Appeal*

If a trial court misstates the legal standard, the appellate court will review the ruling de novo.

If a trial court states the standard correctly, but arguably misapplies it, the appellate court will review the ruling on an abuse-of-discretion standard. Appellate courts grant trial courts wide latitude in such discretionary determinations because such judgment calls are best performed by the trial court, which benefits from viewing the evidence in fuller context and observing the demeanor of witnesses.

     EVIDENCE ON APPEAL CHECKLIST

For Improperly Admitted Evidence

1. Did the mistake in evidence affect the substantial right of a party? In other words, was the error not harmless, but prejudicial?

   If yes: Go to Step 2.

   If no: A procedural mistake was made that did not interfere with justice, and the verdict will not be reversed because of the improperly admitted evidence.

2. Was a timely objection raised at trial to the evidence?

   If yes: Go to Step 3.

   If no: The evidence can only be excluded and the trial court's judgment reversed if there is plain error. Go to Step 4.

3. Was the objection valid and properly presented with the correct grounds for exclusion?

   If yes: The appellate court should reverse the verdict and order a new trial or, in unusual circumstances and depending on what other evidence exists, substitute a new verdict.

   If no: The evidence can only be excluded it if constitutes plain error. Go to Step 4.

4. Was admission of the evidence plain error? In other words, was the error sufficiently obvious and substantial that it would

interfere with justice and perception of fairness of the proceeding?

If yes: The appellate court should reverse the verdict and order a new trial, or, in unusual circumstances and depending on what other evidence exists, substitute a new verdict.

If no: The procedural error in failing to object in a correct and timely fashion waived the objection.

<u>For Improperly Excluded Evidence</u>

1. Was a valid explanation provided to the trial court about why the evidence should be admitted despite the opposing party's objection?

    If yes: Go to Step 2.

    If no: The exclusion of the evidence will stand unless it constitutes plain error. Go to Step 4.

2. Did the party proffering the evidence make an offer of proof?

    If yes: Go to Step 3.

    If no: The evidence can only be excluded it if constitutes plain error. Go to Step 4.

3. Did the incorrectly excluded evidence affect the substantial right of a party? In other words, was the error not harmless, but prejudicial?

    If yes: The appellate court should reverse the verdict and order a new trial, or, in unusual circumstances and depending on what other evidence exists, substitute a new verdict.

    If no: A procedural mistake was made that did not interfere with justice, and the verdict will not be reversed because of the improperly excluded evidence unless the error was plain. Go to Step 4.

4. Was exclusion of the evidence plain error? In other words, was the error sufficiently obvious and substantial that it would interfere with justice and perception of fairness of the proceeding?

    If yes: The appellate court should reverse the verdict and order a new trial, or, in unusual circumstances and depending on what other evidence exists, substitute a new verdict. Note that plain error is more likely in the admission of evidence than in its exclusion.

    If no: The procedural error in failing to object in a correct and timely fashion or make an offer of proof waived the objection.

Standard of Review

1. Did the trial judge state the legal standard correctly?

    If yes: Go to Step 2.

    If no: The appellate court should review the evidence in light of the correct legal standard de novo.

2. Has the trial court, applying the correct legal standard, exercised its broad discretionary authority in a reasonable manner in determining the admissibility of evidence?

    If yes: The appellate court should affirm, even if the judges on the panel might have reached a different conclusion.

    If no: The appellate court may reverse for abuse of discretion.

ILLUSTRATIVE PROBLEMS

■ PROBLEM 16.1 ■

Q: Alice is convicted of selling cocaine. Part of the evidence included a video of Alice conducting the sale. Her attorney correctly objected to improperly authenticated evidence of credit card receipts connecting her to the location where the cocaine was sold, but the trial judge overruled the objection.

A: Even though the evidence of credit card receipts was mistakenly admitted and properly objected to, the appellate court will not reverse unless the error affected a substantial right of Alice. In this case, given the video, the mistaken admission of credit card receipts was harmless error because Alice would have been convicted anyway.

■ PROBLEM 16.2 ■

Q: Alvin was convicted of animal abuse. The evidence connecting him to the injured animal was weak—hearsay from an unavailable witness in the form of an excited utterance. However, Alvin's attorney (who may have been napping) failed to object to evidence that Alvin had tortured a puppy the year before. Alvin had done nothing to open the door to such impermissible character evidence. At closing, the Prosecutor said: "Think of the poor lame puppy that Alvin tortured. Alvin is a serial animal abuser. You must make him stop before he hurts another pet."

A: Alvin's prior bad act was clearly used for the prohibited purpose of propensity. Given the weakness of the rest of the case, the error was not harmless. Given the importance and obviousness of the character rule, there is a strong chance that an appellate court would find the error plain and reverse, remanding for a new trial.

POINTS TO REMEMBER

- Only evidentiary errors that affect a substantial right of a party constitute reversible error.

- Even when improper admission or exclusion of evidence affects a substantial right and thus is not harmless error, a party must generally follow the procedural rules and:

  o Object to improperly admitted evidence in a timely manner; or

  o Make an offer of proof where evidence is improperly excluded.

- In extraordinary cases, even when procedures for objecting to or preserving evidence have not been followed, appellate courts will reverse based on plain error if the error was obvious.

- The standard of review for legal rules is de novo.

- The standard of review for applying evidence rules is abuse of discretion.

CHAPTER 17

Notes on Exam Preparation

The following are suggestions about how to prepare for your evidence exam. Obviously, anything your teacher tells you trumps this otherwise good advice.

- Remember that the goal is to demonstrate your knowledge. Unless specifically instructed, do not give brief "yes" or "no" answers. Naked assertions are not enough. Instead, explain your answers. Offer reasons, support from authority, and policy discussion.

EXAMPLE

Joan witnesses a hit-and-run accident and is very shaken. She screams repeatedly, "It was the man with the snake tattoo!" She is unavailable to testify at the civil trial but the Plaintiff wishes to call another bystander who will repeat Joan's statement. The Defendant sports a snake tattoo on his neck. May the witness repeat Joan's statement for its truth?

Answer 1: Yes. Rule 803(2).

Answer 2: Joan's statement is hearsay because the trier-of-fact is being asked to believe the truth of her out-of-court assertion. Fed. R. Evid. 801. As a general rule, under Fed. R. Evid. 802 such hearsay statements are not admissible because they cannot be meaningfully subjected to cross-examination and the declarant has not taken an oath. However, Rule 803(2) provides an exception for excited utterances made under the stress of a startling event. Joan's statement fits the excited utterance exception because it was made spontaneously under the stress of excitement caused by the accident, and it relates to that startling event. A traffic accident qualifies as a startling event that would cause stress. Historically, such excited utterances have been deemed reliable because of the sincerity wrought by the stressful event and the closeness in time to the event. This common-law exception has been codified in the federal rules even though psychologists have criticized it—the very stress that increases sincerity may also diminish cognitive function, impairing memory and the ability to narrate events. Despite these policy concerns, the categorical approach to hearsay and its exceptions indicates that Joan's statement will be admitted for its truth, even if she is not available to testify or her identity is unknown.

The person who submitted Answer #1 may indeed know everything that the person who provided Answer #2 wrote, but Student #1 has not demonstrated that knowledge. Obviously, time restraints and word limitations will influence the scope of your answer, but when you are given no such guidance, a fuller answer that discusses policy and practical application is the superior answer.

- Avoid even the appearance of wasting time and space.

    o   Never repeat the question at length.

    o   Never copy over large portions of the rules (though citing and selectively quoting the relevant phrase is always a very good idea).

    o   Weave relevant facts from the question into your analysis of the rules that you apply.

- Think about policy and try to put together themes. This may be directly relevant if your exam asks a policy question, but it is helpful even with blackletter doctrine in organizing your ideas and enhancing your understanding of the underpinnings of the evidence rules. Such policies and themes include the following:

    o   The role of the judge as screener of evidence;

    o   The vast discretion afforded to the trial judge;

    o   Rules that express distrust of the jury's ability to handle evidence;

    o   The tendency of the rules towards admission of evidence;

    o   Rules that grant special treatment to the accused or provide variations for criminal cases;

    o   Rules that require advance notice to the adversary;

    o   The pattern of admitting evidence offered for "another purpose;"

    o   Variations on the Rule 403 balance that are sprinkled throughout the rules;

- o   Rules that defer to state evidence law in diversity cases.

- Do not discuss at length policy, politics, or social matters that were not part of the class. If your class readings and discussions only focused on the doctrinal application of the rape shield rules, a long discussion of social attitudes towards rape victims and a feminist analysis of how evidence law ignores the experience of women is interesting, but probably misplaced. You know you are off track if you write extensively about something that was not mentioned in class or included in the readings. On the other hand, if your class read and talked about such policy, your discussion will be welcome.

- Do not copy your notes into your exam.

  - o   It is rarely flattering and often creepy for the professor to hear her words repeated verbatim.

  - o   Other students will provide the same language from *their* notes and it will sound unoriginal and average.

  - o   Your notes, by definition, are not tailored to the individual question being posed on the exam. They will never be as responsive to the question as your targeted answer.

- Despite what some exam prep manuals tell you, ***never underline or bold KEY words.*** (See how annoying that is?) It is insulting to your reader, who is grimly determined to read every word.

- Set yourself a strict schedule at the beginning of the exam, budgeting time for each question and leaving enough time to review everything at the end. Make sure you address every question. An excellent first essay and a blank second essay will never generate a superior grade. If necessary because you are running out of time, outline your answer at the end.

- It is OK to forget obscure case names (and describe the facts instead), but know the major cases, and in an open-book exam, cite them specifically (though correct *Bluebook* form is unnecessary).

- Develop counterarguments where appropriate. Sometimes there is one correct answer, but often in law exams, as in life, there are two sides to the story. The best exams take a position, but acknowledge possible counterarguments where appropriate. In evidence, however, some answers are definite. For example, where an out-of-court statement is hearsay, you get more points for saying so clearly than you do for issuing some mealy-mouthed response like "this is arguably hearsay" or "the judge will probably consider the statement hearsay."

- Read the questions carefully. Twice.

  o Although it is possible that your professor has introduced some irrelevant material to see if you can recognize a red herring, it is more likely that some small, seemingly random fact is actually relevant to the argument you are expected to make. Analyze the question line by line, scrupulously considering each fact to figure out whether it should influence your answer.

  o Pay particular attention to the specific charge at the end of the question. Sometimes the question just instructs you to "discuss the evidence issues." Often, however, a question will have multiple parts. For instance, it will ask you to raise all the objections the accused could make to the testimony, consider the prosecutor's responses, and discuss how the judge should rule. Organize your answer around each sub-part of the question. Pay particular attention to whether you need to take a particular role, such as that of a judge, an attorney, or a junior associate. Even if you represent a party, do not ignore the counterarguments. Explain how your designated party would deal with reasonable objections.

- If something is not an issue, it is sometimes useful to explain why, but beware of going off on a tangent. For instance, noting that an out-of-court statement does not present a hearsay problem because it fits the requirements of Rule 801(d)(1)(A) "prior statement by a witness" is useful. Mentioning that the same out-of-court statement does not trigger the best evidence rule is not useful.

- Do not waste time and space discussing counterfactual hypotheticals. A brief aside is OK, but do not overdo it. For example, in a test question where the witness is clearly available for confrontation, it is a mistake to spend much space discussing whether the confrontation clause would be triggered if the accused were actually unavailable.

- Actually analyze an evidence problem; do not just demonstrate that you can identify the evidence rule the question implicates.

EXAMPLE

Arianna is accused of wire fraud and takes the witness stand to claim that she had no idea the deal she proposed was fraudulent. May the Prosecutor impeach Arianna with her prior conviction nine years ago for drunk driving, punishable for up to five years in prison, for which she received community service?

Answer Version 1: The Prosecutor may be able to impeach Arianna if the Prosecutor can demonstrate that the probative value of the impeachment outweighs the unfair prejudice to Arianna.

Answer Version 2:

Special Rule for Impeachment of the Accused

Rule 609 allows impeachment of any witness, including the accused in a criminal case. Rule 609(a)(2) places the burden on the prosecutor to demonstrate that the probative value of the impeachment outweighs (not substantially, but merely outweighs) the unfair prejudice to the accused.

Applying the Balance—Probative Value

In applying this special test (which, contrary to the traditional Rule 403 balance, favors exclusion), the court will have to assess both the probative value of the impeachment and the unfair prejudice of the evidence. In this case, the probative value of Arianna's drunk driving goes to her credibility. Although drunk driving is not a crime of dishonesty, and hence is not within the purview of Fed. R. Evid. 609(a)(2) (which admits previous convictions without any balancing), a drunk driving conviction bespeaks a willingness to disobey legal rules and social norms. A person who is willing to drive drunk might be less trustworthy and more likely to lie on the stand than the ordinary witness. The jurors might be more skeptical of Arianna's testimony if they knew this about her. The probative value is diminished, however, because the drunk driving conviction was so long ago, close to the ten-year limit after which Rule 609(b) imposes a much more exclusionary balance.

Applying the Balance—Unfair Prejudice

In assessing the unfair prejudice, it is important to note that the prior conviction is not for the same type of crime as the Accused's current charge. There seems to be little chance of jury confusion or distraction. This also avoids an impermissible propensity leap by the jury. Had the prior conviction been for mail fraud, the jury might have been led to adopt a prohibited character theory that Arianna is the type of person who defrauds others. Here, there is no danger of jurors engaging in that logic, but there still might be unfair prejudice because the jurors might abhor the behavior of a person who would drive drunk. Also, in assessing unfair prejudice we would consider whether it is the type of impeachment that might discourage the Accused from taking the stand.

Recommendation to Exclude the Evidence

A trial judge has broad discretion and will probably be affirmed either way, but in my opinion the probative value of a nine-year-old drunk driving conviction says little about Arianna's willingness to lie on the witness stand, and it may be unfairly prejudicial because the crime indicates callousness to human life. Therefore, as a judge I would exclude it.

- Appeal to your professor's vanity and appreciate the ambiguities in the question. Sometimes a key fact will be purposely left out. For instance, your answer may depend on whether a witness is available for cross-examination. If the problem does not tell you, note that fact and analyze the question both ways.

- Although there may be some evidence teachers who insist on hearing their own theories confirmed, I, and I hope most of my colleagues, find it refreshing when a student makes a reasoned argument disagreeing with the professor on a debatable matter of rule interpretation or policy. I admire the student's moxie and flatter myself that she was interested enough to think about the questions raised in the course. Also, the student could not possibly be copying out of her notes.

- Avoid empty phrases and sentences, particularly when there is a word limit. For example: "This question raises many interesting and important questions about evidence that will require careful analysis" does not add anything or garner points.

- Be conscious of how your answer appears on the page. Try to make it as readable as possible.

  o   If possible, use headings and subheadings.

  o   Indent and leave some white spaces.

  o   Type if you possibly can.

  o   If you write by hand, use ink and skip every other line.

  o   Do not write on the back side of the page.

Suggestions for Study:

- Focus on your readings and your class notes. Unless your professor is sadistic, demented, or clueless (possibilities that I cannot entirely discount), the exam will reflect what was assigned and what was taught.

  o   Rarely (and ideally never) will the correct answer involve an obscure rule or principle that was not covered in class.

  o   Do not use outside outlines (including this one!) until you have exhausted your review of class notes, materials, and problems.

  o   Organize your answers and approach to a problem the way your professor modeled in class. Even if you reach a technically correct answer, if it is with terminology and an approach divergent from the class, you telegraph to your teacher that you felt the class was sub-par and you needed to teach the material to yourself via sources other than the ones chosen by your professor.

  o   Whenever possible, take practice exams—ideally old exams from your professor. The way to get the most out of the experience is to take practice exams towards the end of the semester under exam conditions, limiting your time and access to source material in ways that the actual exam will do. If you can convince others to take the practice exam with you, trade answers and discuss your various approaches to the questions.

- Organize your materials so that you can get to them quickly. If there is no limit on the materials you can bring into the exam, there is a danger that you can get bogged down searching for the place in your notes or your outline that might provide the answer. Rarely is your time well spent rifling through your materials during the exam.

CHAPTER 18

Meta Checklist

I. **Consider these questions to help orient your analysis.**

   A. Clarify whether it is a criminal or civil case. This will affect some applications of the rules and govern whether confrontation applies.

   B. Determine whether a live witness with personal knowledge will testify. If it is a criminal case, figure out whether the accused will testify. If the accused does not testify, she cannot be impeached.

   C. Determine whether the witness or declarant is a party. Statements by party-opponents are easily admissible. Remember: victims are not parties in criminal cases.

   D. If this is a civil case, determine whether state law applies to the substantive questions in the case—in other words, is this a diversity case in federal court? If so, state rules of presumptions, privilege, and competence apply, Fed. R. Evid. 302, 501, and 601.

   E. If you are considering the admissibility of a document, which is the most common type of trial exhibit, you must address:

   • Hearsay;

   • Confrontation (if it is a criminal trial and the document is introduced against the accused);

   • Authentication; and

   • Best evidence.

II. Begin with a discrete piece of evidence and consider all the relevant steps of the checklist.

                    RELEVANCE CHECKLIST

1. Is the evidence logically relevant? Does it have any tendency to make a material fact more or less likely? Fed. R. Evid. 401. *See* § 1.1. Because this is an easy standard to satisfy, the answer is probably yes.

    If yes: Go to Step 2 to consider practical relevance.

    If no: The evidence is not admissible.

2. Does the evidence pass Rule 403 balancing, so that its probative value is not significantly outweighed by unfair prejudice, distraction, confusion, or waste of time?

    Note: If there is other, less prejudicial evidence that a party can easily use to prove the same fact, the probative value of the evidence decreases. If there is an effective way of limiting the unfair prejudice through a limiting instruction, the unfair prejudice of the evidence decreases. *See* §§ 1.3–1.4.

    If yes: Continue to character and other relevance rules.

    If no: The evidence may be excluded by the trial judge. However, this is a highly discretionary decision by the trial judge and you should not necessarily stop here. Even if you think the evidence fails Rule 403, you should conduct the rest of your analysis just to cover the possibility that the trial judge might disagree with you.

CHARACTER EVIDENCE & HABIT

<u>Propensity</u>

3. Is the evidence propensity evidence (does it use a trait of character or a prior act to show a tendency toward that behavior)? Fed. R. Evid. 404(a). *See* § 2.1.

    If yes: Go to Step 4.

    If no: Go to Step 5.

<u>Exceptions to Propensity</u>

4. Does the evidence fall under any of the exceptions to the propensity rule? *See* § 2.3.

    •   In both civil & criminal cases:

    o   A witness's tendency to be untruthful, Fed. R. Evid. 608. *See* § 4.4.

    o   A witness's past convictions to show her disdain for abiding by social rules, Fed. R. Evid. 609. *See* § 4.5–4.6.

- In criminal cases only:

    o   A pertinent character trait of the Accused offered by the accused and the prosecutor's evidence to rebut it, Fed. R. Evid. 404(a)(2)(A) *See* § 2.4.

    o   A pertinent character trait of the accused where the accused raised that particular trait of the victim, Fed. R. Evid. 404(a)(2)(B)(ii). *See* § 2.5.

    o   A pertinent character trait of the victim offered by the accused (except in cases of rape) and the prosecutor's evidence to rebut it, Fed. R. Evid. 404(a)(2)(B)(i). *See* §§ 2.5–2.6.

    o   The accused's sexual propensities in rape and molestation cases, Fed. R. Evid. 413–414. *See* § 2.7.

    o   A homicide case where the accused contends that the victim was the first aggressor, Fed. R. Evid. 404(a)(2)(C). *See* § 2.5.

If yes: It is admissible. Proof of propensity, when admitted subject to an exception, is generally restricted to reputation and opinion evidence. Specific instances may only be inquired into on cross-examination, Fed. R. Evid. 405(a). However, for sexual predisposition under Fed. R. Evid. 413–414, extrinsic evidence of specific instances is allowed. *See* § 2.7.

If no: It is impermissible character evidence.

"Other Purposes" Under Rule 404(b)

5.   If the evidence is not being used for propensity, is it being used for "another [non-character] purpose" such as motive, knowledge or opportunity? Fed. R. Evid. 404(b)(2). *See* § 2.11.

If yes: The court must conduct a Rule 403 balance and should exclude the evidence if the unfair prejudice of the character use substantially outweighs the probative value of the other purpose.

If no: Go to Step 6.

Character at Issue

6.   Is this one of the *very rare* circumstances when character is "in issue" and specific-incident evidence of character is admissible

under Fed. R. Evid. 405(b) as direct evidence of character (because the trait or character is an essential element of the claim, crime, or defense)? *See* § 2.10.

If yes: Double check your answer. Very few types of modern cases (all of them civil) put character in issue. If you are sure, it is admissible and specific instances may be used to prove the character in issue.

If no: Go to Step 7.

Rule 406: Habit

7. Does the evidence involve semiautomatic, routinized behavior that is not likely to generate unfair prejudice? Fed. R. Evid. 406. *See* § 2.12.

    If yes: It is admissible as habit.

    If no: It is not admissible as habit.

OTHER RELEVANCE RULES

Rule 407: Remedial Repair

8. Is this a civil case where the Plaintiff wishes to introduce evidence of the Defendant's remedial measure to prove negligence?

    If yes: Rule 407 will exclude evidence of remedial measures taken after the event, but remedial measures offered for another controverted purpose, such as ownership or feasibility of repair, is admissible. *See* § 3.2. Go to Step 13.

    If no: Go to Step 9.

Rule 408: Offers to Compromise

9. Does the evidence relate to the validity or amount of a disputed claim and arise out of a

    *   Compromise,

    *   Offer to compromise, or

    *   Surrounding statements

    in a civil case where there is a genuine dispute as to validity or amount?

    If yes: Rule 408 will exclude the evidence unless it is either offered for another purpose or it involves a claim made to a public office or agency being brought in a subsequent criminal case. *See* § 3.3. Go to Step 10.

    If no: Rule 408 will not exclude the evidence. Go to Step 10.

Rule 409: Payment of Medical Expenses

10. Does the evidence arise out of payment of medical or similar expenses?

   If yes: Rule 409 will exclude the evidence, but surrounding statements are not covered by this rule. *See* § 3.4. Go to Step 13.

   If no: Go to Step 11.

Rule 410: Plea Bargain

11. Does the evidence arise out of a guilty plea or negotiations with the prosecuting attorney?

   If yes: It is inadmissible unless:

   • It serves to contextualize or explain statements already admitted from the same plea negotiation; or

   • The statements are being introduced in a perjury trial if the accused made the statement under oath, on the record, and with counsel present. *See* § 3.5. Go to Step 14.

   If no: Rule 410 will not exclude the evidence. Go to Step 13.

Rule 411: Insurance

12. Does the evidence concern liability insurance offered to prove whether a person acted negligently or otherwise wrongfully?

   If yes: It is prohibited. *See* § 3.6. Go to Step 14.

   If no: Rule 411 will not exclude evidence offered for another purpose, such as proving agency, ownership, control of an item, or demonstrating bias or prejudice of a witness. Go to Step 13.

Revisiting the Rule 403 Balance

13. If you have determined that the evidence is admissible for "another purpose" other than the one prohibited by the rule, conduct a Rule 403 balance. Does the unfair prejudice of the impermissible use of the evidence substantially outweigh the probative value of the other purpose?

   If yes: The evidence is not admissible. Even though you have articulated a valid purpose, the unfair prejudice of the prohibited purpose vastly predominates and admission would subvert the rule of exclusion. Go to Step 14.

   If no: The evidence is admissible. Go to Step 14.

IMPEACHMENT

14. Has a live witness given testimony or has an absent declarant's testimony been offered for its truth?

If yes: Go to Step 15 to begin examining the various available forms of impeachment. The witness can be impeached in different ways.

If no: There is nothing to impeach. Go to Step 23.

Bias

15. Can the witness be impeached for bias?

If yes: Questions regarding bias may be raised on cross-examination and by extrinsic evidence. *See* § 4.2. Go to Step 16.

If no: Go to Step 16.

Sensory Perception

16. Can the witness be impeached for sensory perception?

If yes: Questions regarding her perception may be raised on cross-examination and by extrinsic evidence. *See* § 4.3. Go to Step 17.

If no: Go to Step 17.

Rule 608: Character for Truthfulness

17. Can the witness be impeached for a propensity for non-truthfulness (excluding any issues raised by criminal convictions)?

If yes: The party impeaching the witness may bring opinion or reputation evidence concerning the witness's truthfulness. The impeaching party may also cross-examine about specific instances of the witness's non-truthfulness, but must accept the witness's answer; (extrinsic evidence concerning the specific evidence of untruthfulness is inadmissible). *See* § 4.4. Go to Step 18.

If no: Go to Step 18.

Rule 609: Prior Conviction

18. Was the witness convicted of a crime of dishonesty or false statement, and have fewer than ten years passed since the witness's conviction or release, whichever is later?

If yes: Unless the witness was a juvenile, or the crime was pardoned, the witness may be impeached with the prior crime and the court will conduct no Rule 403 balancing, even if the witness is the accused, Fed. R. Evid. 609(a)(2). *See* § 4.5. Go to Step 21.

If no: Go to Step 19.

19. Was the witness who is being impeached convicted of a crime

- As an adult;

- Not pardoned;

- Punishable by more than a year in prison; and

Have fewer than ten years passed since the witness's conviction or release?

If yes, and the witnesses is the accused: The prosecutor must prove that the probative value of the impeachment outweighs the unfair prejudice to the accused, Fed. R. Evid. 609(a)(1)(B). *See* § 4.6. Go to Step 20.

If yes, and the witness is anyone but the accused: The objecting party can exclude the impeachment by demonstrating that the unfair prejudice substantially outweighs the probative value—a standard Rule 403 test, Fed. R. Evid. 609(a)(1)(A). *See* § 4.6. Go to Step 20.

If no: Go to Step 20.

20. Was the witness convicted of a crime that would have been otherwise admissible as impeachment under Rule 609(a) except for the fact that more than ten years passed since the witness's conviction or release?

If yes: The evidence is only admissible if its proponent can demonstrate that the probative value of the impeachment, supported by specific facts and circumstances, substantially outweighs its prejudicial effect and the proponent gives written notice to the adverse party. This is a very difficult test to pass and favors exclusion of the evidence, Fed. R. Evid. 609(b). *See* § 4.5. Go to Step 21.

If no: Go to Step 21.

Impeachment by Contradiction

21. Is the proposed impeachment independently admissible extrinsic evidence that contradicts a witness's testimony?

If yes: The impeachment by contradiction is admissible as long as it is not so tangential that it fails the Rule 403 balance for waste of time. *See* § 4.8. Go to Step 23.

If no: It is not admissible. Go to Step 22.

22. Is the proposed impeachment of a witness the witness's own prior statement?

    If yes: The witness need not be shown the statement in advance but generally must be afforded an opportunity to explain or deny it, Fed. R. Evid. 613. *See* § 4.8. Go to Step 23.

    If no: Go to Step 23.

HEARSAY

Hearsay Definition

23. Is the statement hearsay at all? Is the finder-of-fact being asked to believe that what the Declarant said in the out-of-court statement is actually true?

    Note: Four classic examples where an out-of-court statement is *not* being used for the truth of the matter asserted are:

    - Circumstantial evidence of state of mind of the speaker;

    - Effect on listener;

    - Impeachment of a witness with an inconsistent prior statement; and

    - Verbal acts.

    If yes: The statement is hearsay, Fed. R. Evid. 801(a)–(c). *See* §§ 5.1–5.7. Go to Step 24.

    If no: The out-of-court statement is admissible, but it is worthwhile to analyze the out-of-court statement to see if it falls under any exemptions or exclusions just in case the judge disagrees with your hearsay analysis. Go to Step 24.

Rule 801(d)(1): Hearsay Exemptions for Prior Statements by Witnesses

Note: To trigger this exemption, the witness must testify at the current trial.

24. Does the out-of-court statement fall under the "not hearsay" exemption for a witness's prior inconsistent statement? To do so the prior statement by the witness must:

    - Be inconsistent;

    - Have been offered under oath, subject to penalty of perjury; and

    - Been made at another trial, proceeding (including a grand jury), or deposition.

Note: the witness must be subject to cross-examination at the time the statement is introduced (at the current trial), but the prior statement itself need not have been subject to cross-examination at the time it was made.

If yes: The prior statement is "not hearsay" and is admissible for its truth as well as for impeachment, Fed. R. Evid. 801(d)(1)(A). *See* § 6.3. Go to Step 26.

If no: The inconsistent statement will be admissible as common-law, but not for its truth. Go to Step 25.

25. Is the out-of-court statement consistent with the witness's current testimony and offered: (1) to rebut "an express or implied charge that the declarant recently fabricated" the current in-court testimony or "acted from a recent improper influence or motive" or (2) "to rehabilitate the declarant's credibility as a witness when attacked on another ground"?

Note: The prior statement need not have been made under oath.

If yes: The consistent prior statement is "not hearsay" and is admissible for its truth as well as for rehabilitation, Fed. R. Evid. 801(d)(1)(B). *See* § 6.4. Go to Step 26.

If no: The consistent statement will not be admissible. *See* § 6.4. Go to Step 26.

26. Is the out-of-court statement a prior identification of someone, and is the witness currently available?

If yes: The prior statement is "not hearsay" and is admissible for its truth, Fed. R. Evid. 801(d)(1)(C). *See* § 6.5. Go to Step 27.

If no: Go to Step 27.

Rule 801(d)(2): Hearsay Exemptions for Statements by Party-Opponents

27. Is a party-opponent offering the statement (direct or adopted) of a party, or of the party's agent, employee, or co-conspirator?

If yes: The statement is admissible and need not be against interest when made or be made with personal knowledge. However, for statements by agents, employees, or co-conspirators, there must be some independent evidence that the relationship existed at the time of the statement (other than the statement itself). Even though you have found a way to admit the evidence, see if it also fits into any of the Rule 803 or 804 exceptions. *See* §§ 6.6–6.10. Go to Step 28.

If no: Go to Step 28.

Rule 804: Hearsay Exceptions in Which the Declarant Is Unavailable

28. Is the declarant truly unavailable? Fed. R. Evid. 804(a). *See* § 7.16.

    If yes: Go to Step 29.

    If no: Skip all the Rule 804 exceptions. Go to Step 33.

Former Testimony

29. Was the statement by the unavailable declarant made under oath, at a prior proceeding or deposition, where the party against whom it is being offered (or in civil cases, also the party's predecessor in interest) had a similar motive and opportunity to cross-examine?

    If yes: The hearsay statement is admissible for its truth under the former testimony exception, Fed. R. Evid. 804(b)(1). *See* § 7.17. Go to Step 31.

    If no: Go to Step 30.

Dying Declaration

30. Was the statement made by homicide victim or a by an unavailable declarant in a civil case, concerning the cause of her impending death with the subjective expectation that she would soon die?

    If yes: The hearsay statement is admissible for its truth as a dying declaration, even if the declarant did not actually die, Fed. R. Evid. 804(b)(2). *See* § 7.18.

    If no: Go to Step 31.

Statement Against Interest

31. Was the statement by the unavailable declarant so contrary to the declarant's financial, legal, or penal interests that no one would have said it unless it were true?

    If yes: The hearsay statement is admissible for its truth as a statement against interest. In criminal cases where the declarant exposes herself to criminal penalty, there must be corroborating circumstances to indicate the trustworthiness of the statement, Fed. R. Evid. 804(b)(3). *See* § 7.19. Note that some declarations against interest are testimonial; even though they pass the hearsay rule, they violate the Confrontation Clause.

    If no: Go to Step 32.

Forfeiture by Wrongdoing

32. Was the out-of-court statement made by a declarant whom a party intentionally made unavailable in order to avoid the declarant's testimony?

    If yes: The hearsay statement is admissible for its truth against the party who intentionally made the declarant unavailable under the forfeiture by wrongdoing exception, Fed. R. Evid. 804(b)(6). *See* § 7.20. Go to Step 33.

    If no: Go to Step 33.

Rule 803: Hearsay Exceptions in Which the Availability of the Declarant Is Immaterial

Excited Utterance

33. Did the declarant make a statement relating to a startling event or condition, and was the declarant still under the stress of excitement caused by the startling event or condition when she made the statement?

    If yes: The statement is admissible as an excited utterance, Fed. R. Evid. 803(2). *See* § 7.6. Go to Step 34.

    If no: Go to Step 34.

Present Sense Impression

34. Did the declarant make a statement describing or explaining an event as she perceived it or immediately thereafter?

    If yes: The statement is admissible as a present sense impression, Fed. R. Evid. 803(1). *See* § 7.5. Go to Step 35.

    If no: The statement is not admissible as a present sense impression. Go to Step 35.

Then-Existing State of Mind

35. Did the declarant make a statement about her current mental or physical condition, sensation, emotion, thought, or plan?

    If yes: The statement is admissible under the then-existing mental, emotional, or physical condition exception unless it was a fact remembered or believed (except for statements made regarding a will, which may include facts remembered or believed), Fed. R. Evid. 803(3). *See* § 7.7. Go to Step 36.

    If no: The statement is not admissible under the then-existing mental, emotional, or physical condition exception. Go to Step 36.

Medical Diagnosis

36. Did the statement describe medical symptoms, treatment, or history made for the purpose of medical diagnosis or treatment, and was the statement pertinent to the diagnosis?

    If yes: It is admissible under the statements for medical diagnosis or treatment exception, even if the doctor was not a treating physician, Fed. R. Evid. 803(4). *See* § 7.8. Go to Step 37.

    If no: It is not admissible under the statements for medical diagnosis or treatment exception. Go to Step 37.

Recorded Recollection

37. Has the declarant made or adopted a record of a matter about which she once had knowledge but now can only partly remember, and was the record made or adopted when the matter was still fresh in the Declarant's mind?

    If yes: The record is admissible as a past recollection recorded, but it will normally be read into the record as testimony rather than entered as a physical exhibit that goes into the jury, unless it is offered by the opposing party. Note: Complete recollection or no memory at all on the part of the person making or adopting the record makes this exception inapplicable, Fed. R. Evid. 803(5). *See* § 7.9. Go to Step 38.

    If no: The exception for past recollection recorded does not apply. Such a document may have a non-hearsay use as a refreshed recollection. *See* § 7.10. Go to Step 38.

Business Records

38. Is the statement a record of regularly conducted business activity where:

    • It was the regular practice of the business to make such a record;

    • The record was made by a person with knowledge or made from information transmitted by a person with knowledge;

    • The source of the information possessed a business duty to speak or otherwise participate in creating the record; and

    • The opposing party cannot demonstrate that source of information or the method or circumstances of preparation indicate that the record is untrustworthy?

    If yes: The exception for business records applies unless this is a police report offered by the government in a criminal case, Fed. R. Evid. 803(6). *See* § 7.11. Go to Step 39.

If no: The exception for business records does not apply. Go to Step 39.

Public Records

39. Is the statement a public record or report setting out any of the following:

    • Activities of the governmental agency;

    • Matters observed pursuant to a duty imposed by law when the public servant has a duty to report, excluding matters observed by law enforcement personnel; or

    • Factual findings resulting from an investigation made pursuant to legal authority?

If yes: The exception for public records and reports applies as long as source of information and the method or circumstances of preparation do not indicate that the record is untrustworthy. The underlying evidence used by public servants in reaching their conclusion need not be admissible, Fed. R. Evid. 803(8). *See* § 7.12. Go to Step 40.

If no: The exception for public records and reports does not apply. Go to Step 40.

Learned Treatises

40. Does the out-of-court statement come from a learned treatise?

If yes: It is admissible once a foundation has been laid that the work is a reliable authority and can be used to impeach experts. If admitted, the treatise excerpts may be read into evidence but may not be received as exhibits, Fed. R. Evid. 803(18). *See* § 7.14. Go to Step 41.

If no: The exception for learned treatises does not apply. Go to Step 41.

Ancient Documents

41. Does the out-of-court statement arise from a document that is 20 or more years old?

If yes: It is admissible under the ancient documents exception, Fed. R. Evid. 803(16). *See* § 7.15. Go to Step 42.

Note: The Federal Judicial Center has proposed abolishing this rule.

If no: The exception for ancient documents does not apply. Go to Step 42.

Residual Hearsay Exception

42. If there is an out-of-court statement for which no exemption or exception seems to apply, does the statement present any unusual circumstances that:

- Provide "guarantees of trustworthiness" that are "equivalent" to those of the established exceptions;

- Offer evidence that is more probative on the point for which it is offered than any other evidence that can reasonably be obtained; and

- Serve the "interests of justice" by its admission?

If yes: The proponent must provide the opposing party with notice or demonstrate to the court that its failure to do so was excusable. The hearsay statement is admissible for its truth under the residual exception, but the ruling will have no precedential value, Fed. R. Evid. 807. *See* § 7.21. Go to Step 43.

If no: The out-of-court statement is inadmissible hearsay.

CONFRONTATION

Note: The right of confrontation belongs to the accused in a criminal case. The confrontation right does not apply to civil cases or to the government.

43. Is the government offering for its truth an out-of-court statement against an unavailable accused that the accused was unable (at any time) to cross-examine?

If yes: *See* §§ 8.1–8.3. Go to Step 44.

If no: There is no Confrontation Clause problem. Go to Step 47.

44. Is the statement "testimonial," i.e., would a reasonable person expect that the prosecutor would use it against the accused in a criminal trial? (Statements made to address ongoing emergencies are not testimonial.)

If yes: Go to Step 45.

If no: Because it is *non*-testimonial, the Confrontation Clause does not apply (but the statement would still be subject to the hearsay rules). Go to Step 47.

45. Did the accused intentionally make the declarant unavailable in order to prevent the declarant from testifying?

If yes: Even though the out-of-court statement is testimonial and would normally fall under the Confrontation Clause, the forfeiture exception applies and the declarant's statements are admissible. *See* § 8.5. Go to Step 46.

If no: There is no forfeiture and the testimonial statement is barred by the Confrontation Clause. Go to Step 47.

46. Is the statement a dying declaration, made by a victim of homicide, concerning the cause of her impending death, with the subjective expectation that she would soon die?

    If yes: The Supreme Court in dicta has stated this may be an exception to the Confrontation Clause. Go to Step 47.

    If no: The statement is testimonial and is barred by the Confrontation Clause. Go to Step 50.

COMPETENCE

47. Is the witness willing to take an oath, able to communicate, and able to understand the solemnity of the oath?

    If yes: The witness is presumed competent, Fed. R. Evid. 601. *See* §§ 9.1–9.2. Go to Step 48.

    If no: The presumption of competence has been rebutted and the witness is incompetent to testify.

48. Is the witness a judge, juror, or attorney testifying as a fact or expert witness in the case?

    If yes: The witness is incompetent, Fed. R. Evid. 605–606. Go to Step 49.

    If no: Go to Step 49.

49. Is the witness a juror testifying about the jury deliberation?

    If yes: The juror is only competent to testify about:

    • A mistake in reporting the actual verdict;

    • The introduction of extraneous prejudicial information; or

    • An improper outside influence.

    Fed. R. Evid. 606(b). *See* § 9.6. Go to Step 50.

    If no: The juror is incompetent to testify. Go to Step 50.

PRIVILEGES

Note: Federal common law applies to privileges in federal court unless state law provides the rule of decision. State privilege law may vary from the federal common law.

Adverse Spousal Testimony

50. In a criminal matter, are parties to a lawsuit or the police attempting to obtain information about a current spouse via testimony, deposition, police inquiry, or other formal mechanism?

If yes: The spouse from whom the information is sought, the holder of the privilege, may assert the adverse spousal testimony privilege and need not take the stand or answer questions. The privilege will apply in federal court unless the privilege has been waived or abrogated. The confidential communication spousal privilege may also apply. *See* § 10.9. Go to Step 51.

If no: The adverse spousal testimony privilege does not apply. Go to Step 51.

Confidential Spousal Communication

51. In a civil or criminal case, are parties to a lawsuit or the police attempting to obtain information about a confidential communication between spouses that occurred when the spouses were legally married?

    If yes: The spouse who made the confidential communication may assert the confidential spousal communication privilege. The privilege will apply in federal court unless the privilege has been waived or abrogated. *See* § 10.9. Go to Step 52.

    If no: The confidential spousal communication privilege does not apply. Go to Step 52.

Work Product

52. Are parties or the police attempting to obtain information about matters prepared in anticipation of litigation?

    If yes: Mental impressions are absolutely privileged and will not be admissible. A qualified privilege exists for tangible work product, but it may be obtainable if the party seeking it demonstrates need for the information that it cannot obtain with undue hardship. *See* § 10.5. Go to Step 53.

    If no: It does not fit within the work product privilege. Go to Step 53.

Attorney-Client Privilege

53. Are parties or the police attempting to obtain information about a confidential communication between lawyer and client relating to legal matters?

    If yes: The attorney-client privilege will protect the communication unless it was disclosed to a third party, waived because of testimony, or is part of a crime or fraud. *See* §§ 10.4, 10.6.

    If no: The attorney-client privilege does not apply. Go to Step 54.

Other Professional Privileges

54. Are parties or the police attempting to obtain information about a confidential communication between an individual and any of the following:

   - A clergyperson or

   - A therapist?

   If yes: The communication will be privileged unless it was disclosed to a third party, waived because of testimony, or is part of a crime or fraud. *See* §§ 10.7, 10.8, 10.11. Go to Step 55.

   If no: No professional privileges apply. Go to Step 55.

Privilege Against Self-Incrimination

55. Are parties or the police attempting to obtain information that could subject an individual to a criminal penalty?

   If yes: The party from whom the information is sought can assert the Fifth Amendment privilege against self-incrimination. If the person asserting the privilege is the accused, she may refuse to take the stand entirely. If the person is merely a witness or a deponent, she will have to do so under oath at the hearing, deposition, or proceeding. *See* § 10.10. Go to Step 56.

   If no: The privilege against self-incrimination does not apply. Go to Step 56.

OPINION AND EXPERT TESTIMONY

Lay Opinion

56. Is lay witness (not testifying as an expert) providing an opinion based on her perceptions that is helpful to the fact-finder in clarifying the witness's testimony or determining a disputed fact?

   If yes: It is a permissible lay opinion under Fed. R. Evid. 701. Note: Sometimes a witness is both a fact and expert witness. *See* § 11.1. Go to Step 57.

   If no: It is not a permissible lay opinion. It may qualify as an expert opinion if the witness has been qualified as an expert. Go to Step 57.

Expert Opinion

57. Is the witness qualified by her education, experience, knowledge, or skill, and does the expert's opinion derive from any of the following:

   - Personal knowledge;

- Any information the expert learned in preparation for testimony; or

- Training and study?

If yes: The witness may be qualified as an expert under Fed. R. Evid. 702. *See* § 11.3. Go to Step 58.

If no: The witness may not offer expert testimony. Go to Step 60.

58. Is the expert opinion based on sufficient facts or data, and is it the product of reliable principles and methods applied correctly by the expert?

If yes: The expert may offer her opinion and rely on inadmissible evidence, if experts in the field reasonably rely on those kinds of facts or data, Fed. R. Evid. 703. *See* §§ 11.4–11.5. Go to Step 59.

If no: The judge as gatekeeper should reject the expert's testimony. Go to Step 59.

59. Is this expert testifying in a criminal case about the mental state of the accused relating to a criminal element or defense?

If yes: That part of the expert's testimony is prohibited by the Hinckley Amendment. Go to Step 60.

If no: The expert testimony is admissible and experts are generally permitted to testify as to the ultimate issue. Go to Step 60.

JUDICIAL NOTICE

60. Is a fact related to the case:

- not subject to reasonable dispute; and

- either

  - generally known in the jurisdiction or

  - accurately and readily determined from reliable sources?

If yes: The judge, after hearing objections, should grant judicial notice or may do so sua sponte. In civil cases, the jury must accept the judicially-noticed fact as conclusively proved. In criminal cases, the jury does not have to accept the fact as conclusively proved, Fed. R. Evid. 201. *See* §§ 12.3–12.7. Go to Step 61.

If no: The court should not grant judicial notice. Go to Step 61.

AUTHENTICATION

Real Evidence

61. Is a tangible item offered by a party what its proponent claims it to be?

If yes: The item has been authenticated and the judge should allow the jury to consider the evidence. *See* §§ 14.1–14.3. Fed. R. Evid. 901(b) provides examples, including the following:

- Testimony of a witness with knowledge;

- Distinctive characteristics and the like;

- Evidence about public records filed in a public office as authorized by law or the office where items of this kind are kept;

- Evidence about ancient documents or data compilations; or

- Evidence describing a process or system and showing that it produces an accurate result.

Go to Step 62.

If no: The judge will sustain an objection for lack of authentication, and the evidence will be inadmissible. Go to Step 62 for demonstrative evidence.

Demonstrative Evidence

62. Is the tangible item offered as demonstrative evidence (such as a chart, map, or replica) authenticated by a witness who demonstrates familiarity with whatever is depicted and who testifies that the exhibit fairly and accurately represents the subject?

If yes: The demonstrative evidence has been authenticated, Fed. R. Evid. 901. Go to Step 63.

If no: The court should not admit the demonstrative evidence and should sustain an objection as to authenticity. Go to Step 63.

BEST EVIDENCE

63. Is the proponent trying to "prove the contents" of a writing, recording, or photo? (Note: Just because a writing, recording, or photo exists does not mean the proponent is trying to prove its contents.)

If yes: The best evidence rule applies, Fed. R. Evid. 1002. *See* § 15.3. Go to Step 64.

If no: The best evidence rule does not apply. Go to Step 65.

64. Is the writing, recording, or photo merely incidental or collateral to the witness's testimony or lost through no fault of the proponent?

If yes: The best evidence rule does not apply, Fed. R. Evid. 1004. *See* § 15.5. Go to Step 65.

If no: The item must be presented to the jury (as opposed to merely having testimony about the item). Unless there is a question about authentication or a duplicate would be unfair, a mechanically- or digitally-made duplicate is acceptable, Fed. R. Evid. 1003. *See* § 15.4. Go to Step 65.

APPEAL

For Improperly Admitted Evidence

65. Was a timely and correct objection to the improperly admitted evidence raised, and did that admission affect the substantial right of a party?

If yes: The court committed reversible error. *See* §§ 16.1–16.3. Go to Step 66.

If no: The court will not reverse unless the admission affected the substantial right of a party and was plain (sufficiently obvious and substantial that it would interfere with justice and perception of fairness of the proceeding), Fed. R. Evid. 103(e). *See* § 16.6. Go to Step 66.

For Improperly Excluded Evidence

66. Was a timely and correct objection raised and an offer of proof proffered at trial regarding the improperly excluded evidence, and did the improper exclusion affect a substantial right of a party?

If yes: The court committed reversible error. Go to Step 67.

If no: The court will not reverse unless the admission affected a substantial right of a party and was plain. Go to Step 67.

Standard of Review

67. Did the trial judge state the legal standard correctly?

If yes: Go to Step 68.

If no: The Appellate Court should review the legal standard de novo.

68. Has the trial court, applying the correct legal standard, exercised its broad discretion in a reasonable manner in determining the admissibility of evidence?

If yes: The Appellate Court should affirm, even if the judges on the panel might have reached a different conclusion.

If no: The Appellate Court may reverse for abuse of discretion.

Table of Rules